ENCYCLOPÆDIA
OF THE
WORLD

Contents

© Macdonald Educational Limited 1979
Printed in Spain by
Printer industria gráfica sa
Sant Vicenç dels Horts   Barcelona 1979
Depósito legal B. 29.225-1979
Second impression 1984

ISBN 0 356 07026 3

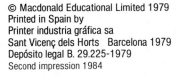

U.S.S.R.

ASIA

Contents

The birth of the Sun and planets

The planet earth is one of nine planets which, along with moons, comets, meteorites and rocky lumps called asteroids, orbit round the Sun. Together, they make up our solar system.

Earth is a fairly small, rocky planet, roughly spherical in shape and 12,800 kilometres in diameter. It takes one year (365¼ days) to complete its orbit of the Sun and as it does so it rotates. Each revolution takes 23 hours 56 minutes (one day). Much of the earth's surface is covered with water and the whole planet is surrounded by an atmosphere rich in oxygen which supports life.

The Sun lies at the centre of the solar system. It is a star with a diameter 109 times larger than the earth's. It consists of a mass of extremely hot hydrogen and helium gas at a temperature of 6,000° centigrade. This heat is created by thermo-nuclear reactions.

The Sun may seem important to us, but it is only one of thousands of millions of stars that make up the Milky Way – our galaxy. Astronomers have detected at least 400 million other galaxies in outer space as large as our own!

The origin of the solar system

No one knows exactly how the solar system formed. Several theories have been put forward by astronomers to explain how it may have happened. The most widely accepted of these suggests that the solar system was formed from the contraction and condensation of an enormous revolving cloud of gas and dust. Most of this matter went to the centre, making the Sun, while the planets and other bodies were formed from the outer part of the cloud.

A second theory suggests that another star passed close to our sun. The gravitational pull of the star attracted a streamer of gas and dust that later condensed to form the planets.

The latest theory is based on the study of stars that are known to have formed recently. New stars are recognized by their irregular, flashing light, and some people think that each flash puffs clouds of gas and dust into space around the new star. These gather into balls that later become planets.

How old is the solar system?

The oldest rocks on earth have been found in Greenland. Scientists calculate that they are between 3,700 and 3,900 million years old. Rock samples brought back from the Moon by the Apollo 15 astronauts have been found to be even older, probably 4,150 million years old. Some meteorites are older still. Such evidence leads scientists to believe that the solar system was formed about 4,600 million years ago.

The infant earth must have been very different from that of today. Its surface was hot, molten rock, which slowly cooled and solidified. The lightest material formed a scum on the surface, later to become the rocks of the continents, while heavier material sank to lower layers and formed the ocean floors.

Even today, man has only penetrated eight kilometres into the earth's solid crust in his deepest bore hole. To discover what lies below this level, scientists must use other means of investigation.

When earthquakes occur their shock waves travel through the earth. The speeds at which these waves travel and the paths they take vary with each different layer they pass through. Scientists can measure these and thus identify the matter that lies below the earth's crust.

The solid outer layer is rather like the wrinkled skin of an old apple, 33 kilometres thick at the most. At the bottom of this layer lies hot, dense basalt, or magma, which forms the mantle. Some 2,900 kilometres below this lies the core. The core consists of very heavy material, and is probably made chiefly of the metals iron and nickel.

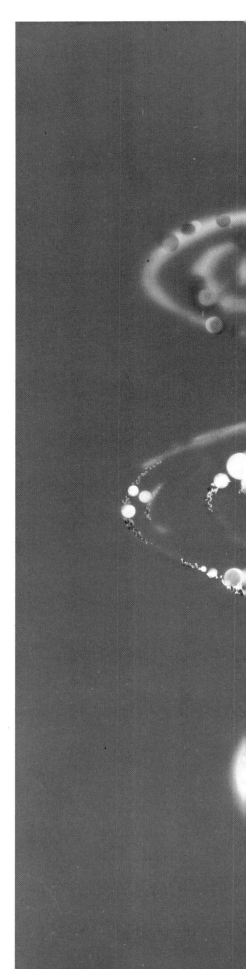

Scientists believe that the earth and the solar system came into being about 4,600 million years ago. There are several conflicting theories that attempt to explain how this happened. The most widely recognized of these is shown in the drawing below. It shows a vast rotating cloud of gas and dust in space which gradually condenses and contracts under its own gravity. The gas at the centre of the cloud becomes hot enough for thermonuclear reactions to start. This gives rise to a new star, the Sun, with the earth and the other planets orbiting round it.

Rocks and volcanoes

The rocks of the earth's crust have been formed in three ways.

Igneous rocks are made when molten magma cools and solidifies. Granite is an igneous rock made from magma that cooled slowly under other rocks. It has large crystals of feldspar, quartz, and other minerals. Basalt cooled fast when magma poured over the crust, and has small crystals.

Sedimentary rocks are layers (strata) of silt, sand, gravel and other materials which have broken off other rocks and been deposited on the beds of lakes and seas. Clay, sandstone and limestone are sedimentary rocks, and often contain the fossil remains of things which lived in the silt and sand when the strata formed.

Metamorphic rocks were igneous or sedimentary rocks which changed under the effects of great heat or pressure. Slate has formed from clay that has been squashed by enormous pressure, and marble from limestone that has been greatly heated or subjected to great pressure.

Over millions of years the earth's surface has been carved into hills and valleys, cliffs and plains. The rocks are broken up by constant changes in temperature, by rain, ice and wind, and by the sea.

Weathering and erosion

This breaking up of the rocks is called weathering. The broken pieces of rock are removed from higher to lower ground by strong winds, rivers and glaciers. They may reach the sea, where they are deposited. The particular way rock weathers varies from place to place.

Through erosion pieces of rock are carried from one place to another. The process is very slow, but if it goes on over vast periods of time, mighty mountains are worn down to flat plains.

Generally, rocks which do not erode easily form the uplands, while the lowlands are made of the more easily eroded rocks, or of the sediments from the higher ground which have been deposited.

Acid rain

Some rocks are also eroded by being dissolved. As rain falls, it absorbs carbon dioxide gas from the air. It becomes a weak acid. Limestone, made of the shells of prehistoric animals, is slowly dissolved by the acid rain as it trickles through cracks in the rock. The limestone is carried away, and pot-holes form.

Below ground, caverns are slowly formed, often containing spectacular stalactites and stalagmites. These are made from the mineral "calcite" which is re-deposited limestone.

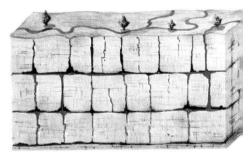

Above: Limestone is full of cracks. Rain water trickles through these.

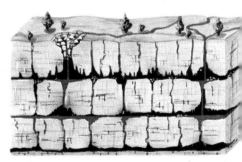

Above: The cracks gradually grow, as the limestone is dissolved away.

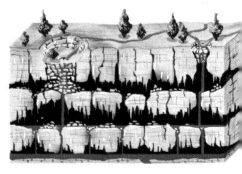

Above: The result is a landscape with pot-holes. Streams may disappear down these and caverns form.

Above: The Grand Canyon in the U.S.A., carved out by the Colorado River, is nearly two kilometres deep.

The rocks the river has eroded clearly show layering typical of sedimentary rock formations.

Volcanoes

Most volcanoes are cone-shaped vents rising up from the earth's crust, mainly along the edges of the rigid "plates" of which the earth's outer shell is made. Matter from inside the earth, mainly hot molten rock (magma), erupts through these vents. Gases, steam, ash and cinders may also be emitted during an eruption.

Lava may also pour out of cracks in the earth's crust, forming a flat sheet.

Lava

Lava is sometimes able to flow long distances before it solidifies, forming a gently sloping cone.

Elsewhere, the lava may be too thick to flow far, and it makes a steep-sided cone. It can plug the vent, causing the volcano to explode violently later on. This happened to Mont Pelée in Martinique in 1902 when more than 30,000 people were killed in a volcanic explosion.

Of course volcanoes can threaten life on earth. But without them there would have been no life on earth. The first living cells were evolved in the conditions provided by the activity of volcanoes, where they could make use of the minerals, water, heat and electrical energy.

Right: This is perhaps the most typical kind of volcanic cone. It is composed of layers of ash and lava that build up with each eruption. The surface quickly weathers, and because it is particularly rich in minerals which are vital to plants, it forms fertile soil.

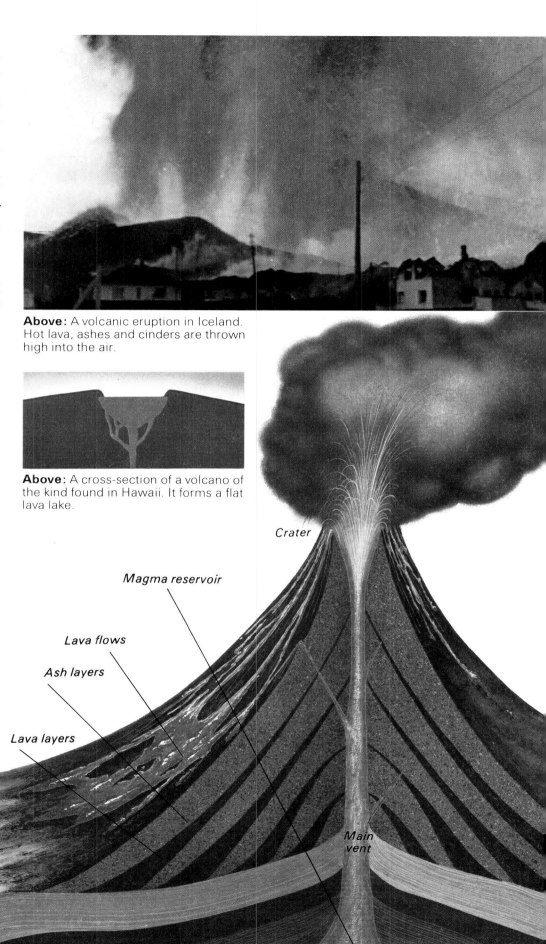

Above: A volcanic eruption in Iceland. Hot lava, ashes and cinders are thrown high into the air.

Above: A cross-section of a volcano of the kind found in Hawaii. It forms a flat lava lake.

Crater

Magma reservoir

Lava flows

Ash layers

Lava layers

Main vent

Weathering and glaciation

Four times in the last two million years, the world's climate has become very cold. It was so cold that the polar ice caps, which now cover most of Greenland and Antarctica, expanded. Glaciers covered the mountains and filled the valleys.

Glaciers

High in the mountains, snow collects in hollows year after year and turns into compacted ice as its weight builds up. Glaciers are great masses of ice which spill out from these permanent snow fields and gradually slide downhill. Today, valley glaciers are still found in high mountain ranges such as the Alps.

As the slow-moving glacier moves across uneven ground huge cracks, called crevasses, occur in the ice. The glacier carries vast quantities of rock fragments with it taken from the rocks it passes over. Fallen pieces of rock, split from the mountainsides by the frost, are taken along. The glacier acts as a massive bulldozer, using the rocky "moraine" as a grindstone to re-shape entire landscapes. Valleys that were once steep-sided or "V"-shaped are scoured to rounded "U"-shaped troughs. New valleys can be formed by the action of the ice.

Icebergs

The glacier ends either when the ice melts or when it reaches the sea, where huge chunks break off forming icebergs.

If the climate becomes warmer, the glacier melts nearer its source, and the end "retreats", dumping all the moraine the ice was carrying. A ridge of "end moraine" may be left across a valley damming the water from the melting glacier and making a lake.

In some cases when glaciers flowed into the sea, the melting ice caused the water to flood inland. This created long, steep-sided inlets, or fjords. There are many fjords along the coasts of Norway, Scotland and British Columbia.

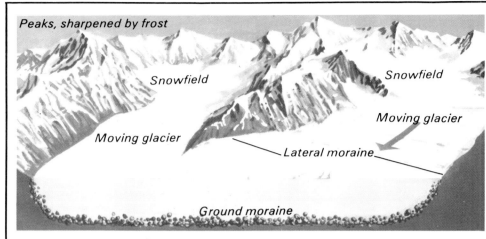

Above: Snowfields occur high in mountainous areas where it is cold enough for snow to gather year after year. The snow, packed hard under its own weight, forms ice. These glaciers are flowing from their snowfields. The jagged mountain peaks are sharpened by the action of severe frosts. The moraine of rock fragments at the sides and below the glacier, scrapes and grinds the rocks, changing the valley to a "U"-shaped trough. When the glacier melts, streams cascade down the sides.

Below: If the glacier does not melt before it reaches the sea, huge lumps break off and float away as icebergs which are dangerous to ships. When the glacier passes over uneven parts of the valley floor, cracks or crevasses form. They are often hidden by freshly fallen snow, and are very dangerous to climbers. Ice falls happen where the valley floor is especially steep.

Above: A fjord in Norway. A glacier moving down from the mountains carved this trough, which was flooded by the sea when the ice melted.

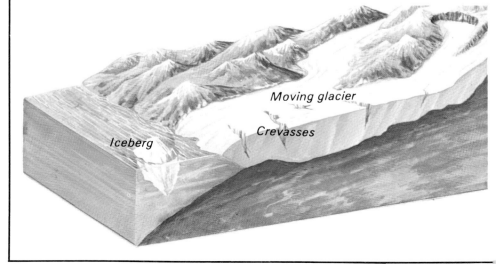

Desert rain

Erosion by water still happens even in hot deserts and other dry areas. Although rain may fall only once every ten years, when it does, it comes as violent thunderstorms. The ground becomes waterlogged and water floods across it, washing loose material with it and tearing gullies. Wadis (valleys that are usually dry) become torrents.

Breaking rocks

Rocks break up as the sun heats them. The minerals in them expand at different rates, and are loosened. At night the temperature drops quickly and the rocks contract. As this happens day after day over a long time, the rocks slowly split into small pieces. They are eventually broken down into sand and soil.

Above: Ayers Rock, near Alice Springs, Australia. This two-kilometre-long, flat-topped hill is an inselberg. It is made of rock which resisted erosion.

Wind

Once a desert storm has ended, the hot sun quickly dries up the water, so the desert is back to normal. Now the wind can get back to work. It gathers up the weathered pieces of rock (hard, sharp grains of sand), and flings them against any object in its path.

Desert rocks are polished and carved into fantastic shapes by the sand-blast. The elephant in the picture on the left was formed in this way.

There are more sand grains near the ground so erosion happens fastest at this level. Rocks are undercut at their bases. Soft rocks are worn away faster than hard ones, and this may also result in unusual formations.

Rounded hills with flat tops are very typical of hot, arid landscapes. These "inselbergs" are all that remains of a higher land surface, which was worn away. The sand removed by the wind is deposited as sand dunes.

Above: Elephant Rock in the Valley of Fire State, Nevada, U.S.A. In arid areas and deserts, wind is a powerful erosion agent. It carries away loose bits of earth and rock in dust storms which sand-blast whatever they strike. Wind-carved rocks can usually be distinguished from other types because they are usually more worn away near their bases.

15

The earth on the move

If you look closely at a map of the world you may be able to see that you can fit the shapes of the continents together like pieces of a jigsaw puzzle.

Drifting

This fact fascinated the scientist Alfred Wegener. He suggested that the continents have not always been where they are now, but are slowly moving about in the oceans. This theory is called "Continental Drift". Wegener first suggested it in 1924, but few people accepted it until recently. Many other clues suggest that Wegener was right.

Clues

The clues include the positions of certain rocks, fossils and land forms that must have been formed very close to one another. Yet today, they are separated by oceans. The best explanation for this is the theory that, 200 million years ago, the continents were all joined as one vast land mass called "Pangaea". Later, this split into two smaller super-continents, "Laurasia" (North America, Europe and Asia, minus India), and "Gondwanaland" (South America, Africa, Antarctica, Australia and India).

They were separated in the east by a sea called "Tethys". Laurasia and Gondwanaland have since split to make up the continents we recognize today.

Still moving

Slowly the continents have drifted apart. This movement is still happening. Studies of the ocean floors, and positions of active volcanoes and earthquakes, all explain how this happens.

Right: 200 million years ago the continents were joined together as one land mass, "Pangaea". Two smaller super-continents existed 135 million years ago, "Gondwanaland" and "Laurasia". They slowly broke apart and drifted to give today's pattern of continents. India drifted into Asia, buckling the plate edges to make the Himalayas.

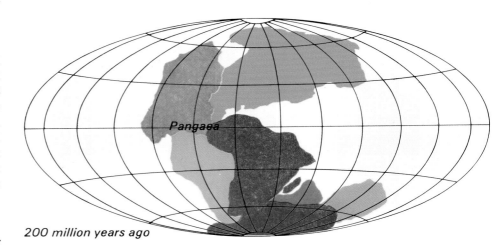

200 million years ago

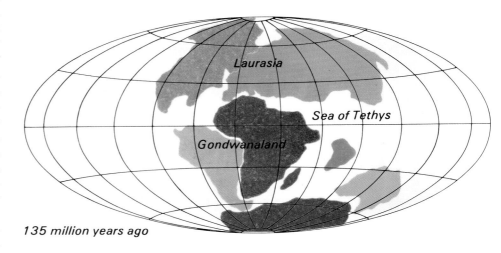

135 million years ago

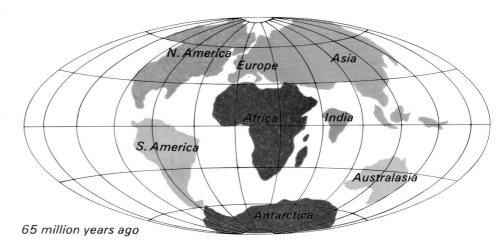

65 million years ago

Continental drift

Recent studies of the earth's crust have shown that the outer shell is made up of a series of large plates called tectonic plates. These float on the molten magma of the mantle below the crust. The continental land masses are made of lighter material than the ocean floors, so they are able to ride on the top of the tectonic plates like piggy-back passengers.

It seems that the earth's crust is like a broken egg shell. The tectonic plates each make up one piece of the shell. They are gradually forced apart from one another by slow-moving convection currents in the molten magma.

Volcanoes

As the cracks widen, molten magma rises upwards to fill the gap. The edges of the plates are marked by active volcanoes. A ring of volcanoes, the "Pacific Ring of Fire", around the Pacific Ocean, marks the edge of the plate that lies under the ocean.

Another crack runs down the centre of the Atlantic Ocean where the edges of the Eurasian Plate and the American Plate meet. It is marked by the Mid-Atlantic Ridge, a series of volcanoes under the sea. These rise above the surface of the ocean in some places, forming groups of volcanic islands such as the Azores and Iceland. One of the world's youngest volcanoes, Surtsey, lies just off Iceland. It first erupted and rose above the sea in 1963.

Buckling

While some of the tectonic plates are being forced apart, others are being forced together. When two cars collide, metal is buckled. In the same way, the edges of the plates are crumpled when they collide, forming ranges of mountains. The Himalayas resulted from India colliding with the Eurasian Plate. Other plates are forced downwards, making deep trenches in the ocean floor.

On land there are mountains, valleys and plains. But 70 per cent of the earth's surface is sea. The ocean floors are as varied as the land. Some undersea mountain ranges are 4,000 kilometres wide, and the Marianas Trench in the Pacific Ocean is over eleven kilometres deeper than the height of Mt Everest!

Atmosphere

Above the surface of the earth is the atmosphere, a mixture of gases up to a height of about 50 kilometres. Above five kilometres the atmosphere is thin. It is mainly nitrogen (78 per cent) and oxygen (21 per cent) with small amounts of other gases such as carbon dioxide (0.03 per cent), water vapour, dust and salt crystals.

Above: A spacecraft photograph of the planet earth. The continent of Africa is in the centre of the picture. Notice the swirling masses of white clouds that cluster over some parts of the earth's surface.

The lower atmosphere is divided into three main layers. The lowest is the troposphere. This reaches up to 15 kilometres, and contains almost all of the air. It gets much colder the higher one goes. The tropopause is a narrow zone where there is a steady low temperature. It divides the troposphere from the upper air, or stratosphere. The stratosphere is a layer of very thin air, where the temperature stays almost constant, and clouds cannot therefore exist.

Causes of the weather

The rays from the sun supply the earth and its atmosphere with energy in the form of heat, but the cloud and dust in the air, and pale surfaces such as snow and ice, reflect some of this heat back into space.

The earth does not now seem to be getting either warmer or cooler. There is a balance between the energy received and that lost. But the different parts of the earth's surface get different amounts of energy.

Winds

Winds are air movements that result from the uneven heating of the surface. Land heats faster than the sea. In daytime, as the sun heats it, the warm air, which weighs less than cool, rises over the land. This reduces the pressure at the surface. Cool air from over the sea blows in to replace the rising air. This causes onshore sea breezes on warm days.

On the global scale, areas near to the equator receive more heat than areas nearer to the poles. In tropical areas cooler air flows in to take the place of air rising at the equator.

The warmed air rises, moves towards the poles, cools and sinks back to the surface. This makes high pressure areas around 30° North and South of the equator. If the earth was not spinning, these winds would simply blow north to south, and south to north, but the spin deflects them. This deflection makes the wind system very complicated indeed.

Rain

Winds flow from areas of high pressure to areas of low pressure. The deflection caused by the spin of the earth results in rotating air masses. Water vapour is carried upwards in rising air and condenses to form clouds and rain.

This is why low pressure areas, or depressions, usually bring clouds, strong winds and rain when they move into your area.

Every day, the sun evaporates

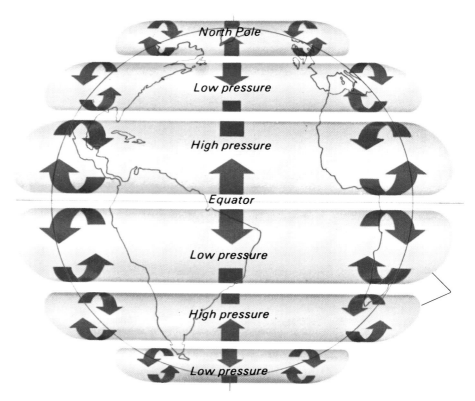

Above: Winds are movements of air from one place to another, caused by uneven heating of the earth's surface. The arrows show how the air rises, moves and sinks in the atmosphere.

enormous quantities of water from the land and the sea. This either stays in the air as water vapour, which is not visible, or cools and condenses, forming tiny droplets of water which we can see as mist, fog or clouds.

Condensation happens because

warm air holds much more water vapour than cold. When it cools, the water vapour changes from a gas to a liquid. Rain falls when the droplets become large and heavy enough to fall back to the earth's surface. Then the cycle starts all over again.

Below: This photograph was taken high over the Pacific Ocean in 1969 during the Apollo 9 space flight. It shows the swirling cloud pattern of a large tropical cyclone.

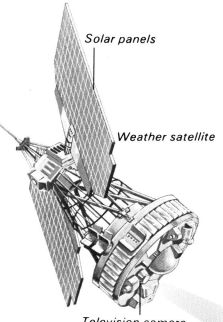

Solar panels

Weather satellite

Television camera

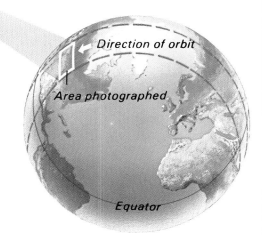

Direction of orbit

Area photographed

Equator

Rain gauge

Above: A weather satellite has a television camera to transmit a continuous picture of the changing patterns of cloud back to earth. It is fitted with solar panels that trap and convert energy from the sun into electricity to power the camera and transmitter.

Far right: A rain gauge.

Above right: Air is forced to rise up mountainsides. It cools and water vapour forms as a cloud near the summit.

Forecasts

A regular weather forecast is important for farmers and those working with aircraft and ships. But it is difficult to predict the behaviour of the atmosphere at any point on the earth's surface for more than a few hours ahead. This is why long-range weather forecasts do not always turn out to be accurate.

Short-range forecasts are better. Meteorologists (people who study weather) collect facts about the atmosphere from weather stations all over the world. Special aircraft, weather ships, radiosonde balloons and satellites with television cameras, all give a picture of the changing weather patterns. The information is fed into computers to produce up-to-date weather maps. Forecasts are made from these.

The basic facts used in weather forecasting are pressure, temperature, the amount of water vapour present in the air, the speed of the wind and its direction.

Pressure

Areas of low pressure often bring windy weather with cloud and rain. High pressure is more likely to give dry weather with clear skies.

Air pressure is measured by a barometer. Some people keep a barometer in their house. Lines on a map drawn to link places with the same pressure are called isobars. These are shown on television weather maps.

Wind speed and temperature

The cups on an anemometer turn in the wind, recording its speed. Temperatures are measured on a thermometer. A special pair of thermometers, with one bulb surrounded by wet muslin, helps the meteorologist work out how much water vapour is in the air.

The sunshine recorder, with its glass ball, focuses the rays of the sun on to a piece of card. When it is bright enough, the sun burns the card.

The rain gauge is one of the simplest instruments. It is a funnel leading down to a graduated tube. The amount of rain that has fallen is measured every 24 hours.

Recording

With the help of these instruments, details of the weather can be recorded daily. After the facts have been collected for a number of years, regular seasonal patterns show up, and it is possible to say if a particular month or season has had normal weather.

Winds and storms

Above: A summer's day in Greece. The climate of the Mediterranean Sea area is noted for its hot dry summers and warm but wet winters. White-walled buildings reflect the sun's heat.

Pictures of the earth from a space satellite reveal a series of distinct zones on the earth's land surfaces which differ in colour and texture. These are bands of various types of vegetation, each the result of a different climate.

Climate

Climate is the average weather found in a place. Usually, it is described by the average monthly temperatures and rainfall. Temperatures become cooler the closer to the poles you get, and as you climb higher above sea level. Rainfall amounts also vary from place to place. This is due to the uneven way the earth's surface is heated and how far a place is from the sea.

Deserts

In hot deserts average weather conditions are hot and arid. At midday, temperatures in the shade may reach 45° centigrade, but at night the temperature drops sharply. Rain may not fall for several years until, at last, the drought is broken by a sudden torrential storm. The few plants that grow in deserts must be able to adapt to withstand long periods without rain.

Temperate climates

In contrast, places like the British Isles enjoy a cool, temperate climate, with moderate amounts of rainfall spread evenly through the year. The rain is brought by "depressions", which are cylindrical areas of atmospheric low pressure that may measure 1,400 kilometres across. Depressions form when warm air masses from sub-tropical areas collide with cold air from the polar regions. The boundary between the two is known as a front. The lighter warm air rises over a wedge of cold air and, as it does so, water vapour condenses into clouds.

The appearance of high, wispy cirrus clouds is the first sign of a depression. The clouds become lower and thicker as the warm front gets nearer and rain falls from thick nimbo-stratus clouds close to the ground. Temperatures rise in the "warm sector" and the weather becomes showery with bright periods. The cold front is marked by towering cumulonimbus clouds often with thunderstorms. Sometimes the cold front "overtakes" the warm front, giving rise to an occluded front which may bring heavy rain that lasts a long time. As the depression moves away, the barometer rises and the skies clear within a short time.

Weather symbols

On a weather map the fronts are marked by symbols. The warm front is shown by a line of semicircles, the rounded side facing in the direction the front is moving. The rounded shapes indicate that warmer air follows. The cold front is shown by a line of triangles, pointing the way the front is moving.

Occlusion

Where the cold front has caught up with the warm front, the occlusion is shown by a combination of triangles and semi-circles. By tracking the movement of fronts, rain can be forecast.

Below: A mid-latitude depression. Low pressure systems of this kind, that move from west to east, bring rainfall to such areas as the British Isles and north-west Europe.

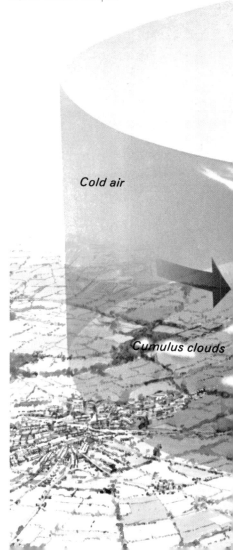

Cold air

Cumulus clouds

Violent winds

Areas of extreme low pressure sometimes occur over tropical oceans. These are hurricanes and are probably the most feared storms in the world. Hurricanes bring incredibly strong winds of up to 250 kilometres per hour, heavy rainfall, thunder and lightning. They can cause terrible damage.

Strictly speaking, hurricanes are tropical storms in the Gulf of Mexico. Similar storms are called cyclones in the Indian and Pacific Oceans, willy-willies in Australia, and typhoons in the China Sea.

Tropical storms can be 80 to 800 kilometres wide, last for several days, and may travel hundreds of kilometres before losing their fury as they pass over a land mass.

The violent winds spiral around a calm centre known as the "eye", and the wind blows from a different direction after the eye has passed. Severe tropical storms cause widespread damage, especially when they pass over islands in their path. Some damage is caused by huge tidal waves whipped up by the powerful winds. The rainfall is torrential – up to 250 millimetres can fall in a few hours.

As such storms are such a threat to human life and property, accurate forecasting of their movements is essential. The first sign of an approaching storm is a rapid fall of pressure. Television pictures from satellites are of great help in tracing their paths. The United States Weather Bureau gives each storm a name, such as Hurricane Debbie and Hurricane Camille.

Above: A satellite picture of the "eye" of a hurricane, showing the calm centre with the destructive winds spiralling round it. The hurricane also brings with it heavy rain.

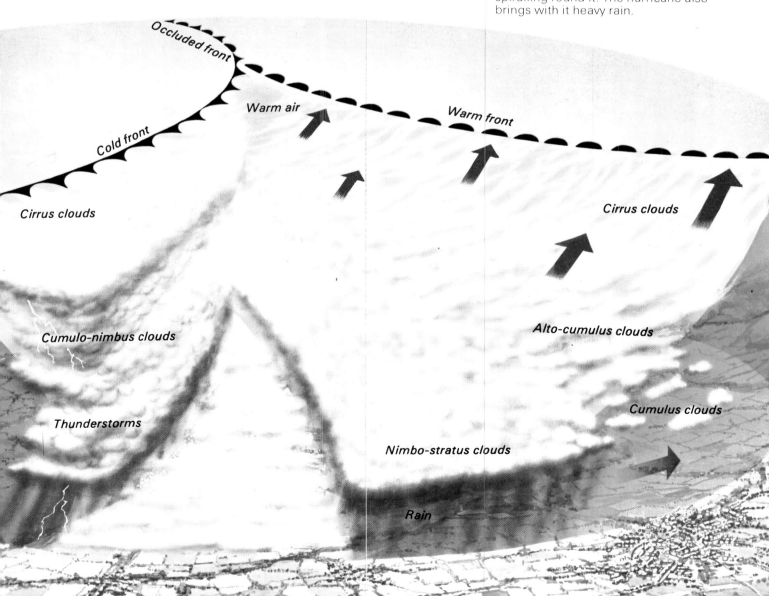

Occluded front

Warm air

Warm front

Cold front

Cirrus clouds

Cirrus clouds

Cumulo-nimbus clouds

Alto-cumulus clouds

Cumulus clouds

Thunderstorms

Nimbo-stratus clouds

Rain

Snow and ice

Water is the commonest substance on the earth, and life cannot exist without it. It can be liquid (water), solid (ice), or gaseous (water vapour) in form.

Liquid form

Nearly 98 per cent of the water on earth is in liquid form. About two per cent is solid (mainly in the form of ice) and 0.001% is gas or water vapour. These percentages may change over a long period of time. Far more of the water must have been locked up as solid ice during the Ice Age. Even now, it has been estimated that if all the ice sheets, snow fields and glaciers in the world today were to melt, then the sea level would rise by as much as 50 metres!

Snow and ice

The glaciers and ice sheets high in the mountains and at the poles result from snow building up year after year. Snow is formed from minute ice crystals which are made when water condenses at temperatures below freezing.

In very low temperatures these crystals fall to the ground as a fine dust or stay aloft. As the temperature warms up, the crystals stick together to make beautiful flowerlike snowflakes.

Single snowflakes may also join together forming large, feathery flakes several centimetres across, a sign that the air is only just cold enough for snow to fall.

Snowflakes melt and become raindrops if the air they are falling through is above freezing point. Sleet is a mixture of snow and rain.

The quantity of snow a place receives and the length of time that it stays on the ground is partly due to its height. As you go higher up a mountain it gets colder and it is more likely that snow will fall instead of rain. If the mountain is high enough, you will eventually climb to a point where it is cold enough for snow to lie all through the year. This is the "permanent snow line".

Blinding snow storms, when a bitterly cold wind blows the snow horizontally, are called blizzards. Visibility is only a few metres at the most, and large snow drifts may occur, especially on higher ground where there are strong winds. When drifts occur across roads they can cause great problems to travellers.

Wheels, feet or sledge runners exert pressure on the fallen snow so that a thin surface layer melts. However, very soon afterwards, it freezes again and forms ice. The compacted ice reduces the friction between the object pressing down and the surface, and causes a loss of grip, or slipping.

Hail

Hail is also water falling as ice. In a thunder cloud, a raindrop may be swept high into the cloud several times. It freezes and the ice pellet grows larger each time it goes upwards. Finally it is so heavy that it falls. Some hailstones are as big as golf balls. Hailstorms happen suddenly and are over quickly.

Right: When blizzards occur in exposed areas, drifts build up and make problems for drivers. Snow ploughs will be needed to release these lorries.

Left: Snowflakes are crystals of frozen water, and form in flower-like shapes like these.

Our changing climate

The patterns of the earth's climate have not always been as they are today. We know this because coal seams, formed from the remains of plants that grew in warm, wet conditions 300 million years ago, are found in Antarctica, now one of the coldest places on earth.

Only 50,000 years ago glaciers covered much of Europe, but even during the Ice Age it was not cold all the time. At least four times the ice advanced and then melted. The climate then may have been warmer than today.

One reason for the changes in climate is the drifting of continents. Another reason is that the earth's orbit and atmosphere may alter from time to time.

Right: The fossil remains of animals such as this extinct woolly mammoth have been found near London. The climate this animal needed was very different from that which London enjoys today.

WORLD CLIMATIC ZONES

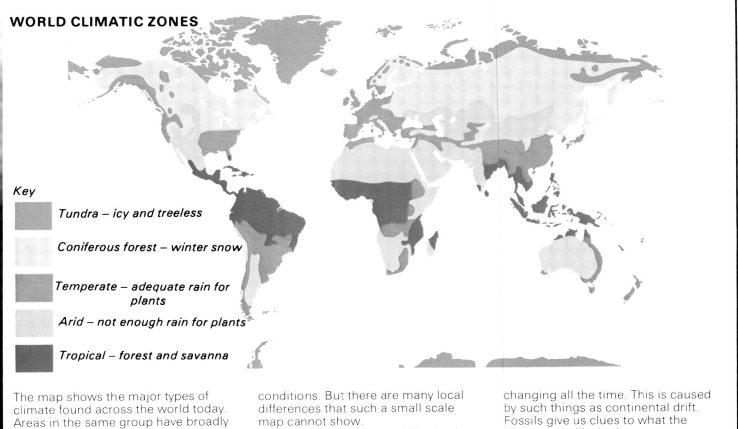

Key

Tundra – icy and treeless

Coniferous forest – winter snow

Temperate – adequate rain for plants

Arid – not enough rain for plants

Tropical – forest and savanna

The map shows the major types of climate found across the world today. Areas in the same group have broadly similar temperature and rainfall conditions. But there are many local differences that such a small scale map cannot show.

The climate of the world is slowly changing all the time. This is caused by such things as continental drift. Fossils give us clues to what the climate was like in the past.

The life-giving soil

In some tropical areas steep hillsides are terraced to retain pockets of soil. The banks must be carefully maintained like those below, or heavy rains will cause gullying, as shown in the picture above.

Soil is the substance in which plants grow. It provides them with food, in the form of minerals and moisture. Plants are the food of all other living things, making sugar and starch through photosynthesis.

Thin cover

Soil forms a thin cover to the surface rocks and is made up of fragments weathered from this bedrock mixed with humus, which is the decomposed remains of plants and minute animals.

In the first place, the soil is built up by hardy plants able to colonize a bare surface. These make direct use of minerals from the rocks. Their filaments and roots anchor the rock fragments together. As they die and decay, the humus layer of the soil builds up, and other plants can grow. More plants, more humus, more soil organisms arrive, including earthworms which keep the mixture well stirred.

Minerals in soil

In some tropical parts of the world soil has been forming for millions

Below: Bare rocks must first be colonized by "pioneer" plants before soil is formed. Hardy grasses are colonizing these bare rocks high in the rugged Andes Mountains in South America.

of years, and is now so thick that the bedrock is too far below the surface for plant roots to reach it. So, most of the important minerals, nitrates, phosphates, potassium, iron and calcium, are in the living vegetation. Only when something, or a part of it, dies, are the essential minerals it contains free to be used again. In the natural world nothing is ever wasted.

A hectare of soil may contain over ten tonnes of living organisms. A fallen leaf becomes food for a host of nature's dustmen: fungi, bacteria and other decomposers that return the vital minerals to the soil.

Erosion

Unfortunately, people often upset nature's finely balanced system for replenishing the soil. In order to grow crops, they remove the natural cover of vegetation. This destroys its store of vital minerals. The bare ground becomes exposed to the sun, wind and rain. It may be baked hard, blown or washed away. Soils that were once highly fertile may turn to dust. Man's ignorance has caused soil erosion to devastate vast areas of the earth's surface.

If soil is eroded away because the land is badly managed, a dust bowl results. Farming is then impossible. Soil can be worn out if

the same crops are grown in it year after year. Its minerals, the nutrients for plants, are used up. They must be constantly replaced, either by the dead plants and fallen leaves, by returning minerals to the soil or by the farmer applying artificial fertilizers.

Shifting agriculture

In many areas of tropical rain forest, shifting agriculture is practised. Trees are cut down and burned, and for a few years the plot can yield a good crop of yams, rice or other vegetables. But soon the soil loses its vital plant nutrients as they are washed away by the tropical rainstorms. Rain can now reach the soil because the sheltering trees have been removed.

The soil can no longer produce a successful crop, and the farmer moves on to destroy another area. It will take many years for the forest to regrow and for the soil to be rich again.

Problems in America

In America the soil has suffered severely from misuse.

Settlers from Europe tried to farm with methods that suited the European climate. When they applied these to the conditions of the U.S.A. they were doomed to failure. They ploughed and felled trees where they should not have done. Soil was exposed to the ravages of wind and rain, and was blown and washed away. In the states of Oklahoma, Kansas and North and South Dakota the drought-ridden 1930s became known as "the dustbowl" years.

Wide-ranging effects

Soil erosion has several effects. If the farmer can no longer grow crops he must leave the land or starve. Mud chokes lakes and reservoirs, pollutes rivers and spoils them for wildlife, sport and water supplies. Soil erosion is still going on in many places, but people have learned from past mistakes. If soil is properly treated erosion can be reduced or prevented.

Prevention

One answer is to use fertilizers regularly, but another is to practise crop rotation. This means growing a different crop each year over three or four years. Plants such as clover have roots with nodules containing bacteria that make nitrates. These improve the soil, and stay in it for a long time after the crop has been harvested. Many farmers grow clover and other crops in rotation. The fields are also left fallow (without crops) for some periods to clean the land.

Some grasses help to prevent soil erosion. Their roots bind the loose particles of sandy soil together. Trees will act as wind breaks, and they also help to stop soil being washed down steep slopes. Building terraces on hillsides keeps pockets of soil in place, and ploughing along the side of a hill, instead of up and down, helps to stop soil being washed away.

New land is constantly being used for agriculture, as swamps and marshlands are drained, and deserts are irrigated.

Below: This tropical swamp is being reclaimed for agriculture. Draining of wetland areas, and irrigating deserts helps to offset the losses of land caused by erosion.

Above: To prevent wind erosion, strips of grass have been planted to break its force and bind the soil particles.

Below: Severe drought dries and cracks the soil, exposing it to attack by winds and the next rain that falls.

The first life

The earth was formed about 4,600 million years ago but it was another 1,200 million years, during which the rocks cooled and the seas formed, before anything that could be said to be living appeared.

The seas and air contained the chemical ingredients from which living things are made – carbon, oxygen, nitrogen, hydrogen and others.

Special conditions were needed before these chemicals could become linked together as molecules of protein able to reproduce themselves.

The energy supply for this process was provided by sunlight, volcanic eruptions and electrical storms which welded the chemicals together to become simple living cells similar to the bacteria and blue-green algae of today.

Early life forms

After the development of the first living cells, another 2,800 million years went by before more complex life forms such as corals, sponges and jellyfish appeared.

Nothing lived on land until about 390 million years ago, when simple plants began to grow in tropical swamps. As time went on the first fish developed, with backbones to which muscles were attached. A few crawled out onto land and developed primitive lungs. Slowly, their fins modified to form legs and they became the first amphibians.

Reptiles evolved from amphibians. Some developed to become the dinosaurs that dominated the earth for 140 million years until

they suddenly became extinct 65 million years ago. That left the land free for the evolving insects, birds and mammals to take over. One of the most recent species to have evolved is man himself.

The scene below attempts to show what the world looked like 300 million years ago in tropical areas. There were giant horsetails and tree ferns that fell into the swamps when they died. They became preserved as fossils, and are mined today as coal.

Evolution

In 1859 Charles Darwin published his revolutionary book *On The Origin of Species* which set out his evidence and ideas for his "Theory of Evolution".

Creation

Today, we accept most of Darwin's ideas but at the time they upset many people, for it was generally believed that each plant and animal species had been created separately by God. Darwin denied this, suggesting instead that all the present-day species, including man, had evolved by a slow process of continual change from primitive species that had lived in the past.

Darwin noticed that individuals of the same species are frequently slightly different from one another, varying in eye colour, leg length and so on. Offspring inherit these features, and all other traits, from their parents.

Survival

The ability to survive is most important. An individual might have a special feature that will give it a better chance of living longer, such as a camouflage or skill in escaping from enemies. A longer life provides it with more time to breed and pass on its advantage. Its offspring are likely to compete successfully with those that do not have the advantage. Only the fittest survive.

Evolution is the constant improvement of living things by natural selection. The environment is always changing, so living things must also change.

Variation and adaptation

Genes form a part of a living cell that passes on a mass of messages to make sure that, when living things reproduce, the offspring resembles its parents. A variation in the genes, due to parents of two different species, will cause a new feature to appear in their offspring. This can be a disadvantage, in which case the new form will soon die. But if it is an improvement, the

Above: A sabre-toothed tiger. Like the woolly mammoth it probably became extinct about 30,000 years ago, unable to withstand the competition from people as they evolved as very skilful hunters.

Below: Darwin suggested that the long necks of giraffes slowly evolved as "improvements" on their fellows by natural selection. The tallest animals survived as they could reach higher branches for more food.

new form will continue, and help to create a new species.

If an animal or plant cannot adapt to meet changing conditions or the arrival of a new competing species, it dies out. The dodo is an example of this. It was a flightless bird, once common in Mauritius. Man arrived in 1598, bringing predators that hunted the bird and destroyed its habitat. By 1688, the

Above: Charles Darwin shown as an ape in a 19th-century cartoon. His theories that people, like other living things, had evolved, and that apes were their ancestors, were greeted with uproar. But Darwin was broadly right, and far more evidence has been found to support his ideas.

dodo was extinct. This is how the saying "as dead as a dodo" arose. Fossils of plants and animals – their shape and structure and the places where they are found – are all clues to evolution.

In the 1830s, Darwin went round the world on H.M.S. *Beagle*. He was particularly fascinated by the animals of the Galapagos Islands, remote islands west of South America. Here there were animals similar to those on the mainland, but many of them had marked differences.

Finches
Darwin found a number of new species, including 14 different finches. Each finch was adapted to a different aspect of the local environment, some eating seeds, others insects or fruit. The woodpecker finch used a thorn to winkle grubs out of holes in trees and cacti. Each species had a different shaped beak and varied in colour to suit its life-style.

Darwin concluded that their ancestors were finches from South America, which must have travelled to Galapagos, perhaps blown off course in a storm. They multiplied and slowly evolved their own improvements to suit the varied environments of their new home.

The peppered moth
The peppered moth is a good example of natural selection. Until the 19th century, the usual form of this moth was pale and speckled, a perfect camouflage against lichen-covered bark. When Britain became an industrial nation, trees near towns were covered in soot from polluted smoke. The pale moths showed up and became easy prey to birds. Occasionally, however, a black moth was produced. These were better camouflaged against sooty bark, and survived. Today almost all the peppered moths in industrial areas are of the black form, although the pale, speckled variety is still common in

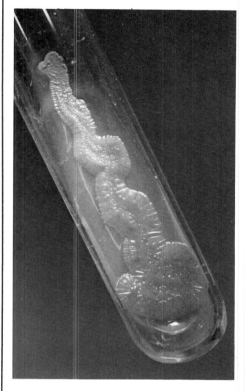

Above: Natural selection is usually a very slow process, but bacteria reproduce very fast indeed, as can be seen from the clock below. The test tube contains a colony of bacteria with several million cells. As some can divide every half hour, a single bacterium will multiply to become one million in ten hours. Penicillin kills most bacteria, but if one individual bacterium, during the course of reproduction, can resist the penicillin, it will pass this "improvement" on to its offspring. In their turn they will divide and produce many millions of individuals that can resist penicillin.

If all the members of a species were exactly alike, survival would be a matter of chance. Only the fittest are most likely to survive and pass on their advantages to their offspring.

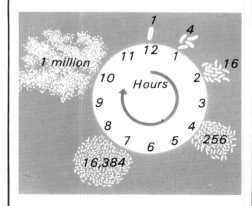

clean, rural areas. Natural selection depends on the chance production of individuals with new features which will help them to survive.

Man
If other living things had evolved from more primitive ancestors, what about man? Darwin suggested that modern man and apes share a common ancestor. Since Darwin's time there has been more and more evidence to back his theory.

Man has also helped in the process of evolution. All the cultivated crops and flowers, domestic pets, and farm livestock have been bred from wild stock. For centuries man has been selecting certain varieties for breeding, to make a rose of a special colour or a pig that grows faster. This is selective breeding, evolution in action.

Below: The two different forms of peppered moth can be seen on birch bark. Against this background the light, speckled form is hard to see. However, the dark, sooty-coloured form is very obvious, and becomes easy food for a hungry bird.

The world's plant life

All living things depend on green plants, for plants alone are able to trap and store the energy in sunlight and make it into food. They do this in the cells of green leaves by a process called "photosynthesis".

Hydrogen from water, carbon dioxide from air, and nutrients from soil are all combined, and the energy is stored in the form of sugars. These are used by the plant to grow and make roots and stems, flowers and fruits. Plants are eaten by animals, which may in turn be eaten by other animals.

Plant diversity

Plants take many different forms – from tall trees to duckweed on a pond. Evolution has made sure that there are few places left on earth where nothing can grow. But plants must have water in liquid form and they must have light. Apart from parts of deserts, the only places without plants are those where the ice never melts, and the ocean depths where light cannot penetrate. Wherever there is potential for growth there is some living thing to exploit it.

A plant's root anchors it to the same spot for most of its life. This means that it cannot move away from bad weather conditions as an animal can, and must survive some other way. A plant may have to live through a cold winter, or a period of drought, and in both these cases, liquid water, which a plant needs, is not available. One way it can survive is as a seed, inside a tough skin. Another is to store food during the better times of year. Potatoes and daffodil bulbs are both food stores.

In arid areas some plants survive long, dry periods by storing food and water in swollen stems. Thorns take the place of leaves as they do not allow much water to evaporate, and a grazing animal is not likely to eat them. After a rare rain storm, seeds and bulbs burst into life and the desert blooms for a short time.

Tropical forests

Trees are the largest plants on earth. Their spreading leaves and branches are supported by trunks,

Right: Plants must have water, and in deserts plants such as cacti survive times of drought by storing water in swollen stems.

Below: Grasses are a vital part of our diet. Today's cereals have been produced by selectively breeding wild forms.

Below: In the cold winds of the Arctic winter tundra plants do not grow. In the short summer they must grow, flower and seed quickly for this is the one way to survive winter's ice.

thickened with wood. They are at their most spectacular in the hot, wet, tropical rain forests as in the Amazon Basin, where they are often more than 30 metres tall.

At ground level the forest is dark and damp, smelling of decaying matter. Overhead the branches and leaves form a dense canopy. This traps most of the light, so that little can grow on the forest floor. To survive, smaller plants and herbs must get to the top, and many of these live high in the canopy as epiphytes on tree branches. Long creepers, or lianas, trail to the ground, entangling the branches.

Only when a giant forest tree dies are seedlings able to struggle upwards, as a new shaft of light penetrates the forest gloom. One by one the competitors fail in their race upwards, and only the fittest survives.

Forests in temperate zones
In colder climates, trees do not grow in the winter months. In Britain most of the original forest cover has been removed, but in surviving woods, broad-leaved

Below: A forest in Canada with a mixture of evergreen and deciduous trees. Evergreen conifers are ready to begin growth as soon as spring arrives.

deciduous trees abound.

In autumn they lose their leaves so that they will not lose water through them while it is in short supply in frosty weather. Deciduous trees can only grow when they are in leaf and, each year, growth rings appear in the timber of their trunks. By counting these rings it is possible to find out how old a tree is. Wide rings indicate a good summer when the tree grew well, and narrow rings a season when there was little growth.

Evergreens
South of the Arctic Circle a broad belt of coniferous trees stretches across the continents of Europe, Asia and North America. They are farther north than the deciduous forests, and farther away from the warming influence of the sea. The area experiences long, cold winters and in summer there is not enough time for the trees to grow new leaves and start a new growth cycle. However, as they are evergreen, they have needle-shaped leaves to avoid water loss. When spring arrives the trees can begin growth straight away.

Both tropical and coniferous forests provide large amounts of commercial timber.

Animal life in cool climates

All animals depend on the process of photosynthesis that can only take place in a green plant.

Many animals eat nothing but plants and are called herbivores. These include rodents, deer, gorillas, cattle and geese. Herbivores have adapted to their way of life. A cow's teeth and digestive system are able to chop and grind grass and break down the cellulose of plant cells.

The energy first trapped in a green leaf during photosynthesis is passed along a living food chain. An example might be: grass – caterpillar – shrew – owl – buzzard.

When an animal dies it decomposes and the minerals and energy of which it is made are recycled.

Flesh-eaters

Flesh-eating birds and animals are called carnivores and include shrews, owls, foxes and wolves. Carnivores usually eat herbivores, but sometimes they eat others of their kind. (For example, a buzzard will eat a dead fox.)

Badgers and man are examples of animals that eat both plants and animals and are called omnivores.

The food-rich oceans

The world's greatest storehouse of food is contained in the seas. Minute plants (phytoplankton) floating near the surface are eaten by tiny floating animals, called the zooplankton. These, in turn, are eaten by small fish, which are preyed on by larger fish. Surprisingly, some large fish and whales – including the largest animal that has ever lived, the blue whale – feed on nothing but plankton.

Adaptations

Adaptation to the environment and a way of life is as vital to animals as it is to plants, and is the result of evolution. For example, predators (carnivorous animals that hunt others), have evolved to make themselves efficient. Owls hunt at night, so have large sensitive eyes to see in poor light and silent wings to enable them to

Above: The elephant seal has a thick layer of blubber as insulation against extreme cold.

Right: The fish-eating razorbills chase their prey by swimming under water using their wings as flippers.

Below right: The Arctic hare is both insulated against the cold and concealed from predators by its thick, white fur coat.

creep up on their prey unheard.

In their turn shrews, often preyed on by owls, are equipped to avoid capture. They feed in the dark amongst rank vegetation and are dark coloured. If shrews could be seen easily by owls, they would quickly be killed and become extinct.

Animals that live in cold climates must be specially adapted to survive the winter weather. Sea-dwellers such as seals and whales are insulated by a thick layer of blubber, while the Arctic hare keeps warm inside a coat of thick fur. In the winter snows the hare grows a snow-white coat as camouflage against predators like the Arctic fox, but in summer when there is no snow the hare changes to a grey-brown colour to match the bare ground.

Close relatives

The domestic dog and the wild red

fox are closely related but have very different histories. For 10,000 years dogs have lived with people both as pets and as working animals. The wild ancestor of today's many breeds of domestic dog is now extinct, but it was probably like a small wolf.

Selective breeding

By deliberately choosing the features that pleased them, like the ability to hunt or act as a guard dog, pleasant colour, size or shape, people have produced many varieties of dog. Man has chosen those that are fittest to survive and breed.

Like the dog, the wild fox is a carnivore, and is well equipped as a predator with a sensitive nose, sharp teeth and stealthy behaviour. It hunts at night, eating small animals such as rabbits and rats, and sometimes poultry.

In recent years, some foxes have changed their habits and they are becoming common in towns where they scavenge among rubbish. Perhaps a new variety of fox will evolve as a result of this new behaviour and change of habitat.

Above: The domestic dog has been bred selectively for centuries to give today's many varieties. The wild red fox has all the features of a predator.

Below: A life among trees means a squirrel must climb well. An adult may carry its young.

Woodland animals

Animals that live in woodland must also be adapted to their kind of environment. Woodpeckers, for example, have chisel-like bills for splitting nuts and hacking into wood in search of grubs or for making a nest-hole. Unlike most birds they have two toes pointing forwards and two backwards to help grip onto the tree bark. Their tail feathers are stiffened to give another form of support.

Squirrels are also tree dwellers. Their sharp claws are an ideal aid for running up and down vertical tree trunks. The red squirrel's colour is good camouflage against the rusty coloured bark of a pine tree. Its long bushy tail helps it to balance as it performs the acrobatics that are needed when it is travelling through the branches. The tail acts like a tight-rope walker's balancing pole.

Squirrels feed mainly on plant food including nuts and shoots. Britain's native red squirrel has become rare because of competition from the grey squirrel, introduced from North America.

Animal life in hot climates

The African tropical grasslands are known as savanna. For most of the year the climate is hot but there are distinct wet and dry seasons. The grasses may grow to heights of two to three metres in the wet season, and scattered clumps of deciduous trees may flourish. But in the dry season the trees lose their leaves, and the grasses dry up and wither.

In Africa the savanna supports large herds of herbivores – zebra, antelope and wildebeeste. Giraffes find food on the upper branches of trees while smaller animals find shade and cover below. All are forced to roam in search of fresh supplies of food and water in times of drought and often gather near water-holes.

Cheating the predators

These herbivores are often killed and eaten by predators including lions and leopards and the "hangers-on" – the scavenging jackals and hyaenas. To avoid them, the grazing animals have evolved a number of defences. Antelopes, for example, possess long sharp horns, long legs for running fast and effective camouflage. Zebras

Left: A leopard is a typical predator of the savanna. It is a member of the cat family. It kills only twice a week.

Below: The Arabian dromedary stores food and water in its hump. Its large feet stop it sinking into the desert sand.

have black and white stripes which may help to confuse the eye of a lion, its main enemy.

The predators are also provided with a camouflage that can help them mount a surprise attack. For example, leopards are dappled with spots which can look like the shimmer of sunlight and shade in the branches of a tree.

Large herbivores, like the elephant and rhinoceros, have little to fear from lions and other meat-eaters; their main threat is man. Hunters illegally kill such animals for ivory and horn, and forest fires and man's herds of cattle and goats have reduced the amount of savanna available.

Life in the desert

Desert regions support a surprisingly large variety of animal life with some amazing adaptations to an arid environment. Many desert animals are only active at night and survive the heat of the day in cool burrows. Others, like the camel, store food and water as fat deposits inside their humps. There are many insects, some carnivorous, which provide food for lizards and birds. Even in the harshest surroundings, complex food chains exist.

Below: The African elephant's trunk is perfect for collecting its food – leaves, grasses and roots. The elephant is too large for most predators and has no natural enemies other than man.

Life at the top

In the tropical rain forests many animals live their lives high in the leaf canopy where there is plenty of light and food. Frogs even live in the tree tops! The frequent heavy rain and mist keep the skins of tree frogs moist and there are often pools of trapped rain where they can spawn.

There is an abundance of insect life in tropical rain forests, which provides food for the frogs. Many of these insects eat leaves, but some are predators. Both frogs and insects are sometimes remarkably camouflaged to avoid detection. There are some butterflies and moths which mimic leaves, and caterpillars that resemble twigs. There is even a species of spider that looks exactly like a bird dropping!

Parrots and other brightly coloured birds are common in the tree tops. They forage for nuts and fruit. As their bright colours might attract the attention of a predator, parrots nest in holes in the bark of trees.

Some mammals also live up in the trees. Monkeys are particularly well adapted – some use their tail as an extra hand. They are very agile and can move about among the branches at great speed. At the opposite speed extreme is the tree sloth.

Above: Tropical rain forests are the home of the colourful and appealing tree frog. A tree frog can change colour to match its surroundings.

Above right: The kiwi is a flightless bird that is found only in the forests of New Zealand.

Separate development

Australia and New Zealand are home to several kinds of animals not found anywhere else in the world. These include the marsupials, or pouched mammals. They became isolated from the rest of the world at an early stage when the continents drifted apart.

In most parts of the world evolution produced a new type of animal that was more successful than the marsupials. These were the placental mammals. They gradually replaced pouched animals. Only in Australasia and parts of America have the marsupials lived on due to isolation.

Another unique creature lives in the forests of New Zealand – the kiwi. It is one of the few surviving flightless birds. Fossils show that such birds once lived in several other parts of the world.

Above right: Brightly coloured birds like this macaw live in the canopy of the tropical forest.

Right: A gall wasp lays its eggs inside a tree bud which the grub then eats.

The first men

Man is a newcomer among life on earth. The fossil record only shows man-like creatures during the last 14 million years.

Man and the modern apes share a common ancestor, but over millions of years they developed quite differently. Man's far distant ancestor, *Ramapithecus*, was a small, ape-like animal that could walk upright. He came down from the trees to live on the open grasslands. From this beginning, two types of ape-men developed.

Australopithecus, who lived about four million years ago, had a small brain, but *Homo habilis*, who lived alongside, was more intelligent. He learned to make simple stone tools, using sharp edges for cutting and scraping.

Australopithecus died out about one million years ago but the descendants of *Homo habilis* gave rise to a new species – *Homo erectus*. His brain was not as large as that of modern man, but he walked upright. He lived in caves and formed hunting parties to trap and kill animals such as elephants.

Modern man, or *Homo sapiens*, is thought to have evolved about 250,000 years ago, during the Ice Age. At Neanderthal in Germany, remains show that he lived as a hunter. His main prey were woolly mammoths, reindeer and bison, but he also attacked huge cavebears. He survived the cold by wearing furs, living in huts and caves and using fire to cook meat and keep warm. He made tools and weapons of flint and bone.

Cro-Magnon man moved into Europe from Africa about 40,000 years ago and replaced Neanderthal man. His physical appearance was very like our own and he was a skilful hunter. He chipped and carved tools from stone and bone, and decorated the walls of caves with paintings.

Modern man owes his success to the evolution of special features not shared by other animals. Walking upright helps him see a long way and forward-facing eyes help him judge distance. He has a well-developed brain and he communicates with others by speech and facial expressions. His hands are also well adapted for gripping the tools he makes.

Left: Neanderthal man had to fight huge cave bears in order to take over the caves where they lived. Bear skins were used to make warm clothing for the winter.

The rise of towns

About 8000 B.C. a discovery was made that completely altered the lives of men. People learned how to grow their own crops, which meant that for the first time they could settle in one place. Until this time humans lived by hunting animals or gathering berries, fruits and nuts, often moving from one place to another in search of new food supplies.

This agricultural revolution probably first took place somewhere in the Middle East, perhaps in the fertile valley between the Tigris and Euphrates rivers. Wild wheat and barley grew here and formed the staple diet of the early farmer. At about the same time he started to domesticate animals such as goats and cattle.

Living together

The new way of life brought other changes. Hunting animals and gathering berries seldom produced enough food to allow people to live in large groups. Meat could not then be kept for long. Grain, however, could be stored throughout the year, and the crop could be tended by a small number of men. This food surplus released many from the need to produce their own food. For example, the best village potter could spend all his time producing pots in exchange for food. In this way a whole range of specialist jobs were developed. Living in one place meant that permanent homes could be built using mud, stone, and wood.

Man also had to organize his life to fit the seasons, with times for planting and harvesting. Villagers needed a leader to make decisions and distribute the food surplus. Trade developed so that materials not available locally could be brought in from outside.

The rule of the Pharaohs

As the new ideas spread, a centre of agriculture and civilization arose in the fertile valley of the River Nile controlled by god-kings (Pharaohs) and religious leaders.

The soils of the Nile valley were

Above: A busy medieval market town. Many people from nearby villages came to visit the market which was held in a wide street. They could buy from the stalls or be entertained by acrobats and other street performers.

fertile and very suitable for growing cereals. As the Nile flooded each year spreading silt over the soil, its fertility was kept up.

The Pharaohs organized the building of great palaces and monuments. Many of these, including the Pyramids, are still standing today. They are symbols of the might and wealth of the Pharaohs. It was a time when the art of the craftsman flourished.

The Far East

Not everyone believes that the agricultural revolution first took place in the Middle East. Some historians favour the Far East, perhaps India or China, for both were early centres of rice cultivation.

But wherever the first farming settlements arose, one thing is certain. A food surplus left men free to invent new and better tools which led to an easier way of life. For the first time the human brain could begin to prove its potential for working out problems. It was not long before the wheel was invented, and craftsmen learned to make use of metals.

The growth of the city

Advances in growing crops and the domestication of farm animals continued. As the idea of agriculture spread, towns were built in many parts of the settled world. In the Middle East, military and trading centres were established by the Phoenicians and Greeks. From the third century B.C. caravans traded along the "Great Silk Route" that stretched from Turkestan to China, and towns grew at oasis sites. As the Roman armies conquered Europe they built fortified towns from which to rule the local people. Their efficient roads linked centre to centre.

But when the Roman Empire collapsed and the Dark Ages began, many towns declined.

They did not revive until the eleventh century when medieval market towns, often protected by walls, spread across Europe. Few had more than 10,000 people but those with favoured sites, such as ports, grew at the expense of others, attracting craftsmen and merchants. Some became religious centres with great cathedrals, others were university cities.

This process continued until the 18th century with its great advances in agriculture – crop rotation, fertilizers, improved live-

stock and machinery. Fewer and fewer people were needed to produce more food.

The Industrial Revolution had begun, with coal its chief source of energy, as steam power was harnessed for railways, factories and ships. The new industrial centres grew rapidly, and were often situated on coalfields. Railways, trams, buses and later the motor car enabled towns to expand.

Further developments in trade and commerce created today's vast commercial cities, such as London and New York, relying on fast international air services and telecommunications.

The population explosion

In 8000 B.C., when man first discovered how to grow crops, fewer than five million people lived on earth (less than half the number that live in Greater London now). Today, the total world population is just over the 4,000 million mark and could reach 7,000 million by the year A.D. 2000. But as recently as A.D. 1800 the total was only 1,000 million. Why has there been such a dramatic increase – a "population explosion" – over the last couple of hundred years?

Limits to population growth

Until man became a farmer his numbers were severely limited by diseases, attack by predators, food shortages and the problems of constantly moving from place to place. Growing crops meant that he had to settle and he built more permanent homes that could be defended. But even with these advantages the population of the world increased only slowly due to a lack of knowledge of medicine and hygiene. Plagues, such as the Black Death that swept through Europe during the 14th century, kept numbers down. Infant mortality was high. In Shakespearean London fewer than 300 of every 1,000 people born reached their fifteenth birthday.

The dramatic population increase since A.D. 1800 coincided with the Industrial Revolution which brought with it a complete change in the way that most people lived.

Effects of industrial growth

Large numbers left the farms to work in the new factories. As transport and communications improved, trade developed with continents such as North America and Australasia, where vast areas were opened up for agriculture. This, and new farming techniques, produced an even greater surplus to feed the growing work force.

But perhaps the most important cause of the population explosion was the rapid advance in the fight against disease. Infant mortality has been greatly reduced and diseases such as malaria have decreased in tropical areas. Housing conditions have improved and modern public water supplies and disposal of sewage have wiped out cholera and typhoid in most parts of the world. Outbreaks of most infectious diseases can be controlled by vaccination programmes. More people survive to have children and people are living

Below: In western countries today it is rare for people to have such large families as the one shown here. Two children per family are generally needed to keep the population of a country static.

Below: The world map shows that there are very high concentrations of people in Asia, but fewer in Australia, Africa and America. But even in a country like the U.S.A. people are not evenly spread. The most densely populated regions are cities and industrial areas.

Right: One reason for the population explosion has been the increase in life expectancy as the rate of infant mortality has fallen. When large numbers of babies were expected to die, people had more children so that at least some survived. Modern knowledge of medicine and hygiene has enabled more babies to survive to have children in their turn, and people now live longer. In most western countries family planning is practised and family sizes are kept small. In many developing countries, however, families are still large. Due to modern medicine facilities, more children survive so that the populations of these countries continue to grow rapidly.

The graph shows just how rapidly the population of the world is increasing. The rate of increase was fairly slow until about 1800 when the population figures rose sharply as a result of the many scientific and medical discoveries that took place around that time.

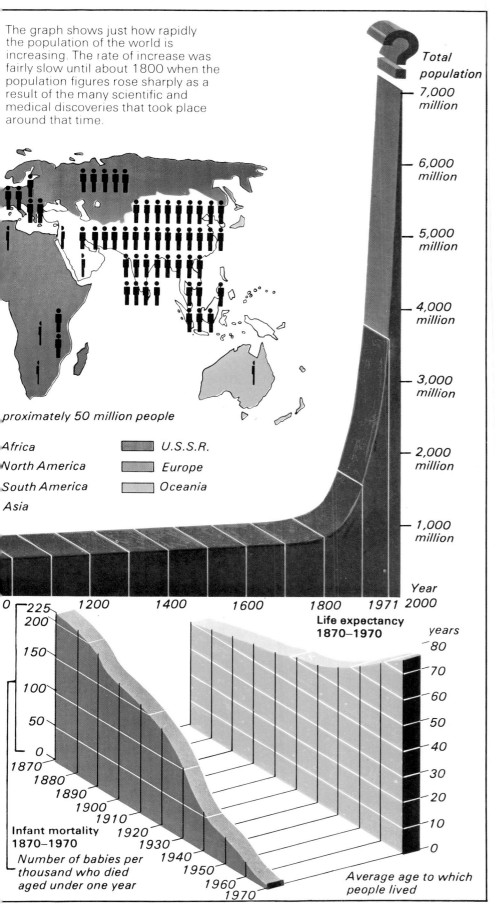

proximately 50 million people

Africa   U.S.S.R.
North America   Europe
South America   Oceania
Asia

Total population

7,000 million

6,000 million

5,000 million

4,000 million

3,000 million

2,000 million

1,000 million

Year

0   225   1200   1400   1600   1800   1971 2000

Life expectancy 1870–1970   years

200   80

150   70

100   60

50   50

0   40

1870   30

1880   20

1890

1900   10

1910   0

Infant mortality 1870–1970   1920

1930

Number of babies per thousand who died aged under one year   1940

1950

1960   *Average age to which people lived*

1970

Above: To keep down the rapid increase in population in countries such as India, people are urged by posters to plan the size of their families.

much longer than previously.

People are not evenly distributed over the land areas of the earth. Desert, mountainous and cold regions are generally sparsely populated. Other areas, particularly some broad river valleys in Asia – the Ganges in India and the Yangtze Kiang and Hwang Ho in China – are very densely populated.

The strain of high population

In countries which have only recently had the advantages of modern medical knowledge and improved standards of hygiene, birth rates are often very high. Reduced infant mortality and improved general health have increased life expectancy. Suddenly these countries are faced with large numbers of young people and even more who are too old to work. They all need food and living space. The young need schools and jobs. This puts a tremendous strain on resources; so the population increase has to be slowed. India publicly encourages family planning.

People on the move

As far back in history as we know about, people have always moved from place to place. Early man evolved as a hunter and gatherer, probably first in Africa, where he led a nomadic life, constantly searching for fresh supplies of food. Now, people occupy all the habitable areas on earth. The highest mountains have been climbed and the ocean floors explored, while a handful of astronauts have even travelled from earth to the moon and back! There is no other animal as adaptable as we are. Even so, people tend to concentrate in those places where it is easiest to make a living and today these are often the world's large urban areas.

Reasons for moving on

Some people have no choice about whether to leave their home and move elsewhere. War, famine or some other disaster may force them to seek a new place to live.

In the 18th and 19th centuries thousands of negroes were taken from Africa to work as slaves on plantations in the West Indies and the southern states of the U.S.A. In 1845 and 1846, blight totally destroyed the Irish potato crop, on which so many families depended. Over one million people died but a million more emigrated, particularly to North America. Similarly in the 1920s and 30s, drought and soil erosion in some mid-American states forced thousands of farmers to abandon the land, and seek new lives in such places as California. And in the early 20th century, Jewish people in Russia and Eastern Europe were forced to settle in other parts of Europe and North America.

Right: This painting by Grant Wood depicts the typical farmers of rural America. They are descended from European immigrants fleeing persecution and hardship.

Depopulation

The prospect of better opportunities elsewhere is a strong lure for many people. Since the Industrial Revolution the more remote rural areas of industrial nations have suffered depopulation, good examples being the Scottish Highlands and Massif Central in France. People from such regions are pushed into moving because life is so hard on their farms and the climate so harsh. The prospect of better wages, housing, education, entertainment and social conditions in the rapidly growing urban areas is not easy to resist. The young people head for the towns leaving the rural areas with an ageing population.

During the 1960s the economy of Europe "boomed" and industrial regions attracted many "guest workers", particularly from Southern Europe. By 1975 it was estimated that West Germany had over four million foreign workers. The United Kingdom has tended to attract migrants from the Commonwealth countries and Pakistan. In the U.S.A., Mexicans and Puerto Ricans have been similarly attracted, and cities like New York have large concentrations of recent immigrants.

In developed countries the move to the towns has been going on for

Above: Rush-hour commuters of an Indian city. Workers travel to work over ever greater distances.

nearly two centuries but it has only been happening more recently in developing nations. With their rapidly growing populations, the countryside of such countries as India and Brazil is rife with unemployment. People therefore flock to the towns, and "shanty towns" of shacks, built of little more than rotten wood and corrugated iron, mushroom overnight. Squalor and disease are rampant.

Commuters

While the central areas of cities have become overcrowded, improved transport systems have encouraged those that can afford it to move to places outside the cities. Most large urban areas of the world are surrounded by suburbs, the dormitories of the city workers. Every morning and evening they clog the traffic arteries – the roads and the railways – in their rush to and from work. Commuting has become the daily pattern of life for many.

However, the advantages of suburban living outweigh the disadvantages. Property is more spacious and has countryside nearby.

In most developed nations more

Above: The shanty town squalor contrasts sharply with high-rise flats in modern Bombay, India.

than 70 per cent of the population live in towns and suburbs. It is hardly surprising, therefore, that most people seek a change of environment for their holidays and leisure time. The better off may have a second home, chalet or caravan in the countryside to which they "escape" at weekends, while tourism has brought money to many rural areas and encouraged more people to stay there.

Today, leisure and the holiday industry have become big business. Large sums of money are spent advertising package tours that encourage people to "migrate" to warmer climates for their holiday.

A place to retire to

Many people uproot themselves yet again when they retire. Large numbers of elderly people are attracted to coastal resorts to spend the last part of their lives there. They look forward to more pleasant surroundings and a healthier climate.

Feeding the world

Growing sufficient food for a rapidly increasing population is one of the major problems facing the world's farmers today. People in various parts of the world have very different diets, and many live close to starvation.

Essential food

There is usually one staple food that forms the bulk of the diet in any region. In China and India this is rice; in Europe, bread and potatoes. But people require other essentials and their staple diet is supplemented by proteins, fats, carbohydrates and vitamins provided by fish, meat, dairy products, vegetables and fruit.

If you look on the shelves in your local supermarket you will discover that your daily food comes from many different countries. Tea from Assam, India, coffee from Brazil or Kenya, lamb from New Zealand, dates from Tunisia – the list seems endless. Even the flour from which your bread is made was probably grown in North America. Food and agriculture are major world trades, especially in the western world, and methods have changed greatly in the last 50 years.

Keeping the land fertile

Vital minerals are taken from the soil by crops and these have to be replaced to avoid soil exhaustion and erosion. In the past, soil fertility was kept up by crop rotation. Crops take different minerals from the soil. By changing the crop planted in a field each year, minerals used by one crop were replaced by another. A field was also rested every three years. Clover played an essential part in crop rotation as its roots put nitrates back into the soil. Manure, seaweed and guano (sea-bird droppings from South America) were also used. Today chemical fertilizers that contain nitrates, phosphates and other minerals are widely used. These, together with selective breeding of plants and animals to give very high yield

Right: By terracing hillsides the amount of farmland is increased. These terraces were constructed centuries ago, but today they are planted with new high-yielding varieties of rice.

varieties, have helped farmers to produce the increasing quantities of food needed for the world's growing population.

Increased production has also been made possible by controlling fungus and insect pests by the use of chemical pesticides, sometimes spread by crop-spraying aircraft.

The amount of land available for farming has been slightly reduced in many parts of the world by soil erosion and by the spread of cities. But in other places new land has been created by reclamation. Swamps and other wetlands have been drained and land reclaimed from the sea, especially in the Netherlands. In some mountainous areas, steep hillsides have been terraced to retain flat pockets of soil. In deserts, agriculture has been made possible by irrigation.

Modern farming

Increasingly, the modern farmer relies on machines. The tractor has replaced the horse and electric milking machines have vastly increased the speed of milking a dairy herd. Combine harvesters must be used in large fields to gather the crops efficiently. New techniques of food storage, from quick drying to deep freeze, ensure that food reaches the shops in good condition.

It is interesting to note that, in most of the advanced countries, the number of people that are actively employed in growing food has been decreasing. From being a simple way of life, farming has become a highly organized and complex business.

Above right: In the Netherlands much land has been reclaimed from the sea. Windmills or diesel pumps are used to pump water off the land.

Right: Irrigated desert areas can produce valuable crops.

Conditions for farming

By no means all the earth's land surface is farmed. Like the human population, good farmland is unevenly distributed. Intensive cultivation can only take place where conditions of soil, slope and climate are favourable. Enough food may be produced from a square kilometre to feed hundreds of people. Examples include most of Denmark and the "corn belt" of the U.S.A.

Other areas produce very little. These include tropical rain forests, which are difficult to clear; areas of very low temperature or rainfall; and mountainous areas with steep, exposed slopes and thin soils. In places like these, barely enough food is grown to feed the farmer and his family.

Sometimes the introduction of new varieties of plants and animals makes it possible to farm a region that was previously unsuitable. However, there are farmers who cling to traditional crops and methods and do not get the best yields from their land. If countries like India are to feed their rapidly growing populations, new farming ideas must be adopted. A programme to educate farmers is now taking place.

Perishable products

The particular crop or stock grown in an area is decided by the local conditions and also by the distance from the place where the produce is sold. Perishable products must be grown near their markets unless some storage method ensures they arrive in good condition. Before the invention of refrigerators New Zealand reared sheep just for wool, but now their meat is exported to Europe.

Above: In the Middle East many areas are too hilly and dry to produce good crops. Here a farmer is threshing wheat by hand.

Below: The prairie provinces of Canada contain very rich farmland. Fields of wheat stretch as far as the eye can see.

Modern agriculture and fishing

In most parts of the world, farming is becoming more and more mechanized. By making use of modern farm machinery, especially tractors, fewer farmers are able to produce more food.

Contour ploughing

Tractors make it easy to plough large tracts of land where natural conditions make good crop yields unlikely. In some areas of Australia and the U.S.A., this has led to soil erosion, however. But by ploughing across the side of a hill (contour ploughing) rather than up and down a slope, such erosion has been reduced.

Bread basket of the world

Much of the world's wheat is grown on the prairies of North America, and this has been made possible by large-scale use of machinery and chemical fertilizers. At harvest time teams of workers operate huge combine harvesters round the clock. The grain is stored in large silos before being exported.

"Factory farming" describes another method used to increase food production on modern farms. Chickens, pigs and even calves and lambs may be raised in this way. Large numbers are kept in huge, windowless houses in which temperature and light conditions are most carefully controlled. The correct quantities of food and water are supplied automatically and the animals grow rapidly. Chickens are closely packed in small wire mesh cages in a "battery" system, and are thus reared for both eggs and meat.

Although some people consider it cruel to keep animals in these conditions, never exposed to the outside world, all their needs are provided. It is efficient and

Above right: Combine harvesters gathering wheat on the prairies.

Right: Battery hens in their carefully controlled conditions. Such methods increase production and cut costs.

Below: Machinery has opened up vast areas of land for farming. Contour ploughing reduces soil erosion.

productive and without such methods food would be scarcer and more expensive.

The harvest of the sea

Fish are a valuable source of food and protein. Man harvests the larger fish and crustaceans which, like all living things, are part of a food web. Light used for photosynthesis cannot penetrate deeper than about 150 metres, so it is in surface waters that solar energy is trapped and stored as food by plant plankton. These minute plants are food for animal plankton, in their turn food for fish and other larger creatures.

Seas cover 70 per cent of the earth's surface but fishing on a large scale takes place mainly in the shallower coastal waters covering the continental shelves.

How fish are caught

Fishing methods vary greatly, depending on the species. Some fish are hunted with spears and harpoons, but the hook and line is an old-established method. Long lines with several hundred baited hooks or trolled lures are still used for catching cod and halibut on a commercial scale. However, nets are the most common method. Floats support the top edge of the net and the bottom is weighted. Drift nets are used to catch fish feeding near the surface, like herring and salmon. Several nets are joined to form a "fleet" several kilometres long.

Seining and trawling

Seine nets also catch fish near the surface. A long net encircles a shoal and the line at the bottom of the net is drawn in first, closing the base of the net like a purse. In the Mediterranean this method is used at night, with powerful lights to lure fish into the net.

A trawl net is used to catch fish that feed on the sea floor. Floats keep the upper part open and weights drag across the bottom. Two flat "otter boards" keep the sides from closing. As the trawler

moves along, the fish are scooped into the small pocket known as the "cod end".

Since the 1940s many fishing boats have been equipped with echo-sounders which locate fish by transmitting short pulses of high-frequency sound into the water. The pulses bounce off any object in their path, including fish shoals. Such methods have proved very successful, especially in the seas around Europe where stocks of herring and cod are now unfortunately declining rapidly.

At present most commercial fishing is limited to wild stocks and few attempts have been made to "farm" sea fish. However, it is very likely that fish farming will become important in the future.

Above: A simple method of catching fish is to drive them into traps.

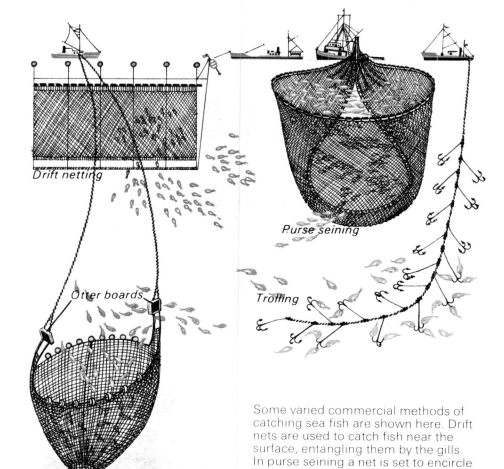

Some varied commercial methods of catching sea fish are shown here. Drift nets are used to catch fish near the surface, entangling them by the gills. In purse seining a net is set to encircle a shoal and is drawn in bottom first like a purse.

Trolling makes use of many baited hooks or lures. In deeper waters a trawl net is used, the funnel-shaped net being kept open by the flat otter boards. The fish are forced into the small "cod end".

47

Fuel and raw materials

Above: High in the Andes of South America ores of precious metals are found. Here miners search for tin and silver at Potosi in Bolivia.

Above: Nigeria is Africa's biggest producer of oil, but such resources may be short-lived. Discovered in 1958, supplies could dry up before the turn of the century.

In the modern world we rely heavily on minerals from the rocks of the earth's crust. Some provide raw materials from which we make things, while others are sources of energy or power to drive machines and provide heat and light.

Fossil fuels

Even among primitive peoples a fire for cooking made use of fuel of some kind, perhaps wood, charcoal or animal dung. Modern man uses fuels of many different kinds to provide power. These include coals (anthracite, bituminous coal, lignite, brown coal and peat), mineral or petroleum oil (called "crude oil" in its unrefined state) and natural gas. These are all "fossil fuels" since they are derived from the remains of animals and plants that lived millions of years ago.

Coals are formed from the fossilized remains of trees and other plants that lived in the past in a moist, mild climate. Oil consists of the remains of plants and animals including Foraminifera. These are marine plankton and are often called "oil bugs".

Because of the changes on the earth's surface over the millions of years, fossil fuels are often found deep underground or even beneath the sea. What is more, some of these deposits have already been exploited and used up. Once used they are gone forever and a constant search has to be made for fresh supplies. Like rich farmland, fossil fuels and minerals are not distributed evenly over the earth's surface.

Uses of raw materials

There are three minerals of vital importance to the limited number of modern industrial nations – oil, coal and iron. Other minerals which are used in rather smaller quantities are only slightly less important, such as tin ore, bauxite, copper and manganese.

Although coal and oil are used mainly as a source of fuel and power, they also form the raw materials from which many products are made. One of the main uses of coal is in the smelting and refining of metallic ores. Most of the world's steel and pig-iron is made by smelting iron ore with coke. The U.S.S.R. and U.S.A. have the largest reserves of coal, although those of China, West and East Germany, Poland and the United Kingdom are also significant. Elsewhere, deposits are smaller or less suitable for coke production. This, and the fact that coal is bulky and difficult to transport, helps to explain why other nations of the world may be less heavily industrialized.

Oil and gas

Oil and natural gas are often found in parts of the world far away from where they are needed. Fortunately they are relatively easy to transport by pipelines over land and by giant supertankers at sea. Several of the world's leading oil-producing countries use only a tiny part of their total output, this being particularly true of the Middle Eastern countries bordering the Persian Gulf.

The discovery of oil and natural gas is a tremendous asset to the economy of a nation. The United Kingdom has been successful in drilling for these fuels beneath the North Sea, but the supply will probably be exhausted by the end of this century.

Electrical power is increasingly the method by which energy is distributed to the consumer, but most of the electricity produced is generated by burning coal and oil.

Above: Hardwood timber such as teak and mahogany is obtained from tropical rain forests then taken to ports at the coast for export.

Above: A Belgian coal miner at work in the Campine coalfield. Coal provides energy and raw materials for chemical products.

Iron ore

The ores from which metals are obtained are also far from even in their distribution. Iron ore is particularly important and many deposits that were mined during the early years of the Industrial Revolution were quickly used up. Large deposits may occur in places far distant from large centres of population and the iron and steel works where they will be smelted and refined. In order to exploit such a resource, special transport facilities may be needed.

In Northern Quebec and Labrador, iron ore deposits could only be obtained after the construction of a main railway line 640 kilometres long, through a barren landscape with a harsh climate. The problems were similar at Mount Tom Price in North-West Australia where deposits have recently been made accessible. The ore from this area is now shipped to Japan to be made into steel.

Searching for gold

Throughout history the search for precious metals and gems has played its part in the exploration and development of new lands and the rapid, if sometimes temporary, rush of people to new areas. The quest for gold and silver, and the story of El Dorado (a king said to rule a legendary city made of gold) spurred on the Spanish Conquistadores in their exploration of South America in the 16th and 17th centuries.

Although it was 800 kilometres from the nearest town, the story of the discovery of gold in the Yukon in 1895 started a gold rush causing thousands of prospectors to pour into the area. Settlements mushroomed, but unfortunately the deposits gave out as suddenly as they had been discovered and within weeks the settlements became deserted "ghost towns".

Timber

Timber is a different kind of natural resource because, unlike mineral resources, it may be renewed. When trees are felled young saplings may be planted to take their place, although they may take many years to reach maturity.

Timber from coniferous trees such as Scots pine and Norwegian spruce supplies valuable softwood. This is used widely in the building industry and can also be converted to pulp for paper. Hardwoods are obtained from broadleaved trees in temperate areas, while teak, ebony and mahogany come from tropical forests.

Above: Unlike the deposits found in the streams that started the Yukon gold rush, South African gold comes from three kilometres below ground

Tomorrow's energy

The fossil fuels and mineral deposits on which we depend so much are being used up, in some cases slowly, but with great speed in others. For this reason large sums of money are being spent on research to discover new sources of power that will not run out.

Water power

For many centuries people have made use of the force of falling water to turn a wheel and create power. In the past waterfalls provided sites for many textile and grain mills. Today, however, hydro-electric power is steadily increasing in importance. So long as a river continues to flow the source of energy is available, and a large waterfall can produce the electricity requirements of a whole town. In many hydro-electric schemes, dams have been built across a river to ensure a constant supply of water to drive the turbines and the electricity generators. In Venezuela, for example, the Guri Dam has been built across the Caroni River.

As hydro-electric power is cheap, and large quantities of electricity are required to convert bauxite (aluminium ore) to metal, such sites have attracted aluminium smelting works. One of the world's largest concentrations of hydro-electric plants is close to the Niagara Falls in North America.

Another form of water power which may be further exploited in the future is the tidal movement of water in estuaries. In France a tidal power station has been constructed on the River Rance near St Malo. As the tides ebb and flow, the water is passed by turbines, and the force of the tide generates electricity. A similar scheme is proposed for the Severn estuary in the United Kingdom. Research is even being carried out to try to harness the potential energy of sea waves.

Wind and solar power

Man has used the energy of the wind with sailing ships and windmills for thousands of years. In the future, energy may be produced using rotating propellers in windy areas.

It is perhaps surprising that more use is not made of the direct energy from the sun, especially in countries with long hours of sunshine. Solar panels fixed to roof tops are now available to boost domestic hot water supplies and solar cells recharge batteries on space satellites. Solar energy is still radiated on cloudy days.

Nuclear energy

Nuclear power is also making a contribution to the world's energy needs. But the cost of developing

Right: Both oil and natural gas have been discovered beneath the North Sea. This discovery will make Britain self-sufficient in oil by 1980. The search continues in other areas.

Above: The Aswan High Dam on the Nile in south-eastern Egypt was built to control annual flooding. It was opened in 1971 and has currently the highest output of any single hydro-electric dam in Africa.

Right: As minerals are being rapidly used up, scientists are constantly thinking of other sources of energy. This is a solar energy research project at Odeillo in France.

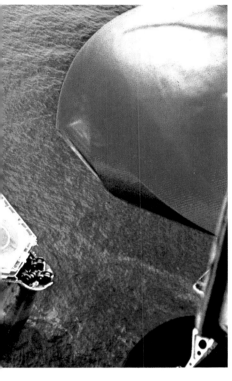

safe reactors and disposing of dangerous atomic waste is enormous. For these reasons, the future of nuclear energy may be in doubt.

Mineral deposits

The reserves of some minerals are vast and there is little chance of them running out for thousands of years. Many known reserves of coal are expected to last for a long time and research is going on to improve the techniques of making oil from coal.

In the meantime, we will have to continue to make use of fossil fuels and the search for new deposits must go on as known resources are

Below: Little is known of the mineral deposits that may be found under the sea bed. New technology enables scientists to carry on the search beneath the waves.

used up. Although offshore drilling is very expensive, rigs are a familiar feature in the shallow waters of the continental shelves in many parts of the world. Over 10,000 holes are drilled every year in search of new oil, but only one in 20 is successful. New technology has been developed so that the sea bed may be explored for other kinds of minerals. But at the moment little is known about this area as a possible new source.

In the case of metallic ores there are good chances of discovering rich deposits in the ancient rocks of Africa, Brazil and Northern Canada. Exploration in these areas has not gone ahead so far due to the remote and difficult environments. Again, new technology has been developed for the purpose, including specially equipped aircraft for tracing mineral deposits.

Industry

Prior to the Industrial Revolution that started in England in the late 18th century, man's only sources of power had been water, wind, animals and his own manual toil. But the invention of the steam engine gave a new use to a rock commonly found in the earth – coal. Coal provided the fuel for the engines that powered factory machinery. In north-west Europe the mills making cloth or smelting iron had been small, usually located beside swift streams that could turn a wheel. But, with steam, the factories could be made much larger. Unfortunately, coal was heavy and expensive to transport, so the coalfield attracted industry like magnets.

Iron and steel

At about the same time, a further use for coal was discovered. Previously charcoal had been used to smelt iron ore and all attempts to use coal as a substitute had failed. By heating coal in huge ovens it becomes coke, and coke proved ideal for smelting. Since iron ore was found close to many coalfields, iron and steel works also developed here.

New improvements in agriculture enabled fewer farmers to produce far more food and people flocked to work in the new indus-

Above: A painting by L. S. Lowry showing a typical 19th-century industrial town.

Left: A modern shipyard in Japan. Japan builds many supertankers.

Below: Much coal is still drilled by hand.

trial towns. These towns grew rapidly and were characterized by rows of terraced houses set among the mines and factory chimneys.

Development of transport

At first manufactured goods were transported by canal. Then steam was harnessed and railways were built linking town to town and industries to markets and ports. People could also travel by rail and villages along the new routes expanded into bigger settlements.

Towards the end of the 19th century scientists discovered how to transmit electricity by cable. The need for industry to be located on the coalfields decreased and many of today's factories are sited by main roads and by-passes and close to motorway junctions. The lorry and car are now important for carrying both goods and people.

Today's fuel

The fuel industry is also changing. Coal remains an important fuel for many electric power stations, but oil and natural gas have also become vital. Oil not only provides fuel for cars and lorries but is an essential raw material for many plastics and chemicals. Huge quantities are imported into Europe and America from such areas as the Middle East and Venezuela. Today, hydro-electric and nuclear power are becoming increasingly important in areas where there are suitable water supplies to work the turbines and for cooling.

Mass production

New industrial techniques have increased production. In the 1920s Henry Ford developed the conveyor belt system. This paved the way for mass production methods. Automation has been introduced, so that electronically controlled machines are able to carry out many routine processes. Such methods have brought down the prices of cars and other manufactured goods so that many people can afford them.

Today's industries depend on a

high degree of technical skill. Years of research were necessary before an aircraft like *Concorde* was ready for production. Research also goes into the marketing of products to create demand.

Problems of pollution

Modern industrial production has its problems, however. The landscape is often spoiled by electric pylons, quarries, pitheads and spoil heaps. Rivers are polluted by poisonous chemical wastes and this problem is made worse by the fertilizers and insecticides that are washed in from farmland.

Because demand for land is high, oil refineries are built beside estuaries that are also the feeding places for millions of birds, which must go elsewhere or perish. The supertankers carrying oil to refineries do sometimes have accidents and thousands of tonnes of tar spoil beaches for holidaymakers and destroy wildlife.

Above: Many years of research are necessary to ensure that an aircraft such as *Concorde* will fly safely. Many of today's products require a high degree of technological knowledge and skill.

Below: The car industry is a good example of the use of mass production techniques. This is the production line of a car factory in the U.S.A. Henry Ford set up the first production line in the city of Detroit to build the Model "T" Ford car.

Trade

Trade developed as man changed from hunting and gathering food to an organized agricultural way of life. The new surplus of food enabled some people to specialize in making things which could be exchanged for food – wheat for pottery or cattle for axeheads. This system of trade is called "barter" and is still found among some of the world's more primitive peoples. But barter became inconvenient if one person did not need the things another was offering. Money was introduced to overcome this problem, although jewels, shells and spearheads were probably used before coins.

Money as we know it was first used around 3000 B.C. in Babylon, where stamped metal bars were exchanged in the temples. The earliest known coins date from the 17th century B.C. and paper money was first used in China, as long ago as the 7th century A.D. Because money acts as a means of exchange, we no longer have to barter to obtain the things we need. In a modern society many people "exchange" their labour for money. Their salary or wages are used to buy the necessities of life. But by the year 2000, money in the form of coins and notes may have disappeared. Instead, transactions will be done by computer, so people will not have to carry any cash to do their shopping.

Expansion of trade

Simple trading began in the Middle East and soon developed over most of Europe. If some item was not found or could not be produced in one place, it was obtained from elsewhere. Sometimes trade came about through military strength. The Romans could import goods from the many remote places that were within their Empire. Wheat was imported from Alexandria and the Romans travelled as far as Britain to obtain some of their needs. Even before the Romans it is known that the Phoenicians obtained tin from Cornwall.

Places where goods could be bought and sold became necessary, so market towns developed at suitable places, such as ports, crossing points of rivers and the junction of two or more routes. Many towns in Britain and Europe still have market squares that date back to the Middle Ages or earlier, for instance Bruges. Throughout the world today towns act as centres for trade and as places to which people go to obtain specialized services – banks, doctors, cinemas and so on.

Worldwide trade

You will notice if you list the things you had for breakfast and the places they come from that a great amount of the food we eat every day has been imported from other parts of the world. Most countries are unable to produce all the goods they need, and rely on purchasing these from other countries. Small industrialized countries like Britain do not have enough land to produce sufficient food for their populations. It has to export manufactured goods to pay for

Above: Barter is one of the oldest forms of trade. This system is no longer used in the Western world, but is still carried out among some of the world's more primitive people.

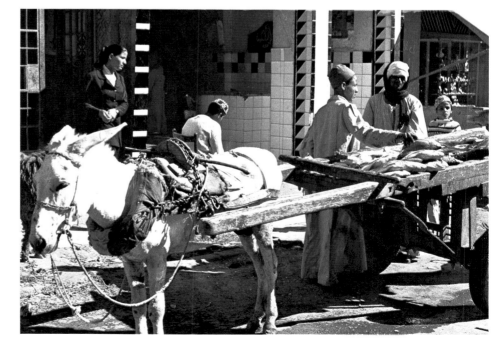

Right: Animals are still used as a major means of transport in Egypt. The donkey is the most common, although the *fellahin* (peasant farmers) use dromedaries (camels).

food from abroad and raw materials that its industry needs. The poorer, mainly agricultural nations export their raw materials to industrialized nations. In exchange they receive advanced equipment which helps to raise their standards of living. Minerals such as oil and precious stones are in limited supply. Africa exports about 75 per cent of the world's diamonds and India grows over 40 per cent of the world's tea. Britain produces neither and must import these.

The difference between the amount a country spends on imports and that received from exports is known as the balance of trade. If there are more exports than imports, trade is good. Until recently Britain imported most of the oil required for her vehicles and industries. Therefore, the discovery of large quantities of oil in the North Sea has been of great benefit to Britain's balance of trade, for, while supplies last, less oil is imported. Exports are known as either "visible" or "invisible". A country's visible exports are the manufactured goods and home-grown produce that are sold abroad. The goods bought by tourists are part of the invisible exports of the country they are visiting.

The goods are not actually being sold abroad but the tourists bring foreign money into the country to pay for them. Other invisible exports include services such as insurance, banking and shipping.

Trade and transport

To support the vast network of trade in the modern world, an efficient transport system is needed. Goods can be transported by road, rail, sea and air, or by pipeline. The method of transport used depends on the bulk and weight of the goods, and on whether they are being taken overseas or inland. Oil may be transported over land by pipeline but must be moved across the sea in vast supertankers. Other cargoes are often carried in containers, which can be easily and conveniently transported on trains, lorries and ships.

Terminals such as ports, airports and stations must be designed so that there are facilities for goods to be transferred from one method of transport to another. An international airport receiving imports which have to be distributed throughout the country must have good road and rail connections. Industries processing raw imported materials are often situated near terminals.

Below: Sydney is a major centre for international trade. Traffic in Sydney harbour is constant, and as can be seen here, her docks are always busy with ships of many nations.

The growth of transport

Above: In Brazil travel to market is often by traditional transport. Cars are expensive and unpaved roads become unusable after heavy rainfall.

In the modern world most countries are dependent on well-developed transport and communications networks. Goods and people have to be transported rapidly from place to place, and

Below: Light aircraft provide vital transport links in the jungles and mountains of Brazil where there are few roads. Flat airstrips are essential.

businessmen have to be able to exchange information instantly by telephone or telex.

Until the 19th century, means of transport were limited to animals such as horses, camels and cattle pulling carts or boats which could be paddled, rowed or blown by the wind. Such means of travel were slow and often hazardous. Only short distances could be covered in a day, and the quantity of goods that could be moved at one time was severely limited. Simple transport must still be used today where the nature of the landscape is not

Above: Los Angeles is a city devoted to the motor car with a criss-crossing network of freeways. This is a freeway interchange.

suitable for a more modern type of transport.

A transport revolution

At the same time as the Industrial Revolution was beginning in the late 18th century, many new kinds

Below: Transporting freight by air is expensive, but is ideal for moving goods that need to be distributed widely and quickly.

Right: Inland waterways are still used to transport heavy goods, particularly in Europe. These push-tows can carry 300 Renault cars at one time.

of transport were being tried out too. They were much faster than methods using animal power.

Early in the Industrial Revolution most heavy cargoes were moved by canal and river, but before long engineers were able to harness the power of steam. The first steam engines were fixed in one place, but in 1811 the inefficient "Puffing Billy" was first used to haul coal. By 1814 George Stephenson had built a much better steam locomotive, and the railway age had begun.

Soon, people were travelling by rail and railway tracks were laid in many parts of the world, opening up empty lands such as parts of North America and Australia. As the rail network grew, so people moved out to the city suburbs and "commuting" to work began. Today steam has largely been superseded by electric and diesel engines.

Motor cars

The steam engine was also used to power ships and road vehicles although at first there were few suitable roads. The invention of the internal combustion engine in 1885 by Daimler, Benz and Butler heralded the motor car era. It was made possible by the use of a much improved system of roads with hard tarmac surfaces, the pneumatic rubber tyre and the mass production line pioneered by Henry Ford for his Model "T" car.

In some parts of the world today, especially Europe, inland waterways are still used to transport bulky goods. By 1985 barges weighing 1,350 tonnes will be able to travel from Europoort in the Netherlands to the Black Sea.

Right: Due to congestion, noise and pollution it is difficult to build new transport systems into an old city. Elevated monorails may be an answer.

The high-speed age

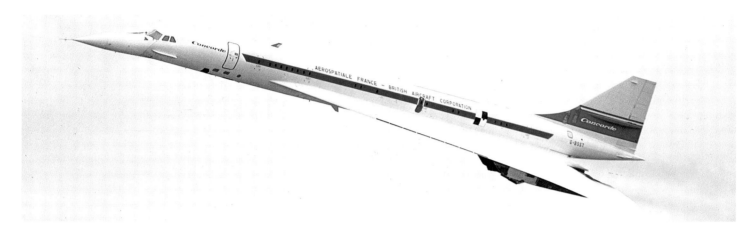

Above: The Concorde supersonic airliner was designed and built jointly by the British and the French. It cut hours off many journey times.

Greater speed is the keynote behind modern developments in transport. In the businessman's world "time is money". The development of jet-powered aircraft reduced the journey between London and New York to about six hours. The supersonic *Concorde* takes less than half that time. Hovercraft take much less time than a conventional ship on a short journey, like the Channel crossing.

The businessman requires up-to-the-minute information to make his decisions. The world-wide exchange of news and vital data has been greatly assisted by recent developments in telecommunications systems. Cables have been laid along the ocean floor to provide an inter-continental telephone link. Messages from one side of the globe to the other may be beamed via space communications satellites. Data is computer-processed and displayed on television screens.

Right: Radio and television provide instant entertainment and vital news and information services in many parts of the world. The pictures and sounds transmitted are controlled by a team of technicians and production staff behind the scenes.

Informing the people

Particularly in developed countries people are better informed than ever before about world affairs thanks to radio, television and daily newspapers. Cities have become centres for the gathering and transmission of facts.

Above: The Pleumeur-Boudou telecommunications station in the west of France receives messages beamed from satellites over the Atlantic Ocean.

Left: The hovercraft transports passengers on a cushion of air. It is quicker than conventional ferry services.

The world

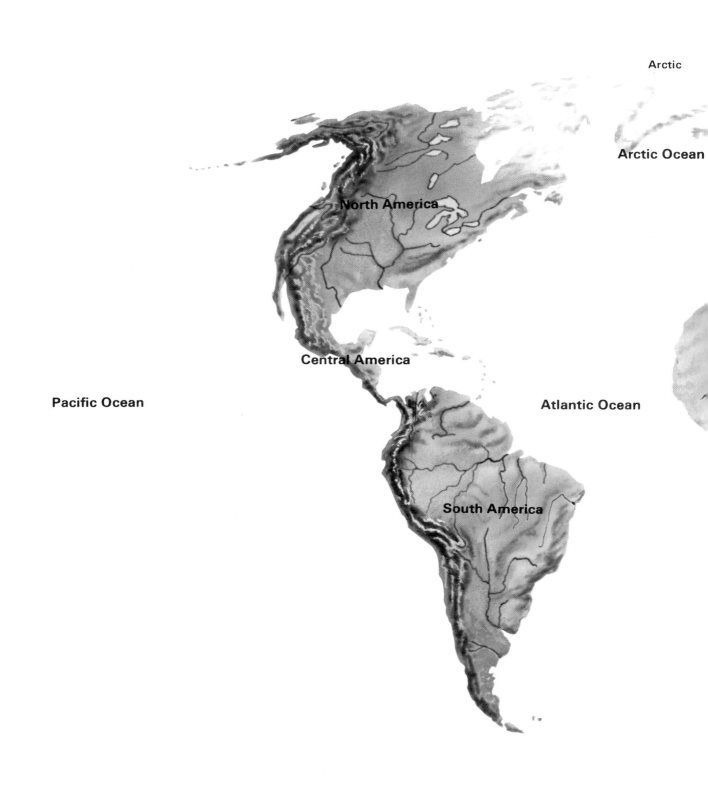

Arctic

Arctic Ocean

North America

Central America

Pacific Ocean

Atlantic Ocean

South America

Antarctic

Europe

U.S.S.R.

Asia

Africa

Pacific Ocean

Indian Ocean

Oceania

Europe, including the European part of the Soviet Union, occupies 9,907,000 square kilometres.
Population: approximately 667,000,000.
There are 34 countries, if the Soviet Union is included.
The **smallest country** is the Vatican City, situated in Rome, which occupies only 0.44 square kilometres, with a population of 1,000.
Discounting the Soviet Union, the **largest country** is France occupying 544,000 square kilometres with a population of 53,090,000.
The **longest river** is the Danube which is 2,700 kilometres long.
The **highest mountain** is Mont Blanc, which is 4,807 metres high.
The **biggest cities** are Paris with 8,424,000 people and London with 7,168,000.

1 Iceland
2 Norway
3 Sweden
4 Finland
5 Denmark
6 United Kingdom
7 Republic of Ireland
8 Netherlands
9 Belgium
10 Luxembourg
11 France
12 Monaco
13 West Germany
14 East Germany
15 Switzerland
16 Liechtenstein
17 Austria
18 Italy
19 San Marino
20 Vatican City
21 Malta
22 Andorra
23 Spain
24 Gibraltar
25 Portugal
26 Poland
27 Czechoslovakia
28 Hungary
29 Romania
30 Bulgaria
31 Yugoslavia
32 Albania
33 Greece

North Sea

Atlantic Ocean

Africa

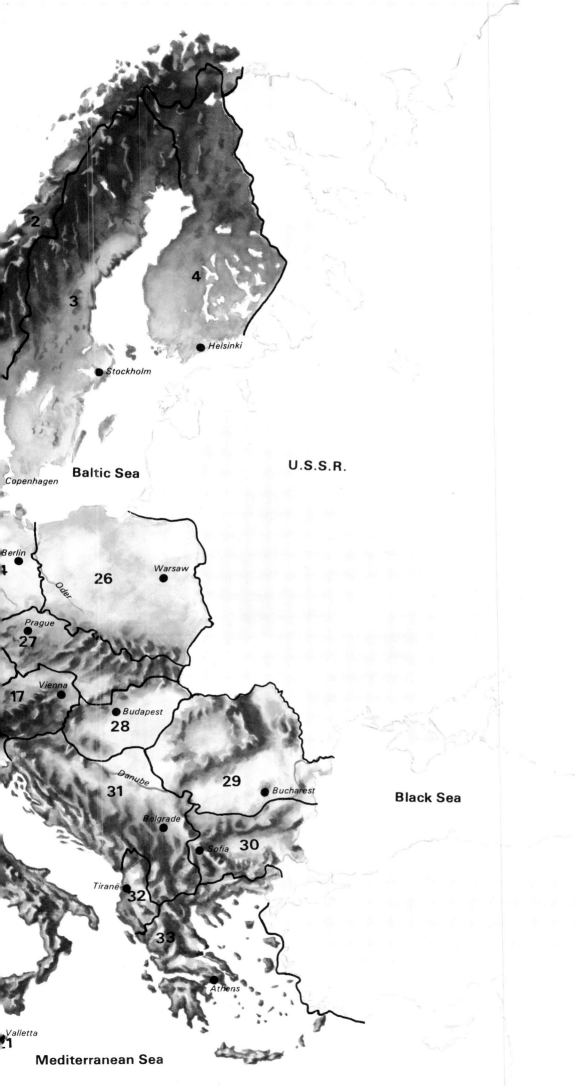

Baltic Sea

U.S.S.R.

2

3

4

● Helsinki

● Stockholm

Copenhagen

Berlin ●

Oder

26

● Warsaw

Prague ●

27

Vienna ●

17

● Budapest

28

Danube

29

● Bucharest

31

Belgrade ●

● Sofia

30

Black Sea

Tiranë ● 32

33

● Athens

Valletta

Mediterranean Sea

Europe

Europe is part of the same land mass as Asia but is always considered as a separate continent. It is the smallest of the world's continents, covering just over 5,500,000 square kilometres. This amounts to about four per cent of the world's land surface. Europe is the "Old World" and for thousands of years has wielded greater cultural and political influence than any other continent.

Above: Corfu is an island off the west coast of Greece. Although the Greek islands are largely unproductive, their great beauty makes them a tourist attraction.

Europe is bounded to the north by the Arctic Ocean, to the west by the Atlantic Ocean and to the south by the Mediterranean and Black Seas. Its eastern boundary is difficult to define, but for the purposes of this book it is taken as the political boundary with the U.S.S.R.

Europe has often been described as a "peninsula of peninsulas". It has a long and complicated coastline and great arms of the sea penetrate far inland. The effect of this is to moderate the climate. A very small part of the continent lies within the Arctic Circle and even here the warming influence of the North Atlantic Drift keeps the coasts ice free. Only in the Baltic where the North Atlantic Drift cannot penetrate and the salt content of the water is low, is the sea prone to freezing in the winter. The influence of the sea also means that all except the most easterly parts experience no great extremes of temperature. There are also no barren deserts.

The size of the continent (some 4,000 kilometres from north to south and 3,200 kilometres from east to west) is small enough for the whole region to be readily accessible. Europe is densely populated and its resources are

Above: A flower market in the Grand Place, Brussels. With its gaily coloured umbrellas, the market makes a brilliant foreground to the ancient buildings.

Above: The City of London, seen from Waterloo Bridge, which spans the River Thames. St. Paul's Cathedral dominates the skyline.

fully exploited. The present population is approximately 462 million, or 12 per cent of the world's population. The density of population is eight people per square kilometre, making Europe the most densely populated continent.

There are 32 separate states in Europe. On its own, each country may be vulnerable to political and economic crises. For this reason many have joined together for their mutual benefit. The North Atlantic Treaty Organization (NATO) and the Warsaw Pact are both defence organizations. The European Free Trade Association (EFTA), Benelux, the European Economic Community (EEC) and Comecon are all designed to provide economic advantages. Although the cherished dream of a united Europe is still far from reality such organizations are beginning to achieve progress in this direction.

Right: The ancient city of Venice in Italy is slowly sinking into its lagoon. Water floods into the ground floors of some of the buildings.

Europe

Iceland

Area:	102,846 square kilometres
Population:	220,918
Capital city:	Reykjavik
Language:	Icelandic
Currency:	Króna

Iceland is an island in the North Atlantic, its northernmost tip lying just inside the Arctic Circle. It is a mountainous, barren and infertile island. In glacial times Iceland was covered by the ice cap, and features of glacial erosion are visible today. Remnants of ice cap still cover the highest ground. The island is entirely composed of volcanic rocks. There are more than 200 volcanoes. The best known is the still active Mt. Hekla (1,491 metres) in the south. Other evidence of vulcanicity includes geysers, mud flows and hot springs. Some of the hot springs have been harnessed to produce geothermal electricity.

The climate is cool and wet but less severe than might be expected because of the warming influence of the North Atlantic Drift.

Farming in Iceland is limited both by the climate and the poor infertile soils. Some potatoes and

Above: Curing herrings. Traditional methods of preserving fish are being replaced by freezing.

Above: Geiranger is a very spectacular fjord in Norway. Mountains rise up sheer out of the water to a height of 1,000 metres.

hay are grown but sheep rearing is the main farming activity. Wool, skins and frozen meat are exported. Some of the wool is used in local clothing factories.

Fishing is the major industry. Fish and fish products, mainly fertilizers, account for 90 per cent of exports. It is hardly surprising that the Icelandic government is so concerned with the conservation of fish stocks. This has led them in recent years to extend their exclusive fishing limit to 320 kilometres from their coasts. The fishing industry is highly organized. Many Icelandic fleets are now found fishing in waters thousands of kilometres from Iceland.

In modern times Iceland had political associations with Denmark, but it became an independent republic in 1944, with a democratically elected government. Iceland is a member of EFTA and NATO.

Norway

Area:	323,884 square kilometres
Population:	3,973,000
Capital city:	Oslo
Languages:	Nynorsk and Bokmål
Currency:	Krone

The kingdom of Norway forms the western part of the Scandinavian peninsula. The Norwegian landscape shows all the typical features of highland glaciation. High rugged mountains rise sharply from the west coast which is deeply indented with many fjords. The longest is the Sogne fjord which is over 150 kilometres in length. The fjords provide sheltered, deep-water harbours, and many tourists are attracted by the spectacular scenery. Due to the fjords Norway has an extremely long coastline. It is estimated that if the fjords were straightened out the length of the Norwegian coastline would be equal to half the equatorial circumference of the globe. Parallel to the coast lie some 150,000 islands known as the Skerry Guard. With the exception of the Lofoten Islands these are mostly small and uninhabited but they help to protect coastal shipping from Atlantic storms.

The climate is cold in the mountains and the north with a high rainfall. However, the coastal regions are mild for their latitude due to the North Atlantic Drift, and the west coast is ice free.

The seas off the coast of Norway are rich in plankton which attract large stocks of fish. Cod abound in the north, herring and mackerel in the south. As many as 35,000 Norwegians earn their living as fishermen although many combine this with farming on a part time basis. About 80 per cent of the fish caught is turned into fish meal for fertilizers or oil for margarine. Only a small proportion is used for direct human consumption.

The natural resources of Norway include dense coniferous forests, especially in the south. These are exploited for their timber, but the Government makes sure that re-afforestation is practised so that there will be plentiful supplies for the future. The main mineral deposits found in Norway include iron ore and copper. Norway has no coal, but fast-flowing rivers rushing down the steep mountain sides are harnessed to make cheap hydro-electricity. This provides the power for mining, sawmills, pulp and paper making, railways and the home. It has also given rise to a number of electro-chemical and electro-smelting industries. Bauxite is imported to be made into aluminium.

Only four per cent of Norway is cultivated. The most important farming area is around Oslo fjord in the south. Dairying is the main agricultural activity.

In recent years large deposits of oil have been discovered off the west coast of Norway. Despite the difficulties of drilling in the North Sea, the Ekofisk field is already in production. Revenue from the export of oil has helped to strengthen Norway's economy.

Norway has a democratically elected government. She applied to join the EEC but after a referendum held in 1972 decided not to do so. Norway is a member of EFTA and NATO.

Sweden	
Area:	449,750 square kilometres
Population:	8,240,000
Capital city:	Stockholm
Language:	Swedish
Currency:	Krona

Sweden is the largest country in Scandinavia. The most northerly part, lying within the Arctic Circle, is a barren inhospitable wilderness. The most southerly part, called Scania, is intensively cultivated. Between these two areas lie densely forested uplands. The most southerly part of Sweden has a temperate climate but it becomes increasingly colder in the upland

Above: A Lapp camp in the far north of Norway with a herd of reindeer. Reindeer live off moss buried beneath the snow.

areas and towards the north. The Gulf of Bothnia is frozen for several months each winter.

Arctic Sweden, lying within the Arctic Circle, is the land of the midnight sun. It is a harsh, uninviting landscape, crossed occasionally by nomadic Lapp herders. This region is of great economic importance to Sweden. Vast deposits of high-grade iron ore are mined around Kiruna and Gällivare. The ore used to be exported from the Baltic port of Lulea. But this is icebound for five months every year, so a railway line was driven across the mountains to Narvik in Norway. Over 60 per cent of the ore exported passes through Narvik, mainly to Germany, Belgium and the U.K.

The upland region that makes up the bulk of Sweden is known as Norrland. The uplands are highest and most barren along the border with Norway. Where they slope down to the coastal plains in the east and south they are covered with dense coniferous forest, and timber products account for 40 per cent of exports. The government maintains careful reafforestation schemes. Some of the rivers in the uplands are used after the spring

Above: Stockholm is the capital of Sweden. It is a mixture of old and new, with the narrow streets of the Old Town and huge modern skyscrapers.

Above: A Finnish market. Because of the cold climate most vegetables have to be grown in glasshouses or are imported from other countries.

thaw to transport timber.

The fast flowing Swedish rivers are doubly valuable as they provide hydro-electric power. Some of the most important sites for production are waterfalls (as at the Trollhattan Falls on the Göta) or where rivers drain away from lakes. Even so Sweden has to import most of its fuel supplies.

Southern Sweden is mainly lowland with a temperate climate. There are three large lakes. Lakes Vanern and Vättern are joined by the Göta canal. This runs from Göteborg to Norrkoping providing a water route right across the country. Lake Mälaren lies farther east. Southern Sweden is the most prosperous and densely populated part of the country. Deposits of copper, silver, zinc and iron ore are found here and provide the basis for many manufacturing industries.

Sweden has a reputation for high-quality goods, and a large proportion of all products made are for export. The steel mills produce high-quality alloy steels but much of the ordinary steel used in engineering is imported. Engineering industries are well represented in Sweden: shipbuilding on the coasts, cars (Saab and Volvo),

aircraft, machine tools, cutlery and ball bearings. Electrical engineering (Electrolux) is also widespread, as are textile, chemical and timber-using industries.

Scania in the extreme south of Sweden has the best agricultural land. Wheat and sugar beet are grown but the emphasis is on cattle rearing and milk production.

Sweden's two main cities, Stockholm and Göteborg, are also its chief ports.

The country, which has a tradition of neutrality, has a monarchy and a democratically elected government. It is a member of EFTA.

Finland	
Area:	337,032 square kilometres
Population:	4,750,000
Capital city:	Helsinki
Language:	Finnish
Currency:	Finnish mark

Finland is situated across the Gulf of Bothnia from Sweden. It is a sparsely populated country, a wilderness of lakes and pine forests. The native name for Finland is Suomi which means

"Lakeland". There are some 60,000 lakes in the country, gouged out of the flat land surface when a gigantic ice sheet swept over it. The ice sheet also removed most of the soil and replaced it by infertile glacial deposits.

As in other Scandinavian countries, railways came relatively late to Finland but have played an important part in the country's development. The lines are built on the Russian gauge, which is wider than the ordinary European gauge, so passengers must change trains at the Swedish border.

The climate is severe with long bitterly cold winters and short warm summers. Coastal waters freeze during the winter months.

Agriculture is difficult in Finland. In the north of the country pioneer farmers are trying to carve farms for themselves out of virgin forest. In central Finland, the area with the largest lakes, the forest is dotted with farm clearings. Hay, oats and potatoes are the main crops and practically every farmer has some dairy cattle.

Only the coastal lowlands in the extreme south-west of the country have a growing season longer than 175 days. The most fertile soils are also to be found on the coastal

Below: In Finland, the sea freezes in winter. Anglers break a hole in the ice and are then able to catch fish through the hole.

lowlands so this is the main farming area in Finland. Rye and wheat can be grown here, but in recent years dairying has become important. Milk is sent to co-operative creameries to be made into butter.

Forests cover 65 per cent of Finland and forestry is the main source of livelihood. Most farmers take up lumbering as a part-time occupation in the winter months. Lumber and timber products, including paper, chemicals and furniture, make up 95 per cent of Finnish exports. There are also textile, metal, engineering and electrical industries, which have to rely mainly on imported raw materials. Industry is fairly new to Finland, which until World War Two was a largely agricultural country. After the war, Finland had to make huge reparations to the U.S.S.R. in the form of manufactured goods, and so industry developed. Much of the power for industry comes from hydro-electricity. An enormous terminal moraine called the Salpaus Selkä runs across southern Finland. Many of the streams which plunge southwards over the edge of this are used to produce hydro-electricity.

Below: Farming in Denmark is extremely efficient. Danish farmers use advanced agricultural machinery.

Fishing is important around the Aland Islands off the south-west coast.

Finland is a democratic republic with a freely-elected government. As a neighbour of the U.S.S.R. she has adopted careful political policies since World War Two which are designed to offend neither the free nor the Communist world. The country is an associate member of EFTA.

Denmark	
Area:	43,074 square kilometres
Population:	5,036,000
Capital city:	Copenhagen
Language:	Danish
Currency:	Kroner

Denmark is a small country in north-west Europe. It consists of the peninsula of Jutland and about 500 islands, the largest of which are Zealand, Funen and Lolland. Jutland is separated from Norway by the Skagerrak and from Sweden by the Kattegat. These channels together with the Sound, a narrow stretch of water lying between Zealand and Sweden, form the passage between the North Sea and the Baltic.

Denmark's capital, Copenhagen (its name in Danish means Merchant's Haven), is strategic-

Above: The famous statue of the Little Mermaid in Copenhagen harbour commemorates the birth of Hans Christian Andersen.

ally sited on Zealand guarding the Sound. For hundreds of years it was in an excellent position to control trade in the Baltic Sea. The Great and Little Belts are only shallow passages and of no great importance to shipping.

Denmark is a low-lying country. A line of low hills, rising to about 150 metres, runs north to south through the centre of Jutland. These are a terminal moraine marking one of the resting places of the edge of a great ice sheet. To the west are infertile sands and gravels of the outwash plain. Much of this area was covered with heath and bog, and despite large-scale reclamation West Jutland remains the least productive part of Denmark. Most of the land is devoted to pasture. To the east of the terminal moraine are boulder clay deposits of the ground moraine. The boulder clays contain fragments of chalk, so they produce an extremely fertile soil. East Jutland and the islands are the main arable area of Denmark.

On the east coast of Jutland are several fjords. The longest, the Lim Fjord, extends virtually all the way across the peninsula almost cutting off its northern tip. The Tyboron Canal has been cut to provide a

Europe

passage through to the North Sea.

Denmark has a temperate climate, and is renowned as a dairy farming country. High-quality butter, cheese, bacon, eggs and poultry are exported to other European countries. However, until 100 years ago, Denmark relied upon exporting wheat for its revenue. Then cheaper grain grown on a vast scale in North America flooded the market and deprived Danish farmers of their livelihood. So they turned to dairy farming instead. Much of the land is still arable, but it now produces barley, oats, hay, sugar beet and clover as feeding stuffs for the livestock. Some of the barley grown is used in the brewing of lager. Carlsberg and Tuborg are world famous.

Despite the fame of Danish farming only eight per cent of the population are employed in agriculture. Manufacturing is the largest employer, despite Denmark having no mineral resources of any importance. The raw materials have to be imported, so industry is concentrated in the ports, particularly around Copenhagen. Engineering, ranging from shipbuilding to electrical engineering, is the chief industry. There are also a large range of products based on imported oil seed. Fishing is another source of revenue. Esbjerg on the west coast is the chief fishing port.

Due to the structure of the country, communications in Denmark are difficult. The problem has been met by a remarkable series of ferries, road and rail bridges.

Denmark has a constitutional monarchy and a democratically elected government. In 1973 it became a member of the EEC and is also a member of NATO.

United Kingdom	
Area:	244,013 square kilometres
Population:	56,000,000
Capital city:	London
Language:	English (a little Welsh and Gaelic)
Currency:	Pound sterling

The United Kingdom of Great Britain and Northern Ireland includes all the British Isles except the Republic of Ireland. Great Britain comprises the countries of England, Scotland and Wales. The United Kingdom, which once had a huge empire in Africa and Asia, still has some overseas possessions and is the centre of the Commonwealth.

Most of Scotland and Wales and northern England are composed of ancient uplands. The North-west Highlands lie in the remotest parts of northern Scotland. These are separated from the Grampians to the south by the long narrow valley of Glen More. The highest peak in the United Kingdom, Ben Nevis (1,343 metres), is in the Grampians.

There are many long narrow lakes called lochs in the Scottish highlands, which are noted for their spectacular beauty. Most of the highlands support only rough grazing for sheep. The highest, most exposed parts are covered by heather and grouse moor. There has been an extensive programme of reafforestation in sheltered areas in recent years.

The central lowlands, drained by the Clyde and Forth, lie south of the Grampians. These are the most extensive area of lowland in Scotland. The land then rises to the Southern Uplands which are lower and less rugged than the highlands. The great ridge of the Pennines (often called the "backbone of England") extends from the Southern Uplands southwards into England. To the north-west lies the Lake District, an area noted for its beauty. The highest point in the Cumbrian mountains is Scafell Pike (978 metres). The largest lake is Windermere, which is 16 kilometres long.

The Cambrian mountains, rising to 1,085 metres in Snowdon, cover

Left: Stonehenge on Salisbury Plain. The stone blocks may date from about 2000 B.C. It is believed that ancient peoples worshipped the sun there.

Above: Active outdoor holidays are popular with many people in Britain. This camp site is in the Lake District.

situated on the European continental shelf where conditions are right for prolific plankton growth. Therefore there are a number of excellent fishing grounds. There has been much concern in recent years about overfishing and the depletion of fish stocks. Fishing is becoming strictly controlled and catches of certain fish are limited.

The United Kingdom has a maritime climate. It is greatly influenced by the sea. In general, temperatures are moderate, with warm summers and cool winters. It is colder in the north and warmer in the south. The temperatures are mild for the latitude due to the warming influence of the North Atlantic Drift. There is a plentiful rainfall well distributed throughout the year. Rainfall decreases to the east as the prevailing winds are from the west.

Agriculture in the United Kingdom is very productive. About 50 per cent of the total area is in some kind of agricultural use.

Farming is intensive and heavily mechanized. Great use is made of scientific methods of farming such as fertilizers, insecticides, selective breeding of stock and use of high-yielding strains of crops. Many farmers are owner-occupiers or long-term tenants. Unfortunately population pressures and soaring land values of recent years have led to good farm land being sold for building development.

The lowlands are the most intensively cultivated areas. Most farmers practise mixed farming – they grow arable crops and raise stock, although there is often an emphasis upon one or other.

Wheat, barley, sugar beet and main crop potatoes are the chief crops of southern and eastern England. The deep fertile soils of the East Anglian lowlands are especially productive. Barley, oats and seed potatoes predominate in the cooler north.

As far as stock farming is concerned, dairying is most important

60 per cent of Wales leaving just a coastal rim of lowland. There are also large areas of rugged upland in the south-west peninsula of England.

The most extensive areas of lowland lie in eastern and southern England. Even here there are ridges of low chalk and limestone hills.

Northern Ireland consists mainly of areas of low hills surrounding Loch Neagh (396 square kilometres), which is the largest lake in the United Kingdom.

There are a great many rivers in the United Kingdom. The most important are those which drain into the four main estuaries: the Humber, Thames, Severn and Mersey.

The United Kingdom has a long indented coastline with many good natural harbours. The islands are

Right: The statue of Eros stands in Piccadilly Circus in the heart of London. There are many theatres and cinemas in this part of the capital.

Europe

on the lush pastures of the wetter west. Fluid milk is the main product from farms close to the large cities. Elsewhere butter and cheese are made.

Pigs are reared in association with dairying as they are fed on the skimmed milk returned from the creameries. In the drier east of the country, in hillier districts and remoter areas, beef cattle are reared but they are sent to the lusher pastures of the lowlands for fattening before marketing.

Sheep, especially for wool production, predominate on the large hill farms of the Southern Uplands, Pennines and the Cambrian Mountains.

There are some areas of specialist farming in the United Kingdom. Early season vegetables and flowers are grown in the south-west peninsula, soft fruits are grown in Kent, Hampshire and the Vale of Strathmore, hard fruits are grown in Kent, Hereford and Worcestershire and bulbs in the Fens. Market gardening is found in many areas close to large cities.

Industry is important in the United Kingdom. The country has a long tradition of inventiveness and a skilled labour force. The range of industries is enormous: metallurgical industries, especially steel manufacture, are very important. Much of the steel produced is used within the United

Kingdom, the rest is exported.

Every aspect of engineering is represented. Shipbuilding and associated industries are important on the Clyde, at Belfast and in north-east England. Vehicle manufacture predominates in the Midlands. Electronics and electrical engineering are also important, as are textiles in Yorkshire and Lancashire, and chemicals, plastics and paper.

Industry had a good start in the 18th century as there were plentiful supplies of coal and iron ore. Early on, the coalfields became the main location for heavy industry, but these are now declining areas and modern lighter industries need to be attracted there to absorb the surplus labour available.

Local mineral resources are less important than previously. Most of the iron ore used is now imported; which accounts for the modern coastal locations of huge integrated iron and steel works. Much coal is still mined mainly for electricity production, but the United Kingdom relies heavily on imported oil to power its industries.

Oil refineries and petro-chemical works are also found in coastal locations. Recent discoveries of oil and natural gas in the North Sea has been a great boon to the country. Some hydro-electric power is produced in

Above: Bosham harbour in Sussex. Peaceful scenes such as this typify the lure of the rural south of England.

Scotland, but there are few suitable sites. Bauxite smelting has been attracted by the locally abundant electricity. There are also a number of nuclear power stations.

Tourism is well developed. Visitors are attracted by the wealth of historical treasures and the pageantry of traditional ceremonies. London is the main tourist centre as well as being the leading industrial and commercial centre.

Communications are well developed in the United Kingdom. There has been an extensive programme of motorway building in the last 20 years and more are planned for the future. The railway network has been curtailed for greater efficiency and British Rail have developed a high speed "bullet" train.

The United Kingdom lives by foreign trade. Despite the productivity of British farms, much foodstuff still has to be imported, as do many of the raw materials for industry. These imports have traditionally been paid for by the export of manufactured goods, largely to the developing countries. However, these countries are now establishing their own industries and the United Kingdom is faced with the daunting task of finding new markets.

The United Kingdom is a constitutional monarchy, with Queen Elizabeth II as Head of State, and has a democratically elected government. It is a member of the EEC and NATO.

Republic of Ireland (Eire)

Area:	70,285 square kilometres
Population:	3,190,000
Capital city:	Dublin
Languages:	English and Gaelic
Currency:	Irish pound

Ireland is the second largest island of the British Isles. Six counties in the north-east, which are part of the province of Ulster, are politically within the United Kingdom. The rest of the island forms the Republic of Ireland or Eire in Gaelic.

The Republic of Ireland is composed of a wide lowland plain fringed by a number of low mountain ranges. The highest peak in Ireland is Carrantuohill (1,040 metres) in the MacGillycuddy's Reeks in the south-west. The central plain is limestone, but it is covered by boulder clay. This impedes drainage, so there are great expanses of peat and bog and many lakes, called loughs. The two largest are Lough Corrib and Lough Derg. There are a number of long narrow inlets on the south-west coast of Ireland. They provide excellent sheltered, deepwater harbours. Bantry Bay has become the site of a great oil terminal and distribution centre.

Ireland has a mild climate, warm in the summer, with plentiful rain throughout the year.

Agriculture is the mainstay of Ireland's economy. The soils and climate encourage grass cultivation and cattle rearing is the most important farming activity. Dairying predominates in the south-west and beef farming in the more remote areas. Some cereals are grown but they do not ripen easily. Potatoes are the chief vegetable crop.

Apart from the Tynagh Mine in County Galway producing silver, lead and zinc, Ireland has few mineral resources. For centuries peat has been used as a fuel. It can be used in special power stations to produce electricity.

Manufacturing industries in the Republic of Ireland are limited. Processing of farm products is important. Fertilizers and agricultural equipment are also produced.

The Republic of Ireland, which had previously been politically joined to England, Scotland, Wales and Northern Ireland, achieved independence in 1921. It is a member of the EEC.

Netherlands

Area:	33,811 square kilometres
Population:	13,810,000
Capital city:	Amsterdam is joint capital with The Hague; the seat of government is at The Hague
Language:	Dutch
Currency:	Guilder

The Netherlands is situated in north-west Europe. The country is often called Holland but correctly this refers only to two coastal provinces. It is a low-lying country,

Right: Amsterdam is a city of canals and narrow streets. Barges play an important part in city life, as here at the Singel flower market.

Europe

the highest point, in the extreme south-east in Limburg, being only 132 metres. In fact much of the country is below sea level.

There is a saying "God made the world but the Dutch made the Netherlands". This refers to the fact that almost half the country consists of polders, land painstakingly reclaimed over the years from the sea, rivers, lakes and swamps.

Polderlands lie right along the coast and in a broad belt along the valleys of the Rhine, Maas and their tributaries. Many polders are as much as six metres below sea level and are protected from flooding by dykes. Drainage water is pumped into canals which also serve as communication routes.

Between Den Helder and the Hook the polders are protected on their seaward side by a belt of sand dunes. Elsewhere artificial sea walls have to be built. The dunes are doubly protective as they are also used to store rain water, which holds back the salt water, preventing it from seeping inland through the soil so spoiling it for farming. The largest reclamation area is around the Ijsselmeer in the north of the country. This was formerly a shallow bay of the North Sea called the Zuider Zee.

In the south of the country three of Europe's greatest rivers, the Rhine, Maas and Scheldt enter the sea via deltas. This region known as the Delta district is a network of waterways and islands. In 1953 violent storms breached the sea defences here causing widespread flooding and drowning 1,800 people. Now a tremendous engineering project, The Delta Plan is sealing off the region by building a series of massive dams connecting the islands. It should be completed by 1980 and will bring greater security to the region, prevent salt water seepage, improve communications and provide fresh water supplies for Rotterdam.

South and east of the polders lie areas of higher sandy heathlands. Much of the heath is too dry for cultivation as rain drains quickly through the sands. Elsewhere there are peat bogs where the drainage is impeded. Since the 19th century reclamation has been going on here. The addition of marl and fertilizers has changed the composition of the soil and improved its fertility. There are still extensive areas of forest in the heathlands.

The Netherlands has warm summers, cold winters and a moderate rainfall throughout the year.

Agriculture in the Netherlands is highly organized and scientific. Crops and milk yields are among

Left: The Dutch bulb fields lie between Leiden and Haarlem. There is a big export trade in bulbs and cut flowers.

Above: The open-air cheese market at Alkmaar in North Holland. Edam and Gouda cheeses are on the sledges.

Above: Windmills were originally built in the Netherlands to pump water from the polders into the drainage canals.

the highest in the world. The high quality of the farm produce is maintained by rigid government inspection. The polders are one of the richest farming regions in Europe. Arable farming is important in the north and south. Wheat, barley, sugar beet, potatoes and fodder crops are grown in rotation. In the provinces of Holland permanent pasture predominates.

Everywhere in the polderlands dairy farming is important. Butter, cheese, condensed and powdered milk are processed for export. Alkmaar and Gouda are famous cheese markets.

There are two areas of specialist farming in the polders. South of The Hague are vast areas of glasshouses producing such crops as tomatoes, cucumbers, lettuce, melons, peaches and grapes mainly for export. Between Leiden and Haarlem inland from the dunes lies a belt of light sandy soil. This is the famous bulb growing area.

Arable farming predominates on the fertile loess soil of south Limburg and also in the improved areas of the heathlands. Hardy crops are grown in the heathlands and stock rearing is practised.

The Netherlands have enormous deposits of natural gas in the province of Groningen. There is a small oilfield at Schoonebek near the German border, and a coalfield in south Limburg. However, due to difficulties of mining here, the coalfield has recently been closed. Natural gas supplies the country's domestic needs and there is plenty left for sale to the neighbouring countries of Belgium, France and Germany. The revenue earned from this helps the Dutch balance of payments.

From the start of exploitation of the gas field, the government decided the gas should be used to attract industry to the lesser developed parts of the country. One such example is the bauxite smelter at Delfzyl.

Industry employs over 40 per cent of the Dutch population, making the country one of the most industrialized in Europe. In the 18th century Dutch industry was confined to shipbuilding and repairing. Then with the growth of a colonial empire, new industries developed including chocolate making, sugar refining, vegetable oil processing and diamond cutting.

All these industries still flourish, but there has been a great expansion of industry since the 1930s. This was brought about by a rapid growth of population which could not be absorbed into farming. The main "new" industries are oil refining, petrochemicals (fertilizers, insecticides, detergents and synthetic rubber), iron and steel and engineering.

Many of these industries have coastal locations because of the need to import the raw materials. Inland the only industrial towns of note are Eindhoven, where DAF cars are made and the headquarters of Philips, the electrical engineering company, is situated; and Utrecht specializing in heavy chemicals and electrical switchgear. Cotton textiles are made near the German border.

The Netherlands' two major ports, Rotterdam and Amsterdam, are linked to the sea by deepwater canals, the New Waterway and the North Sea Canal respectively. Mobil's oil refinery is on the North Sea Canal and the iron and steel industry is centred at Velsen near the entrance to the canal.

Amsterdam still handles and processes many tropical imports, and has ship repairing yards and a car assembly plant. It is the headquarters of Dutch banking and many commercial organizations. There is a canal linking Amsterdam to the river Rhine.

Rotterdam is the most important port in the world. Situated on a distributary of the Rhine and with canal links to the Maas, it handles goods for many places in Western Europe. In recent years port facilities in Rotterdam became inadequate and the out-port of Europoort has been built at the seaward end of the New Waterway. There is now a continuous line of docks and industrial development along the south bank of the canal.

Above: The main dam across the Ijssel Meer which protects the lake from the North Sea.

There are five oil refineries here (owned by Shell, a Dutch company, Esso and Chevron), their associated petrochemical plants, shipbuilding and repairing yards, marine engineering, flour milling and tea packing industries.

Both road and rail systems are highly developed, but the Netherlands is a country of canals. The larger canals carry much industrial transport. Many towns have more canals than roads. Amsterdam is often referred to as the "Venice of the North". Though these towns are picturesque, roads are narrow and congested. No wonder so many Dutch people prefer bicycles to cars.

The Netherlands is a constitutional monarchy and has a democratically elected government. The government is concerned that the whole of the country should enjoy a high standard of living. National planning therefore encourages development in the remoter areas and also ensures that some land be kept free for recreational purposes in the built-up industrial regions. The country was a founder member of Benelux, and is a member of the EEC and NATO.

Left: The Freyr Rocks near Dinant, Belgium. Where the River Meuse has cut through the limestone uplands it has produced attractive scenery.

northern parts of Belgium are part of the Great European Plain. This lowland is drained by the River Scheldt and tributaries. Belgium has a short coastline on the North Sea. Sand dunes fringe the coast behind which lies a narrow belt of polders reminiscent of the scenery

in the Netherlands.

Belgium has a mild climate with warm summers and damp winters.

In agriculture, Belgium is almost self-sufficient in foodstuffs. This is achieved despite large tracts of infertile soils and the small size of many Belgian farms. Where agriculture is possible, the land use is intensive and yields are high.

The Kempenland in north Belgium is an extensive area of sands and gravels. Naturally this is heath country, but marling and the use of fertilizers has brought some of this area into cultivation. Even so only hardy crops such as rye and potatoes grow well. Dairying on improved pastures is important around Antwerp. Elsewhere there has been much reafforestation.

The central plain of Belgium lying between the Ardennes and the Kempenland falls into two farming regions, divided by an imaginary west-east line running through Brussels. North of this lies

Belgium	
Area:	30,513 square kilometres
Population:	9,865,000
Capital city:	Brussels
Language:	Flemish in north; French in south
Currency:	Belgian franc

Belgium is situated in north-west Europe. In the south-east of the country lie the rain- and wind-swept uplands of the Ardennes. Belgium's highest point, Signal de Botrange (694 metres) is here. The exposed parts of this ancient plateau are peat covered. The sheltered, steep-sided valleys are densely wooded. The northern edge of the Ardennes is marked by the valleys of the Sambre and Meuse.

The lower and central and

Above: Brussels is the capital of Belgium. The magnificent belfry of the Town Hall dominates the 17th-century houses surrounding the Grand Place.

the province of Flanders. Although the soils here were originally poor they have been laboriously improved since the Middle Ages. The Flemish peasants mixed the surface sands with the underlying clays and added manure to the soil. This is an area of tiny farms, some little more than allotments. There is much hand cultivation. Many of these small holdings are owned and worked in their spare time by factory workers and provide an additional income.

Market gardening is the most important type of farming although wheat, rye and fodder crops are also grown. Most small holdings have a few cows. Flax is grown on the clay soils of the Lys and Escaut valleys.

To the south of Flanders lie the best agricultural lands in Belgium developed on fertile loess soils. Farms here are much larger and more heavily mechanized. Wheat and sugar beet are the main arable crops. Permanent pasture predominates on the heavier soils of the valleys where dairying is important.

There is a specialized market gardening zone around Brussels. South-east of the town is a huge glasshouse development where black grapes and vegetables are grown, largely for export.

Belgium is a highly industrialized country although most of the raw materials have to be imported. The only large-scale mineral resource is coal. This has been mined in the Sambre-Meuse valley since the 19th century and more recently around the town of Genk in the Kempenland. Although the presence of coal in the Sambre-Meuse valley has been a tremendous stimulus to industry in the area, mining conditions have always been extremely difficult here.

Production from this coalfield has been steadily contracting and may soon cease altogether. The region already has many of the problems of a declining industrial area. Power for Belgian industry now comes from imported oil, Dutch natural gas, German and American coal. The country also has several nuclear power stations.

Iron and steel manufacture is an old and established industry in

Above: The Belgian motorway system is linked to German and French motorways. Vehicles can be driven from the Channel ports into the heart of Europe.

Below: Flax fields in Flanders. The waters of the River Lys are used for retting the flax.

Europe

Above: A sailing lesson for children in the yacht basin of Ostend harbour.

Ostend is an important channel port and holiday resort.

Belgium. It developed in the coalfield towns of Liege, Mons and Charleroi originally using local ores. These were soon exhausted and replaced by low-grade ores imported from France and Luxembourg. Recently the industry is coming to rely more on high-grade ores imported from West Africa and Brazil. This accounts for the newest iron and steel mill being built at Zelzate on the Ghent-Terneuzen ship canal.

This trend is reflected in all Belgium's industries. The old established "heavy" industries – coal-based chemicals, glass-making, heavy engineering producing such items as diesel engines, boilers, railway equipment – are found in the Sambre-Meuse valley. The "newer" industries are located on navigable waterways and in the slightly less developed Kempenland.

Antwerp is Belgium's main port and the third most important port in the world. It handles 90 per cent of domestic traffic and also serves northern France, Luxembourg and western Germany. Antwerp is situated on the Scheldt estuary. Although the mouth of the estuary is in Dutch territory the Belgians have a right of way.

Antwerp's industries include car assembly from imported parts, light and electrical engineering, sugar refining, flour milling, copper refining and diamond cutting. Much of the industry and port has been developed since World War Two.

Antwerp specializes in bulk liquid storage and this has given rise to the port's main industry – the production of an enormous range of petrochemicals. Unfortunately the Scheldt cannot take the huge modern supertankers, so much of the oil used now comes by pipeline from Rotterdam.

The Albert Canal runs from Antwerp through the Kempenland to the Meuse. It has helped to bring industry to this once sparsely populated area. Zinc refining, car assembly and dangerous and noxious industries such as explosives and chemicals have developed. Glass-making using the local silver sands is also important.

Textile production is another old-established industry in Belgium. Bruges and Ghent have been textile centres since the Middle Ages. At that time locally-grown flax was used in lace making and wool was imported from England. Much of the textile industry is still located in Flanders, but newer developments have taken place in the east of the country. Woollen and cotton goods are produced and the industry has expanded to include a range of man-made textiles. Communications in Belgium are well developed.

Belgium is the crossroads of Western Europe, and lorries from all over the continent, the Middle East and beyond have to pass through the country. The rivers and canals help to carry much traffic, and motorways of a high standard have been built in recent years.

Belgium has the oldest railway on the European continent, which is now one of the densest railway networks in the world. Like many other countries, Belgium has its own national airline, Sabena.

Belgium became an independent country in 1830. European statesmen at the time saw the country as a "buffer state", a means of separating two ambitious neighbours. The country contains two distinct groups of people who have different languages, cultures and religions. In the north are the Flemings who speak a Dutch dialect and in the south are the French-speaking Walloons. Both groups are jealous of their own identity and suspicious of the other. They have never become completely united and this remains one of the biggest problems facing the country. Originally French was made the official language but in 1963 it was agreed that Flemish should become the "official" language in the northern part of the country. All public notices and official documents are printed in both languages, and there are two television services, one in Flemish and one in French.

Belgium has a constitutional monarchy and a democratically elected government. The country was a founder member of Benelux and is a member of the EEC and NATO.

Luxembourg

Area:	2,586 square kilometres
Population:	356,400
Capital city:	Luxembourg City
Languages:	Luxembourgeois, French and German
Currency:	Luxembourg franc

Above: A street café in Luxembourg City. Open-air cafés shaded by trees or colourful umbrellas are characteristic of many European cities.

The Grand Duchy of Luxembourg lies between Belgium, West Germany and France. Although it is a land-locked country, the canalized river Moselle which forms the eastern border carries barge traffic to and from Luxembourg. The river port of Mertert handles most of this.

Physically and economically Luxembourg falls into two regions. In the north the land rises to over 500 metres in the wooded hilly country of the Ardennes, where farming is difficult. Rye, oats and potatoes are grown.

The southern half of the country is part of the lower plateau of Lorraine. The climate here does not have the extremes experienced in the Ardennes, and farming is more important. Farms are small and there is little mechanization, but production is such that Luxembourg is almost self-supporting in food. Wheat and dairy farming are most important, and vines are also grown.

The mainstay of Luxembourg's economy is its iron and steel industry. The country has large deposits of low-grade iron ore in the south along the border with France. About half a million tonnes of ore are mined each year, but as much again is imported, especially high-grade ores. The chief mining towns are Rodange, Differdange and Dudelange. All these towns have iron and steel mills but the main centre of the industry is Esch-sur-Alzette.

Luxembourg is a very prosperous country. It has a

Below: Luxembourg City is situated on the River Alzette. Originally there was a great fortress on its site.

democratically elected government. It is a member of Benelux, the EEC and NATO. Luxembourg City is the seat of several international bodies, the Secretariat of the European Parliament, the EEC Court of Justice and the European Coal and Steel Community.

France

Area:	544,000 square kilometres
Population:	53,090,000
Capital city:	Paris
Language:	French
Currency:	French franc

France is the largest country in Europe. It is a land of many contrasts. The island of Corsica is part of France.

Physically the heart of the country is the gently rounded upland of the Massif Central. It lies in south central France and rises to 1,885 metres. It is composed of extremely ancient rocks as are the Vosges to the north-east and the Armorican peninsula in the west.

The French Alps in the south-

east are sharply pointed fold mountains. France's highest peak, Mont Blanc (4,807 metres), is in the Alps. The Pyrenees, which form the border with Spain, are also fold mountains.

A narrow basin drained by the rivers Rhône and Saône separates the Massif Central from the Alps. To the west of the Massif Central lies a more extensive area of lowland, the Basin of Aquitaine. This is drained by the rivers Garonne and Dordogne. To the north of the central uplands lies the Paris Basin, the most extensive area of fertile lowland in France. It is drained by the rivers Seine and Loire.

France has a long coastline on the Atlantic and a shorter coastline on the Mediterranean. There are wide climatic variations. In general it is cooler in the north and warmer in the south. As the prevailing winds are from the west, rainfall decreases to the east. Local altitude, aspect and shelter have considerable influence on the climate.

Agriculture is very important in France, some 15 per cent of the population being employed in

Left: A street market in Marseilles. The variety of fruit and vegetables on sale illustrates the range of food produced in France.

Left: The French buy a great deal of their fresh food, especially fruit and vegetables, in street markets. This onion stall is in Normandy.

Central. Thirty per cent of France's electricity is made from water power. There is a tidal power station on the Rance estuary in Brittany, a solar power station in the Pyrenees and many nuclear power stations.

With the exception of Paris, the long established major industrial districts in France coincide with the location of coalfields and iron ore deposits. The two chief areas of heavy industry are the Nord

farming. Traditionally French peasant farmers worked small scattered plots of land. Much of the work was done by hand. Since World War Two the French government has made great efforts to improve farming. They have reorganized the distribution of land into compact farms and encouraged amalgamation to create larger, more economic units. Mechanization and the use of scientific methods of farming have increased enormously.

The lowland basins are the most important farming areas. Much of the Paris Basin is covered by fertile loess making this one of the richest farming areas in Europe. Many cereal crops are grown, but the region is particularly noted for wheat and sugar beet production.

Dairying is practised on the wetter clay vales. In Aquitaine polyculture is dominant. This is mixed farming with arable farming, animal rearing and fruit growing being equally important. Rice is grown in the Rhône delta. The coastal lowlands of southern France are an important fruit and vegetable growing area. Brittany is noted for early season market gardening and dairying.

Fishing is important off the Brittany coast. In the Alps and the Massif Central dairy farming is dominant, giving way to sheep

rearing in the marginal areas.

France is only just second to Italy as the world's leading wine producer. Vines are grown wherever conditions are suitable. In Languedoc in southern France there is almost a monoculture of vine growing. This is where the bulk of the "vin ordinaire" is produced. Aquitaine produces many of the speciality wines, particularly claret.

Cognac comes from the Charente district north of the Gironde. South-facing slopes east of Paris are almost at the northern limit of vine cultivation. Small acid grapes are grown here which are used to make champagne.

France possesses large deposits of coal and has much smaller oil and natural gas fields. Mining conditions are difficult and coal production has declined since the 1960s. There is insufficient home-produced oil and natural gas to meet all the country's requirements, so France has to rely heavily on imported fuels.

This heavy dependence on imported fuel is a constant drain on the French economy, so there are great efforts to develop alternative sources of power. Hydro-electric power is extensively developed in the Alps along the rivers Rhône and Saône and on the rivers draining from the Massif

Above: Grapes are still harvested by hand, but today most crushing is done mechanically.

Europe

Above: The church of Sacré-Coeur dominates Montmartre. Once a peaceful village, it is now noted for its artists and night life.

The city's industries are varied and include engineering, chemicals, furniture, food and luxury goods. Paris is also the main commercial centre of France.

Marseilles is France's leading port. Its main imports are oil, bulk minerals and tropical goods. The coastal region west of Marseilles has developed as a massive oil refining, petrochemical and special steel production complex.

The tourist industry is important in France. The Mediterranean coast is the main tourist area but Brittany also has a flourishing tourist trade. In the south the Côte d'Azur, the coastal region east of the Rhône, caters mainly for wealthy visitors. Luxury hotels and shops, casinos and yachting harbours flourish here. To the west of the Rhône in Languedoc and Roussillon, tourism has been developing since the 1960s.

France is a republic with a democratically elected government. The country is divided into departments for administrative purposes. In the last 20 years the government has set up major schemes to modernize the country. In particular it is trying to rectify the imbalance of prosperity between different parts of the country and attract people away from Paris.

One of the major schemes is the Rhône-Saône Improvement Scheme. By linking them, it has created one of the longest rivers in Europe. Until recently they were of little use. There are seasonal variations in river level and the rivers flow through a series of small basins and narrow gorges. The scheme aims to improve navigation by cutting canals to by-pass the most dangerous sections. There is also a canal link to the Rhine.

Enormous amounts of hydro-electric power are being developed and water is being drawn from the Rhône for irrigation, especially in Languedoc in order to improve farming in the region.

France is a member of the EEC and NATO.

(along the border with Belgium) and Alsace-Lorraine. Traditionally these areas produce iron and steel, chemicals and textiles, but now in common with many other long established industrial areas in Europe they are suffering decline.

The Nord coalfield is becoming worked out and will probably be closed altogether in the 1980s. It is now uneconomic to bring half finished iron and steel from Lorraine. So new mills are being built in coastal locations such as Dunkirk, to use high-grade imported ore.

Lorraine is still a major iron and steel producing area, but even here imported ore and American coal have replaced local minerals. Many small mills have been closed and the industry reorganized into larger, more economic units.

Textiles have suffered from severe foreign competition and the introduction of man-made fibres. The government tries to attract new industries to these declining areas. It offers grants as an incentive and has built new roads to improve the communications.

In areas where hydro-electric power is plentiful, bauxite is smelted and special steels are made.

Paris and the surrounding area is the leading industrial region in France.

Industry has been attracted here by a plentiful labour supply, the enormous market created by the city and the ease of distribution to other areas. The river Seine is navigable by barge as far as Paris.

Monaco

Area:	1.9 square kilometres
Population:	25,000
Capital city:	Monte Carlo
Language:	French
Currency:	Franc

The tiny country of Monaco is an enclave of France. It lies on the Mediterranean coast at the eastern end of the French Riviera. Almost the whole area is urbanized, with hotels, luxury shops, casinos and private villas predominating. Tourism is the main source of revenue. There is an excellent yachting harbour, and the Monaco Grand Prix and the Monte Carlo Rally take place annually.

The country is ruled by an hereditary prince.

West Germany

Area:	248,624 square kilometres
Population:	61,400,000
Capital city:	Bonn
Language:	German
Currency:	Federal German Deutsche Mark

There are three different physical regions in West Germany. In the north are large areas of lowland which form part of the North European Plain. Central Germany is a region of valleys, hills and plateaus

Left: The Brandenburg Gate and part of the Berlin Wall. The gate is one of the frontier posts between West and East Berlin.

known as the Mittelgebirge. In the south there are Alpine fold mountains. The highest peak, the Zugspitze (2,963 metres), is in the Bavarian Alps.

The Rhine, Germany's greatest river, rises in Switzerland. At Basle on the Swiss border it turns abruptly northwards and flows through a broad, flat-floored rift valley to the town of Bingen. Between Bingen and Bonn, it cuts through the central highlands by a narrow gorge. From Bonn the river flows across the northern lowlands before reaching the sea in the Netherlands.

West Germany has coastlines on the North Sea and the Baltic Sea. The Kiel canal cuts across the narrow Jutland peninsula and provides a route between the two.

Hardly surprisingly, there are contrasts of climate within the country. The north-west has mild summers, rather cold winters and adequate rainfall throughout the year. Further east the climate becomes more continental with greater extremes of temperature

Above: A shopping precinct in Munich. Munich is the largest city in southern Germany.

and maximum rainfall in summer.

The varied landscapes found on the North German Plain are due to the last retreat of the Scandinavian ice sheet. Long, undulating grass-covered ridges rising to 150 metres are the moraines marking successive resting places of the ice sheet. Between the lines of moraines are broad marshy depressions called *Urstromtäler*.

These are the routes by which melt-water drained away from the ice sheet. Many are now occupied by rivers and they provide excellent routeways for canals. Huge spreads of sand and gravel cover and intermingle with tracts of more fertile boulder clay. These regions are known as geest. Parts of the geest lands have been reclaimed for agriculture by marling and the heavy use of fertilizer. Cereals, mainly rye, potatoes and sugar beet, are grown.

Large areas such as Lüneburg Heath have been planted with coniferous plantations but heath still remains on the most infertile soils. Cutting across the geest are the broad valleys of the rivers Elbe, Weser and Ems. Along these

Europe

valleys and the North Sea coast-lands are large areas of low-lying marsh called *Watten*. These have been drained like the Dutch polders and are important dairy farming areas.

The southern edge of the North German Plain merges with the foothills of the Mittelgebirge. This region, known as the Börde, is covered by thick deposits of loess which produce fertile soils. The Börde is intensively cultivated and crop yields are high. Wheat and sugar beet are the main crops. Pulp from the sugar refineries is used to fatten cattle.

The Mittelgebirge is a region of great complexity. Blocks of upland are separated from one another by lowland basins and river valleys. Generally the uplands are less than 1,000 metres high and have gently rounded outlines. Soils are thin and infertile and the climate is cold, wet and windy. Most of the uplands, such as the Black Forest, therefore remain densely forested and supply timber.

In contrast the valleys and basins within the Mittelgebirge are fertile and intensively cultivated. Wheat, oats, rye, potatoes and sugar beet are grown. In particularly sheltered areas orchards, hops and tobacco thrive.

Vine cultivation is a specialist form of farming practised in the Mittelgebirge wherever conditions are suitable. Sunny, south-facing valley slopes are terraced. Every available site is used, even the almost vertical sides of the Rhine gorge. German quality wines come from the Moselle valley, the Rhine gorge and the Rheingau. But the most prolific producers are along the Main and Neckar valleys.

In the foothills and valleys of the Bavarian Alps pastoral farming predominates.

West Germany is one of Europe's leading industrial countries. Large deposits of coal gave it a head start. There are also deposits of iron ore, potash and oil.

The industrial heartland is the

Above: Hamburg on the River Elbe is West Germany's main port. The modern dock basins have been reclaimed from river marshes.

Below: The Pfalz is built on an island in the middle of the Rhine. It was built in 1326 to collect customs from merchants travelling by river.

Rhine-Ruhr complex. The Ruhr coalfield with its associated iron and steel, chemical and heavy engineering industries became important in the 19th century when its coals were used to smelt local iron ore. Mining has progressed steadily northwards across the coalfield to tap increasingly deeper seams. Although there are still considerable reserves of coal, output has decreased since the 1960s due to competition from imported oil, natural gas and coal. American and East German coal can be imported more cheaply than Ruhr coal can be mined.

The iron and steel industry has faced similar problems. High-grade ores are imported from South America and Africa, but the industry has to compete with the newer coastal steel mills. But much steel is still produced in the Ruhr and a comprehensive range of heavy engineering products are made. The government has offered numerous incentives to attract new industry into the Ruhr.

Oil refining, car manufacture, electrical engineering and clothing are some of the new developments. The textile industry is also well developed.

Above: The Bavarian Alps are a popular winter tourist resort in West Germany for skiing. There are slopes suitable for beginners and experts.

Below: Fine sandy beaches along West Germany's Baltic coast attract many holidaymakers in the summer months.

Wolfsburg, the home of Volkswagen cars, is an exception. Hamburg is West Germany's chief port. In 1945 Hamburg lost much of its natural hinterland to communist states.

West Berlin stands on the river Spree. It is situated 160 kilometres inside East Germany. All the food, fuel and raw materials the city needs have to be imported, along three air/ground corridors. Berlin's main industries are electrical engineering and machine tools.

Communications in West Germany are among the most highly developed in the world. Navigable rivers supplemented by a vast network of canals carry much industrial traffic. Autobahns (motorways) link all major cities and there is also an excellent railway system. In the post-war period the line of communications has had to be changed. Before the war communications ran east/west across the whole of Germany, but now the main line is north/south, within West Germany.

West Germany has a democratically elected government. For administrative purposes the republic is divided into ten provinces plus West Berlin. Each has its own assembly but the federal government meets in Bonn. West Germany is a member of the EEC and NATO.

The importance of the Rhine as a navigable waterway is emphasized by the amount of industrial development between Wessel and Bonn. Iron and steel mills, car factories, petrochemical plants, dyes and pharmaceutical factories line the banks of the Rhine.

In southern Germany there are several isolated highly industrialized districts. For centuries this was an area of wood carvers, clock, watch and toy makers. Improved communications, modern power sources, such as electricity and oil and a surplus of labour from agriculture have helped attract industry here. A wide range of engineering products are made. Cars are made at Russelheim and Stuttgart.

Precision engineering, including aircraft engine making, is important in Munich. Saarbrucken and Mannheim have steel and chemical plants. Local deposits of coal in the Saar coalfield and the ease of transporting iron ore along the Rhine account for the location of these industries.

Industry on the northern plain is located in inland market towns and the ports. The inland centres are noted for agricultural processing.

East Germany	
Area:	108,179 square kilometres
Population:	16,800,000
Capital city:	East Berlin
Language:	German
Currency:	Mark of the German Democratic Republic

Structurally East Germany is very similar to West Germany. Most of the country is composed of the North European Plain with an arc of higher land in the south. The highest point is Fichtelburg (1,214

Europe

metres) in the Erzgebirge. In the north the country has a coastline on the Baltic Sea. The climate becomes increasingly continental in East Germany. In winter, bitterly cold winds sweep across the country from the U.S.S.R. Rivers freeze and snow covers the ground for months. Summers are hot and dry.

As the structure of the land is similar to West Germany, the types of farming found in each region are similar. The coastal lowlands which are more extensive in East Germany than West are largely devoted to the production of fodder crops supporting dairy, beef and pig rearing.

Farming is collectivized. Until recently the average size of the collectives was about 400 hectares. Now there is a drive to amalgamate the collectives into even larger units of about 6,000 hectares. This makes mechanization more profitable. Despite these changes crop yields have not increased and agricultural production remains comparatively low.

East German industry suffered greatly in World War Two and the immediate post-war period. Those factories that escaped the wartime devastation were deliberately dis-

mantled by the Russians. Since then industrial redevelopment has gone on under a number of five- and seven-year plans. Industry is nationalized and the emphasis was placed first on heavy industry rather than on consumer goods.

East Germany has large deposits of lignite and potash. There is a small bituminous coalfield lying between Zwichau and Dresden, and some rock salt in the foothills of the Harz. All other raw materials have to be imported, mainly from the U.S.S.R., Czechoslovakia and Poland.

Most of the lignite is excavated from highly mechanized open cast pits, and used on site as it is not economical to transport. On the Leipzig field it is used in chemical production, as are the potash and rock salt. Halle is the main chemical producing town. Leipzig, Magdeburg and Erfurt are noted for engineering. The lignite from lower Lusatia is not suitable for chemicals and is compressed into briquettes and burnt in gigantic power stations to produce electricity. There is a bauxite smelter at Lauta. Textiles and precision light engineering are also important.

Communications in East

Germany have been reorganized along Russian lines. Most traffic goes by railways which lead eastwards to Poland and the U.S.S.R. and northwards to the Baltic ports. The canals which led mainly to the west have greatly declined in importance. There is an Autobahn network but many roads are in a poor state of repair.

East Germany has a communist controlled government, is a Warsaw Pact country and a member of Comecon. After World War Two there were such radical changes that millions of people fled to the west. To prevent this the government closed the border, but there is still a labour shortage.

Switzerland

Area:	41,284 square kilometres
Population:	6,350,000
Capital city:	Berne
Languages:	German, French, Italian, Romansh
Currency:	Swiss franc

Switzerland is a small land-locked country in Central Europe. It is a

Below: Picturesque rural Switzerland. In the last 50-60 years the population in many Alpine villages has declined.

Right: Davos is one of the main winter sports centres. The brilliance of the winter sun, the clear air and the crisp snow make the area popular.

confederation of 22 small states called cantons. It is bordered by Germany, France, Austria and Italy, hence the different languages spoken in the country.

Over 75 per cent of Switzerland consists of mountain ranges. The Jura, rising to over 1,600 metres, lies in the north-west. The Alps, rising to over 4,000 metres, extend across the south of the country. The highest parts of the Alps are covered with permanent snowfields. Glaciers extend down the valleys. Two of the best-known peaks in the Alps are the Matterhorn (4,478 metres) and the Jungfrau (4,166 metres).

Between the Jura and the Alps lies the central plateau of the Mittelland. This is the most densely populated part of Switzerland.

There are a number of lakes. Lake Constance, on the West German border, and Lake Geneva are the largest. Two major European rivers, the Rhine and the Rhône, rise in the Alps.

The climate is one of mild summers and cold winters with heavy snowfalls. The direction of slope of a mountain is vitally

Below: In Alpine villages many people keep goats because they can survive on the poor mountain pastures.

important. It determines the amount of precipitation and sunshine, which affects the way land is used in the valleys and on the mountains. Forests clothe the sheltered north-facing slopes, while the sunny south-facing slopes are often terraced for vines and orchards. Occasionally a warm dry wind, the Föhn, blows down the Alpine valleys and on to the Mittelland, bringing with it a rise in temperature.

Farming is difficult in Switzerland, yet farms are efficient and productive. The majority of Swiss farmers specialize in dairy farming and cattle rearing. The cattle are kept in barns and stall fed throughout the winter, but they are left outside in the summer. Rich grass grows quickly in the moist warm weather. Cattle are taken to high mountain pastures to graze in the summer and return to the valley farms in the winter. Hay is the main crop of the upland areas.

Arable farming is more widespread in the Mittelland. Even here the crops grown, hay, oats and lucerne, are for fodder. About 25 per cent of the milk produced is used at home. The rest is used to produce butter, cheese, condensed milk, tinned cream and

chocolate, Nestlé, Tobler and Lindt are well-known manufacturers.

Pig rearing is closely connected with dairy farming. Pigs are reared and fed on skimmed milk, which the creameries return to the farms after the cream has been extracted. Pork products are an important part of the Swiss diet.

Switzerland is one of the leading manufacturing countries in Europe. This is remarkable for a land-locked country with no mineral resources of any importance. In fact Switzerland's only natural resource is a plentiful supply of hydro-electric power. All the raw materials for industry have to be imported. Barge transport along the River Rhine to Basle is Switzerland's industrial lifeline.

Because of these difficulties, the Swiss have specialized in making high-quality goods where the size is small in relation to the value. Clocks and watches, optical instruments and highly specialized engineering products are typical.

Engineering is the most important industry, accounting for 35 per cent of the country's exports. Turbines, marine diesel engines, sewing machines, typewriters and micro balances are made. Textiles

Europe

are an old-established industry while the development of cheap hydro-electricity has attracted electro-smelting, especially aluminium, and electrochemical industries. The chemicals produced range from pharmaceuticals to dyes, insecticides and fertilizers.

Switzerland's tourist industry is famous, but accounts for only five per cent of its income. As Switzerland is a remote, mountainous country, tourism only developed with the coming of the railways after 1850. Winter sports have extended the tourist season throughout the year.

Communications are extremely difficult between Switzerland and her neighbours. The problems have only been overcome by tremendous feats of engineering. As far as possible, both roads and railways follow the line of valleys. Roads negotiate the Alps in spectacular series of hairpin bends. For railways, which can only tolerate gently sloping gradients, tunnelling through the Alps was necessary. As some of the high passes still become blocked by snow in the winter, road tunnels are now being built. The new St. Gotthard tunnel will be 16.3 kilometres long. It should be open in 1980 and will have taken eleven years to build.

The Swiss Confederation can trace its origins back to A.D. 1291 but it was not officially recognized as an independent state until 1815. Throughout its long history Switzerland has rigorously pursued a policy of neutrality. It is a member of the UN and EFTA, but not of any international organization with political or military purposes. This neutral stance has protected the country from the ravages of war and allowed it to become one of the most prosperous countries in the world. The Swiss franc is one of the world's most stable currencies and the country is famous for its international banking activities. Switzerland is the home of the Red Cross and the World Health Organization.

Liechtenstein

Area:	161 square kilometres
Population:	24,169
Capital city:	Vaduz
Language:	German
Currency:	Swiss franc

Liechtenstein is a tiny principality lying in the upper valley of the river Rhine between Switzerland and Austria. It is an upland country with no land below 400 metres. The most densely populated part of the country is the plain bordering the river Rhine in the west. To the east the land rises steeply to 2,440 metres in the Rhaetian Alps, which form the border with Austria.

Farming is the main occupation on the plain. Farms are small. Mixed crops are grown and hay harvested for fodder. There are many orchards and terraced vineyards cover the sunny south-facing slopes. Dairy cattle are raised on the lower mountain pastures.

Tourism and the sale of postage stamps are both important sources of revenue.

Liechtenstein is ruled by an hereditary prince, but has very close ties with Switzerland. There is a postal and customs union and the country uses Swiss currency. The population is mainly of Austrian origin. Vaduz is the only town in Liechtenstein – all other settlements are farming villages.

Austria

Area:	83,846 square kilometres
Population:	7,500,000
Capital city:	Vienna
Language:	German
Currency:	Schilling

Austria is a land-locked country situated in central Europe. It is a mountainous country similar in structure to Switzerland. The Alps cover 70 per cent of the country. The highest peaks are the Grossglockner (3,798 metres) and the Wildspitze (3,774 metres). Roads wind their way across the Alps by way of spectacular passes. The Brenner and Grossglockner passes are the best known.

In the Alps winters are long and cold; there are heavy snowfalls. Unlike their Swiss counterparts, Austrian peasant farmers try to grow a variety of crops (maize, wheat, fruit, vines and tobacco). However, most of their farms are extremely small.

Left: The Houses of Parliament and Town Hall in Vienna, the capital of Austria. The city contains many elaborate baroque buildings.

Above: The Grossglockner is the highest mountain in Austria. Spectacular scenery such as this is typical of the Tyrolean Alps.

In the remote higher valleys much of the arable land is rugged, steep and infertile. There is still much hand cultivation and crop yields are low. Depending on the aspect and steepness of the slope, the valleys can be cultivated to a height of 1,500–2,000 metres. Only in the province of Tyrol does pastoral farming predominate, but even here the profits are small. People are leaving the rural areas more and more and many isolated villages have been saved from decay by the winter sports trade.

Towards the east the mountain ranges gradually fan out and basins between the ridges become wider and lower. These basins contain fertile soils and are intensively cultivated. The isolated towns of Klagenfurt and Graz have grown up in the two largest basins.

To the north of the Alps the land becomes lower through the Alpine foreland to the valley of the river Danube. The foreland consists of gently rolling countryside with occasional wooded ridges. The valleys contain rich farmlands devoted to cattle raising, and fodder crops are also grown. Two particularly beautiful lakes, Atter and Traun, are situated in the foreland. The Danube valley broadens around Vienna to form the Vienna Basin which is the most productive area of lowland in Austria. Here the largest farms in the country are to be found, growing a variety of arable crops (wheat, oats, maize, potatoes) in rotation, as well as fruit and vines.

North of the Danube the land begins to rise again to the Muhl-viertal, a flat-topped plateau. This area has only thin infertile soil and a severe winter climate. It is mainly forested.

East of the Alps is another lowland area called the Burgenland. Despite its gravelly soils, low rainfall and raw winter climate, this area contains the highest proportion of improved farmland in Austria. Stock rearing and wheat cultivation predominate with vines and orchard fruits grown on the sunny hill slopes.

Austria has a number of minerals. Iron ore is mined in the province of Styria. There are also deposits of lead, zinc, copper and bauxite.

There are small deposits of coal, lignite, oil and natural gas, but these fossil fuel resources are rapidly becoming worked out. Hydro-electricity provides about 60 per cent of Austria's domestic power needs and is also used to refine steel and non-ferrous metals.

Manufacturing industry in Austria is concentrated on the lowlands of the north and east. Iron and steel is an old established industry which is still important, the main centres being Donawitz-Leoben and Linz. Sixty per cent of the ore and all the coke used is imported. Thus Austrian steel is very expensive and the industry only remains competitive by producing very high-quality steels.

For centuries the River Danube has carried trade between central and eastern Europe, and it remains a vital link today. Many Austrian towns have developed along its banks, including Vienna, the capital, and Linz, an important river port and industrial town.

Tourism is an important source of income in Austria. As in Switzerland, the tourist season extends throughout the year. In the summer, visitors are attracted by the spectacular mountain scenery, picturesque towns and villages. In the winter, skiing and other winter sports are the main attractions. The Salzburg music festivals attract music-lovers from all over the world.

Austria is a republic and has an elected government. Before 1918 it was the most important part of the Austro-Hungarian Empire. The grand baroque buildings of the major towns date from this time. Between 1918 and 1938 economic development was hindered by political unrest. In 1938 Austria became part of Germany and at the end of World War Two shared her devastation.

In 1955 Austria once again became an independent neutral state. In the last 20 years the government has made great efforts to increase industrial development and improve farming. Austria is a member of EFTA.

Europe

<table>
<tr><td colspan="2">Italy</td></tr>
<tr><td>Area:</td><td>301,245 square kilometres</td></tr>
<tr><td>Population:</td><td>56,320,000</td></tr>
<tr><td>Capital city:</td><td>Rome</td></tr>
<tr><td>Language:</td><td>Italian</td></tr>
<tr><td>Currency:</td><td>Lira</td></tr>
</table>

Italy is a long peninsula projecting into the Mediterranean. The Tyrrhenian Sea lies off the west coast and the Adriatic off the east. The islands of Sicily and Sardinia are part of Italy. There are enormous differences in economic development and standards of living between the prosperous north and the poor underdeveloped south. Between these two extremes lies the broad transitional zone of central Italy.

Physically, Italy can be divided into three large sections, the Alps, the basin of the River Po and the peninsula and islands.

The Alps are a series of ranges of fold mountains forming a complete arc around northern Italy. They rise to over 4,000 metres and form a barrier between Italy and her northern neighbours. There are a number of passes through the Alps of which the Brenner and St Bernard passes are the best known. On the southern flanks of the Alps, are four large moraine dammed lakes – Maggiore, Lugano, Como and Garda. Dairying is important in the Alps. Vines, fruit and vegetables are grown on the terraced lower slopes.

The Po basin lies south of the Alps. It is the most extensive area of lowland in Italy. It is the most densely populated and productive part of the country, both in terms of agriculture and industry.

The Po basin was originally an arm of the sea which has been progressively infilled by debris brought down from the Alps. It is drained by the Po and Adige.

The peninsula is a complex region of hills and basins. The Apennines run as a great ridge, average height 1,500 metres, throughout the length of the peninsula. There are a number of basins within the Apennines and coastal lowlands separated by projections from the main ridge.

There are active volcanoes in Italy. Vesuvius lies east of Naples, Etna is on Sicily and Stromboli is one of the Lipari Islands.

There are great variations of climate. The north has hot summers and cold winters with an adequate rainfall. The peninsula has hot dry summers and warm wet winters. Drought occurs in the extreme south.

The Po basin is the most productive area but even here not all the soils are naturally fertile. There are broad deposits of coarse sands along the Alpine foothills which require irrigation. Elsewhere as in the Po delta there are marshes which need draining before they are suitable for cultivation.

The main crops of the basin are wheat, maize, sugar beet and fodder crops but there are several areas of specialized farming. Rice

is grown in the Po delta and to the south-west of Milan. Vines are important south of Lake Garda and in the Monferrat Hills south of Turin. In the Bologna and Forli areas fruit and vegetables are grown while east Piedmont and west Lombardy are important dairying regions. Parmesan and Gorgonzola cheeses are made here.

Mulberry trees (for silkworm raising) are grown throughout the northern part of the basin, mostly by the roadside or in field boundaries.

The hill lands of central Italy have been intensively cultivated since before the foundation of Rome. Many of the hillsides are terraced and the marshes which once covered the Arno and Tiber valleys have been drained. Wheat, sugar beet and fodder crops are intermingled with vines, olives, fruit trees and chestnuts. Most of the farms here are small holdings worked by tenant farmers.

The plain of Campania around Naples is physically, but not economically, part of the south. It is composed of fertile volcanic soils. Irrigation is used to supplement the scanty rainfall and the area produces high yields of fruit and vegetables, many for export.

Southern Italy, the region south of Rome and including the islands, is known as the Mezzogiorno. It stands in complete contrast to the rest of Italy. Poverty characterizes the area, making it more akin to some of the Third World countries. Some 22 million people live here, about 30 per cent of them employed in farming. Emigration from this region is continuous. Many of the soils are infertile and summer droughts hinder farming.

For centuries much of the land was divided into "Latifundi" or large estates. They were owned by absentee landlords and worked by poverty-stricken peasants. Since the 1950s the government has introduced a system of land reform and many schemes to improve farming. The latifundi have been broken up and the land redistributed in small holdings among the peasant farmers. Many irrigation schemes have been initiated and the farmers now concentrate on fruit and vegetable production.

Industrial development in Italy dates only from the 19th century. The country lacks any major coalfields so most of the development took place in the suburbs of existing towns. Many of the old established rural craft industries such as leather (shoes and gloves), pottery, glass and high class textiles still exist throughout Italy.

The Po basin is the leading industrial region in Italy. This area has been able to take advantage of local fuel resources. Hydroelectric power is generated in the Alps and methane gas is found south-east of Milan and in the Bologna and Forli districts. In addition, large quantities of oil are imported via Genoa and distributed by pipeline. High quality alloy steels are made at Turin,

Europe

Above: Rome is one of the most famous cities in the world. The Forum in Rome is visited by thousands of tourists every year.

Communications in Italy are well developed and are continually being improved. Sixty per cent of Italy's railways were destroyed in World War Two, but there has been extensive rebuilding, and more than 50 per cent of the tracks are now electrified.

One of the most spectacular motorways is the Autostrada Del Sole, which runs from Milan to Calabria. It was a great feat of engineering to build, with 113 major viaducts and 38 tunnels.

The main ports are Genoa and Naples, but others include Trieste, Venice, Palermo, Ancona, Leghorn, Bari and Sarona.

Italy is a republic with an elected government. There are many problems facing the government from the severe underdevelopment of southern Italy to the city of Venice which is slowly sinking.

Italy is a member of the EEC and NATO.

Monza, Bergamo and Brescia.

There are many engineering industries using the locally produced steel. These range from cars (Fiat at Turin and Alfa Romeo at Ferrara) to refrigerators and sewing machines. Oil refining and petro-chemicals are other rapidly expanding industries in the Po basin. They are located mainly at Genoa and Port Marghera near Venice.

Genoa is not physically within the basin, but is closely linked with it economically. There are ship building and repairing yards and a new iron and steel complex at Cornigliano to the west.

Milan is Italy's leading industrial and commercial city. It is the focus of the north Italian railway system and commands a number of trans-Alpine routeways.

In central Italy most industry is still confined to small scale enterprises or long established craft industries. Rome has a number of luxury industries and Florence specializes in making scientific instruments. Only in port locations (Leghorn, Piombino and Naples) is there a heavier concentration of industry.

The Mezzogiorno has never been an industrial region. However, since the 1950s the government has tried to encourage industry to develop here in order to give the south a sounder economic basis.

Tourism is well established in Italy. The country has much to offer, from a warm climate and beautiful beaches to the glorious remains of Rome, Pompeii and Herculaneum and the wealth of the artistic and architectural treasures of the Renaissance cities such as Florence and Venice.

Right: San Marino is a tiny city state perched on a mountain top in central Italy. It is an independent country excluded from the unification of 1870.

San Marino

Area:	61 square kilometres
Population:	19,200
Capital city:	San Marino
Language:	Italian
Currency:	Italian lira

The tiny country of San Marino is

Above: Vatican City. On special occasions the arena is crowded with people waiting for the Pope's blessing. The curved colonnade is by Bernini.

an enclave of Italy. It is situated in northern Italy on the eastern slopes of the Apennine Mountains, near the Italian town of Rimini.

Most of the people, known as Sammarinesi, are peasant farmers. Olives, vines and orchard fruits grow on the slopes and some cereals are cultivated in the valleys. Wine and olive oil are produced.

Tourism and the sale of postage stamps are the chief sources of revenue.

Vatican City

Area:	44 hectares
Population:	1,000
Language:	Italian
Currency:	Papal lira and Italian lira

The Vatican City, the headquarters of the Roman Catholic Church, is the smallest independent state in the world. It is situated within the city of Rome on the right bank of the River Tiber. The state also has jurisdiction over Castel Gandolfo, the Pope's summer palace and a number of other churches and palaces in Rome. It is administered by a governor and council on behalf of the Pope.

The Vatican City is an enormously wealthy state. It has its own police, postal services, radio station and newspaper. It also issues its own money, stamps and passports.

Malta

Area:	316 square kilometres
Population:	305,000
Capital city:	Valletta
Languages:	Maltese and English
Currency:	Maltese pound

Malta is strategically situated in the Mediterranean Sea, 93 kilometres south of Sicily. The country is made up of a number of islands. Malta and Gozo are the largest and Comino, Cominotto and Filfla are much smaller. The islands have rocky coastlines with a number of good anchorages. In particular Valletta, the largest town, has a magnificent deep-water harbour. Overlooking the harbour is a massive fortification dating from the days of the Knights of St. John. Between 1814 and 1964 Malta was a British colony.

Since then, it has been an independent country within the Commonwealth, and an important naval base. Dry docks and ship repair yards were constructed at Valletta for the maintenance of shipping. During World War Two, the island was awarded the George Cross medal because of the people's bravery in the face of constant aerial bombardment. The dockyards have been nationalized, and ship repairing and engineering industries are the mainstay of the Maltese economy. At present the Chinese are helping to build a major new dry dock which will accommodate some of the largest ships afloat.

Physically the islands are low and rocky. The soil is thin and is retained by terracing. The climate is hot and dry in the summer and warm and wet in the winter. The islands lack rivers, springs and trees. Despite these difficulties many people still live by farming. The holdings are small and there is little mechanization. The main crops are fruit, potatoes and other vegetables, some of which are exported. Apart from the dockyard, industry is limited. There are breweries and textile mills and a number of craft industries (glass, pottery, lace making) still flourish.

In recent years tourism has increased tremendously although the country lacks good beaches. Modern villas, hotels and holiday villages are springing up in the coastal areas.

Europe

Andorra

Area:	465 square kilometres
Population:	30,700
Capital city:	Andorra la Vella
Languages:	Catalan, French and Spanish
Currency:	Franc and peseta

Andorra is a small mountain republic situated in the eastern part of the Pyrenees.

The climate is severe especially in the winter. Some farming is possible in the valleys where fodder crops are grown. Sheep and goats are reared on the higher ground.

The French President and the bishop of Urgel in Spain have a joint nominal control over the country.

Spain

Area:	504,750 square kilometres
Population:	35,760,000
Capital city:	Madrid
Languages:	Spanish, some Catalan and Basque
Currency:	Peseta

Left: Horse-drawn carriages take visitors for a ride past Seville's Giralda tower. The city retains much of its southern charm.

Above: A great variety of fruit, vegetables and salad greens can be grown on the fertile irrigated Huerta lands of Valencia.

Spain and Portugal together form the Iberian peninsula. Spain is the larger country. The Canary Islands in the Atlantic and the Balearic Islands in the Mediterranean are also part of Spain.

The country has long coastlines on both the Mediterranean Sea and the Atlantic. The Pyrenees form the border with France.

Most of Spain is composed of a vast upland known as the Meseta. Much of this is an arid barren plateau rising to over 1,000 metres. Above this stand the "Sierras", ridges of even higher land running in a west-east direction.

The Meseta is dissected by a number of rivers, the chief of which are the Douro, Tagus, Guadiana, Guadalquivir, Ebro and Minho. The river valleys and the narrow coastal plain which surrounds the Meseta are the only areas of lowland available for cultivation. Consequently they are also the most densely populated parts of the country.

The Meseta has a continental type climate with hot summers, cold winters and a low rainfall. The Atlantic coastlands have milder temperatures and an adequate rainfall throughout the year. The Mediterranean coastlands have hot, dry summers and warm, wet winters.

The severity of the climate on the Meseta and the thin infertile soils make cultivation difficult. Very large areas support only poor pasture for sheep and goats. Low yielding wheat and barley are grown in a few places.

In the better watered areas, such as the upper Tagus basin, good crops of cereals, fodder, olives, vines and sugar beet are grown.

The Mediterranean coastlands are the most productive farmlands of Spain, thanks largely to irrigation. Water is drawn from a number of small rivers to irrigate huertas (gardens). These are divided into small plots and are intensively cultivated by peasant farmers. The range of crops grown is enormous: vegetables of all kinds, vines, citrus fruits, apples, pears, almonds, dates, figs, olives, maize, rice, cotton and mulberry trees for silkworms. Much of the produce is exported.

Similar stretches of irrigated farmland are found along the

Above: Harvesting garlic. Although Spanish agriculture is still not fully developed, mechanization has increased tremendously.

Guadalquivir valley (noted particularly for citrus fruit) and along the Ebro valley where wheat and sugar beet are most important. The coastlands of the Gulf of Cadiz are low lying and marshy. This area known as La Marismas is where the bulls are reared for the Spanish bull-rings.

There are thousands of hectares of vineyards in Spain. Vines are grown throughout the country, with the exception of the northern coastlands, wherever conditions are suitable.

On the northern, Atlantic coastlands maize, oats, barley and root crops are grown. Dairying is also practised here. Fishing is important off the northern coasts.

Many aspects of Spanish agriculture still require considerable improvement. The overwhelming need is to increase crop yields because agricultural exports earn a great deal of foreign currency. It is also necessary to increase the area under irrigation, introduce more mechanization and a greater use of fertilizer.

Spain has a number of mineral resources including coal, iron ore, lead, zinc, copper, wolfram and mercury. The main mining areas are around Linares (lead) and Rio Tinto (copper and manganese) in the south, but the bulk of the minerals occur in the north in Asturias and the Basque provinces. Coal is mined at Oviedo and iron ore at Bilbão. This explains the concentration of heavy industry in the north. Iron

Right: Beating olives out of the tree. This is the traditional method of collecting the fruit which grows mostly in the southern part of Spain.

and steel, engineering, chemicals, textiles, glass and paper industries are found here.

Elsewhere, Spanish industry suffers from lack of power resources. Even in the north, American coal is imported to supplement local supplies. There has been a tremendous increase in hydro-electric power production in recent years, but imported fuels figure largely in Spain's trade. There is a large oil refinery at Escombreras. Spain has an ambitious nuclear power programme which aims to produce half the country's total energy needs by the mid 1980s.

The necessity of importing raw materials accounts for the presence of industry in the major ports. Thus Barcelona is Spain's most important industrial and commercial centre. Its industries include textiles, engineering (diesel engines, vehicles, electrical equipment), chemicals and paper.

Valencia is also an important industrial centre with food processing, textiles, leather, engineering, chemical and ship building industries. Sagunto to the north has the largest steelworks in Spain.

The area around Cadiz is noted for its arsenals and shipyards.

In recent years Madrid has experienced a minor industrial "boom". Labour has been attracted to the city from the poorer country districts. The reason for the industrial development is improved road and rail communications. Vehicle manu-

Europe

facture, electrical engineering and textiles are found in Madrid.

Agriculture based industries such as food processing are widespread through Spain. Olive oil production is one such industry; the oil being a well-known export extensively used for cooking. Wine, of course, is made from the large number of grapes that are grown. Some is also used for sherry, which is made from dried grapes and spirits, and left to age.

The tourist industry is well developed and has become a key factor in the Spanish economy. There are many beautiful and historic cities, but the majority of visitors are attracted by the climate and sandy beaches. Cheap air transport and the introduction of the "package" holiday have done much to boost the Spanish tourist industry. The Costa Brava, Costa del Sol and the Balearic Islands, especially Majorca, are the main holiday areas. New hotels and holiday apartments appear each year. In winter the Pyrenees are a popular ski resort.

Internal communications in Spain are notoriously poor, although there has been some improvement in recent years. The main reason is the difficult physical nature of the country.

The state railway, R.E.N.F.E., runs the trains. R.E.N.F.E.'s equipment ranges from very old to high speed trains. Some steam trains are still used on local lines but ski trains are among Europe's fastest and most modern. Nevertheless, the mule- or horse-drawn *carreta* can still be seen on country roads.

The relief also helps to explain the disunity of the country. Settlement and economic development has taken place in isolated patches of lowland often separated by vast stretches of barren upland. The inhabitants are very patriotic to their own regions. Some areas even retain their own language. Catalan is spoken around Barcelona, and Basque in the Basque Provinces.

Attempts by a centralized government in Madrid to impose its authority over remote areas

such as the Basque Provinces or Barcelona are bitterly resented, and separatist movements are still strong in some provinces.

For centuries Spain has been plagued by internal jealousies between the different regions. These culminated in a disastrous Civil War between 1936 and 1939. The war started as an army rebellion against the government at the time. The government had been making an effort to redistribute the nation's wealth and diminish the power of the Church.

The rebels, with the help of Nazi Germany, were led by Generalissimo Franco. They were superior in training and discipline to the government forces, and eventually won power over the whole of Spain. Spain was then a military dictatorship until the death of Franco, who had become the leader of the country. Following Franco's death in 1976 moves were made towards turning the country into a democracy. The first free elections were held in 1979.

The country hopes to become a member of the EEC, but still faces many political and economic problems.

Gibraltar

Area:	6.5 square kilometres
Population:	29,000
Language:	English
Currency:	Pound sterling

Gibraltar is a tiny British colony situated at the southern end of the Iberian peninsula. The Strait of Gibraltar, the channel connecting the Atlantic to the Mediterranean, is only 22 kilometres wide.

Gibraltar is a peninsula joined to the Spanish mainland by a low isthmus. The most famous feature is "the Rock", composed of limestone and 429 metres high.

Gibraltar was seized by the British in 1704. The town which grew up on the western slope of the rock has remained a British fortress and naval base ever since.

Portugal

Area:	91,631 square kilometres
Population:	8,750,000
Capital city:	Lisbon
Language:	Portuguese
Currency:	Escudo

Portugal is situated on the west of the Iberian peninsula. The Atlantic islands of Madeira and the Azores are part of Portugal. Like Spain, the country is economically backward with a heavy dependence on agriculture.

Portugal has a long coastline on the Atlantic. Fishing, especially for sardines and tuna, is important. Many of the sardines are canned for export.

The uplands of the Spanish Meseta extend into northern and central Portugal. As in Spain they are barren and scantily populated. They are dissected by a number of rivers notably the Douro and Tagus. There are some mineral deposits in the north including iron ore and wolfram, most of which is exported. There are extensive cork oak forests in the uplands.

The Douro valley is intensively cultivated with vines, for the production of port.

The coastal lowlands are the most important farming areas.

Below: The spectacular Rock of Gibraltar rising sheer from the waters of the Mediterranean makes an impressive sight.

Above: Poland is still a land of many peasant farmers. These are typical peasant houses in the farming community of Kuznice.

Areas of marsh along the coast and in the river valleys have been reclaimed. Rice is the main crop here. There is some dairying and bulls are reared for the bull-rings. Elsewhere wheat, barley, maize, potatoes and beans are grown. Olives, figs, citrus fruit and almonds are grown on the hill slopes. The area under irrigation has been much extended in recent years. Manufacturing industries are not well developed. There are a number of small hydro-electric power plants, but the bulk of Portugal's fuel has to be imported. There are a number of food processing industries, and textiles, steel, engineering and electrical equipment, chemicals and ceramics are made. The ports are the main industrial centres.

For much of this century Portugal has been ruled by a dictatorship. However, there is now an elected government and the country is moving towards democracy. Portugal is a member of NATO and EFTA but hopes eventually to join the EEC.

Poland

Area:	312,677 square kilometres
Population:	34,500,000
Capital city:	Warsaw
Language:	Polish
Currency:	Zloty

Poland is situated in eastern Europe. The country has a long coastline on the Baltic Sea. The word "Pole" means plain and this aptly describes the structure of the country. The North European Plain covers all but the southernmost fringe of the country, where the land rises to the Sudeten highlands and the Carpathian Mountains. The plain is drained by the Vistula river, which flows north to the Baltic, the Oder, and its tributary the Warta.

Throughout history, invading armies have swept across the plain, conquering the country. Between 1795 and 1919 the Polish state ceased to exist, but it was re-created after World War One. After World War Two some Polish

Europe

Above: The Old Town of Warsaw was devastated in the war but has been rebuilt almost to its original design.

territory was ceded to the U.S.S.R., but much former German territory was added to the country.

The Polish climate is warm and wet in the summer, but bitterly cold in the winter. Some rivers remain frozen for several months.

Agriculture in Poland is similar to that in East Germany. The northern part of the plain is covered with hummocky boulder clay, and moraines. The soils are not particularly fertile and there is much woodland. Dairy farming and pig rearing are the main farming activities. Some rye, potatoes and sugar beet are grown where the soils have been im-

proved by fertilizers.

The central part of the plain has stretches of boulder clay interspersed with glacial sands. Rye, oats, and potatoes are the main crops. To the east there are great tracts of bog which merge into the Pripet Marshes of the U.S.S.R. The southern part of the plain is covered by fertile loess soils and is the principal farming region, giving high yields.

Attempts to collectivize agriculture in Poland met with so little success that they were abandoned in 1956. Seventy-five per cent of the farmland is still privately owned. Most farms are very small and often in isolated strips.

Poland has rich mineral deposits, particularly coal and also lignite, sulphur, copper and iron ore. The main coalfield is in Upper

Silesia, but another potentially very rich field has recently been discovered near Lublin.

The Upper Silesian field is easily worked; it is highly mechanized and has huge reserves. The field already provides 75 per cent of Poland's total energy needs and the country is able to export surplus electricity. Poland has to import iron ore to supplement local supplies, but the country has flourishing iron, steel and numerous engineering industries.

Shipbuilding is important in the Baltic ports. Vehicles, machinery and electrical equipment are also made. In recent years there has been a great increase in light engineering and the production of consumer goods. Other important industries in Poland are textiles, chemicals, non-ferrous metal

refining and food processing.

Poland has a communist system of government and is a member of Comecon (Eastern Europe's trade organization) and the Warsaw Pact (Eastern Europe's defence organization).

Czechoslovakia

Area:	127,877 square kilometres
Population:	14,860,000
Capital city:	Prague
Languages:	Czech and Slovak
Currency:	Koruna

Czechoslovakia is a land-locked, mainly mountainous, country in east central Europe. The state was founded in 1919 after the collapse of the Austro-Hungarian Empire.

Two of the newly freed national groups, the Czechs and Slovaks, united to form Czechoslovakia. There are three provinces.

Bohemia in the west is economically the most important. Moravia is the central province and Slovakia lies to the east.

Bohemia consists of a basin-shaped plateau ringed by mountains. The Sudeten mountains and Erzgebirge are in the north; the Bohemian forest and Moravian mountains in the south. The low Polabi Plains in the centre of the basin are drained by the Elbe and its tributaries.

Moravia contains the famous "Moravian gate", the lowland corridor connecting the North European Plain to the Danube basin. The River Moravia, a tributary of the Danube, flows

Above: Wenceslas Square in Prague, the capital of Czechoslovakia. Trams are a common sight in the city.

through the province. Slovakia is dominated by the high ranges of the rugged Carpathians. The High Tatra, famous for its beauty, contains the country's highest peak, Gerlachovka (2,663 metres).

The Czechoslovak lowlands have hot summers and cold winters. The climate is more severe in the mountains and they receive very high rainfall.

Many of the mountain areas are heavily forested, and traditional timber-using industries flourish.

Lower, sheltered valleys have been cleared for farming. Rye, potatoes and hay are grown and dairy farming is important.

The lowlands are the main agricultural regions, being covered by fertile loess and alluvium. Wheat, barley, sugar beet, potatoes, flax, hops and tobacco are grown.

In the Carpathians fruit and vines are important on south facing slopes. Nearly all farming in Czechoslovakia is collectivized and mechanization has increased.

Czechoslovakia has a number of mineral deposits including coal, lignite, iron ore, uranium, non-ferrous metals, kaolin and silica sand (for making glass). These provide the raw materials for industry although extra supplies have to be imported to supplement local resources.

The major industries are iron and steel, heavy and light engineering, cars (made at the Skoda works in Prague), chemicals, textiles, leather goods (Bata shoes), paper, porcelain and glass. There are also many food processing industries.

The main industrial centres are Prague, Brno, Plzen, Bratislava Morava-Ostrava and Košice. Prague on the Vltava and Bratislava on the Danube are both

Below: Lumbering and timber industries are important in the mountain areas of Czechoslovakia.

important river ports. Water transport in Czechoslovakia is hampered by the fact that the bitterly cold winters cause the rivers to freeze. The Elbe and Vltava are the most important waterways.

Czechoslovakia now has a communist system of government. It is a member of Comecon and is a Warsaw Pact country. Consequently the road and rail routes linked to the U.S.S.R. have been improved. Czech trade with Western Europe is slowly increasing.

Hungary	
Area:	93,030 square kilometres
Population:	10,670,000
Capital city:	Budapest
Language:	Magyar
Currency:	Forint

Hungary is a land-locked country in central Europe. It became a separate state after the break-up of the Austro-Hungarian empire at the end of World War One.

Hungary is mainly lowland. There are two plains. The Little Alföld lies in the extreme north-

west. The Hungarian plain or Great Alföld covers most of the rest of the country. The wooded hills of the Bakony forest separate the two areas.

South of Bakony forest lies Lake Balaton. This is the largest lake in central Europe. There is a further area of highland in the north of the country along the border with Czechoslovakia. Here the Matra mountains rise to 1,015 metres in Mount Kekes, Hungary's highest peak.

The country has a continental climate with cold winters, hot summers and a light rainfall occurring mainly in the autumn.

Due to the climate, the Great Alföld was once covered in steppe grasslands and devoted to the rearing of horses, cattle and sheep. Now most of this has been ploughed up and large square fields of the collective farms dominate the scene.

Cattle, sheep and pigs are reared in most parts of the plain, but they are now stall fed.

The Great Alföld is drained by the rivers Danube and Tisza, a major tributary. The land along the rivers is low-lying, swampy and liable to flood, suitable for growing rice.

Reclamation of this land is providing areas of pasture for intensive livestock production. Between the two rivers the land is higher and covered by infertile sandy soils. Rye is the natural crop, but much of this area has been improved by irrigation and the use of fertilizers and other foodstuffs can be grown. Good crops of potatoes, tobacco and melons are produced. Fruit (peaches and apricots) is an important cash crop and large areas are devoted to vines.

The north and east of the Great Alföld have fertile loess soils, and many crops are produced. Maize, wheat, barley, sugar beet, hemp and flax are all grown here.

Hungary's most important mineral resource is bauxite, but as the country lacks power resources

most of this is exported to the U.S.S.R. for smelting. Imported oil supplies almost 50 per cent of Hungary's power. Some hydro-electric power is produced, especially along the Tisza. Most of Hungary's industrial raw materials are imported. Despite this, manufacturing industries are rapidly expanding. Engineering, particularly vehicles, rolling stock and farm machinery, and electrical industries are well developed. Textiles, food processing, brewing, tobacco and leather industries are also important. The River Danube is an important east-west trade route .

Budapest remains the country's major industrial centre despite the government's policy of deliberately siting new industries in less developed regions. It is also the major commercial centre and the heart of Magyar culture.

Hungary has a communist system of government. It is a member of Comecon and is one of the Warsaw Pact countries.

Below: Many Hungarian peasants still dress in this traditional manner. They sell the produce of their small holdings in the local markets.

Europe

Romania

Area:	237,500 square kilometres
Population:	21,250,000
Capital city:	Bucharest
Language:	Romanian
Currency:	Leu

Romania is a mountainous country in south-east Europe. It has a short coastline on the Black Sea.

The Carpathian mountains and Transylvanian Alps form a great arc running from north to west. They enclose the plateau of Transylvania to the north west.

The major lowlands are the plain of Moldavia in the east of the country and the plain of Wallachia, which is part of the Danube basin, in the south. The Danube forms the border with Bulgaria.

Romania has a continental climate with hot summers and cold winters, which are particularly severe in the mountains. Rainfall is light and decreases to the east.

The main agricultural areas of Romania are the lowland plains.

Below: Although religion is not encouraged in Communist states, many of the older generation still cling to their beliefs.

The uplands are forested and provide valuable timber products.

In Transylvania, the western plains are covered by fertile loess. Wheat and maize are grown but the government is encouraging the production of industrial crops such as sugar beet, sunflowers and hemp.

Moldavia is a poor region hampered by drought in the north and bad drainage in the south. Maize is the chief cereal crop, but the area does produce some excellent wines.

The plains of Wallachia are also covered by fertile loess soils where a number of crops can be grown, and this area is intensively cultivated. Irrigation becomes essential to the east. Maize, sunflowers and sugar beet are the chief crops and market gardening is becoming increasingly important.

The outstanding product of its fishing industry is caviare (sturgeon roe), much of which is exported.

In common with most communist countries, farming in Romania is collectivized. Mechanization has increased tremendously, although it is still possible to see peasant farmers

Above: Consumer goods are becoming more readily available in the Communist states, but there are still few private cars.

using out-dated hand methods of cultivation.

The farming community as a whole has a very strong sense of tradition and still faithfully preserves many of its ancient customs.

Romania has rich mineral deposits, especially oil and natural gas. The largest oilfields are in the south around Pitesti and Oltenia. There are also smaller deposits of rock salt, coal and non-ferrous metals.

Below: Oil refining and petrochemicals are important industries in Romania. A lot of money has been invested in the oil industry.

The country's major industries are oil refining and petro-chemicals. There are six fully automated refineries and crude oil is also imported from the U.S.S.R. and the Middle East. Refined petroleum and petro-chemical products are exported to other Comecon countries.

Iron and steel is also well developed in Romania. The most important centre is at Galati on the Danube near the Soviet border, as both ore and coke are imported from the U.S.S.R. There are many engineering industries, notably producing refining and drilling equipment. Locomotives, machine tools and tractors are also made.

At present the government is greatly expanding production of light engineering and consumer goods.

Romania has a communist system of government and is a member of Comecon and is a Warsaw Pact country. The people are racially very mixed, being descended from many groups of invaders and settlers who crossed this part of Europe. The Romanian language has developed from Latin, taken to the area by the Romans in the third century B.C.

Above: The beautiful beaches of the Black Sea coast are a rapidly developing tourist area in Eastern Europe.

Bulgaria

Area:	110,912 square kilometres
Population:	8,730,000
Capital city:	Sofia
Language:	Bulgarian
Currency:	Lev

Bulgaria lies in the east of the Balkan peninsula. The country has a coastline on the Black Sea fringed with many beautiful beaches. In recent years a tourist

Below: Clothes bought in shops are expensive in Communist countries. Private stall-holders sell similar items at a cheaper price.

Above: Rural life in Bulgaria is simple, and old methods of transport are still common. Agricultural production has been improving, though.

industry has developed in Bulgaria. The visitors are attracted to the Black Sea resorts and also to inland centres because of the spectacular mountain scenery.

Much of the country is mountainous. The Balkan mountains run from west to east through the centre of Bulgaria and the barren, rugged Rhodope mountains occupy most of the south. The climate in the mountains is particularly severe and they are thinly populated. However, there are valuable forests here.

Between the Balkan and Rhodope mountains lies the broad valley of the River Maritsa. Winters are mild here and summers hot and dry. Farming is intensive. Although cereals are still grown the emphasis is on market gardening and high value industrial crops such as tobacco, cotton, sugar beet and sunflowers, whose seeds are used for making into vegetable oil.

Near Kazanlik there are extensive rose gardens. The rose petals are used to make Attar of Roses perfume.

North of the Balkan mountains lies a flat plateau. This drops by way of steep cliffs to the River Danube which here forms the boundary with Romania. The climate of the northern plateau is continental with cold winters and hot summers.

The main crops grown here are barley, maize, rye and wheat. Sheep and other livestock are also

Europe

Above: Yugoslavian peasant farmers rejected the state's idea of collective farms and retain their independence. Here, boys tend the family's sheep.

Yugoslavia

Area:	255,804 square kilometres
Population:	21,560,000
Capital city:	Belgrade
Languages:	Serbo-Croat, plus a number of minority languages
Currency:	Dinar

Yugoslavia is the "country of the Southern Slavs". It was formed in 1918 from a number of small Slav states. Some of the minority groups, especially those in remote upland areas, are still not fully assimilated. The country is situated in the west of the Balkan peninsula and has a long coastline on the Adriatic. There are a number of offshore islands.

Most of the country is mountainous. Along the coast is a narrow plain where the typical range of Mediterranean crops are grown. Behind this the land rises steeply to the Dinaric Alps, then drops slightly inland to form a vast broken plateau. Most of the upland area is composed of pure white limestone and there are large areas of bare rock with no soil. The climate of the uplands is one of extremes, and a low rainfall adds to the natural aridity. Within the barren uplands (karst scenery) are occasional clay-lined basins called polje, which support fertile farming oases. Irrigated crops of wheat, maize, tobacco and fodder grasses are grown. Cattle and pigs are raised.

raised in this region.

Bulgaria is primarily an agricultural country. Forty per cent of its land is cultivated. The country is politically very close to the U.S.S.R., and is an agricultural pioneering area for Comecon. Since 1970, collective farms have been abolished and replaced by agro-industrial complexes. These are huge farms, in excess of 20,000 hectares, and tend to specialize in one activity. The industrial plants associated with them are mainly for processing the agricultural products. By contrast, each farm worker is allowed a 1.25 hectare plot for his own private use.

Most of Bulgaria's manufacturing industries have developed since 1947. Agriculture-based industries still figure largely, but other industries are expanding.

Metallurgy, engineering, textiles and chemicals are important industries. The main industrial area lies between Sofia and Pernik. The port area around Varna is growing rapidly. Bulgaria has deposits of lignite and small quantities of iron ore, lead, zinc, copper and manganese in the mountains. Hydroelectric power is produced to supplement power supplies.

Bulgaria has a communist system of government and is a member of Comecon and the Warsaw Pact. The Bulgarian people are made up of two main races, Bulgar and Slav.

Below: Dubrovnik on the Adriatic coast is a popular tourist resort. The ancient city walls are still intact.

The largest area of lowland in Yugoslavia lies in the north-east of the country. This is drained by the Danube and its major tributaries the Drava, Sava, Morava and Tisza. The climate here is hot in summer and cold in winter. The Danube basin contains Yugoslavia's best farmlands. Broad river terraces covered with fertile loess and alluvial soils are intensively cultivated. Wheat, maize, tobacco, hemp, sugar beet, sunflowers, and olives are grown. There are many vineyards and plums are grown to make slivovitz, a plum brandy.

Collectivization of farming was introduced in Yugoslavia in the 1950s but proved to be unsuccessful. The state still owns about 30 per cent of the land but it is mostly farmed by individual peasant farmers on a semi-subsistence level. Many farms are extremely small. Only in parts of the Danube basin has collective farming proved suitable.

Yugoslavia has sizeable deposits of lignite and metal ores including bauxite, iron ore, chromium, copper and mercury. There are also small deposits of coal, oil and natural gas. Hydro-electric power is well developed. The country has a share of the Iron Gate hydro-electric power project on the Danube. However, there is a lack of coking coal and this hampers industrial development. Steel is refined around Sarajevo using imported coal. Bauxite is refined at Mostar and the refining of non-ferrous metals is also important. Engineering industries are expanding and include machine tools, shipbuilding, electrical equipment and motor vehicles assembled from imported parts. The main industrial centres are at Belgrade and Zagreb. Yugoslavia is one of the least industrialized countries in Europe.

The country does have a flourishing tourist trade. The Adriatic coast is particularly beautiful, but there is also some spectacular scenery inland, including many picturesque towns. The

Above: Albania is one of the least developed countries in Europe. Peasant farmers still use hand tools for most jobs.

offshore islands in particular have a thriving tourist industry. Many new hotels have been built and this has boosted the region's income greatly. There are a few modern motor roads, but many of the methods of transport are still primitive.

Although Yugoslavia has a communist government, it is not as ideologically strong as many of the other countries of Eastern Europe. In order to maintain its independence from the dominating influence of the U.S.S.R., Yugoslavia is neither a member of Comecon nor the Warsaw Pact, arrangements to which the other countries of Eastern Europe belong.

Albania	
Area:	28,748 square kilometres
Population:	2,430,000
Capital city:	Tiranë
Language:	Albanian
Currency:	Lek

Albania is a small and mainly mountainous country. It is situated on the west side of the Balkan peninsula and has a coastline on the Adriatic Sea. The Albanian Alps, which cover most of the country, are drained by a number of rivers including the Drin.

Development is concentrated on the coastal lowlands. Drainage and pest control schemes have made considerable areas suitable for agriculture, which is organized on a collective basis. Maize is the main crop grown, but cotton, tobacco, sunflowers, sugar beet and citrus fruit are becoming increasingly important. Recent industrial development, centred around Durrës and Tiranë, is based on local deposits of oil, salt and brown coal.

Albania is isolated from the rest of Europe both physically and by political ideology. Albania is a communist state. Between 1946 and 1962 it was a satellite of the U.S.S.R. It was a founder member of Comecon, but withdrew in 1962 breaking all ties with the U.S.S.R. and aligning with the Chinese People's Republic.

Greece	
Area:	131,986 square kilometres
Population:	9,200,000
Capital city:	Athens
Language:	Greek
Currency:	Drachma

Greece is the southernmost country of the Balkan peninsula and also includes about 400 islands lying in the Aegean and Ionian Seas. Crete is the largest of these islands. The southern part of mainland Greece, known as the Peloponnese, is almost an island. It is joined to the rest of the country by a narrow neck of land, the Isthmus of Corinth, through which runs the Corinth Canal.

Most of Greece is mountainous. Even the islands are rocky. The rugged, barren limestone uplands

Europe

Above: One of the greatest treasures of Classical Greece is the Acropolis which dominates the modern, bustling city of Athens.

of the Pindus mountains run from north to south through the country. Farther east, in a parallel range, lies Greece's highest peak, Mount Olympus (2,917 metres). Between the main mountain ranges a number of lowland basins are found. In classical times it was these isolated lowlands that became the sites of the famous city-states. The most extensive area of lowland occurs in the north-east of the country. This is often referred to as "New" Greece because much of this territory has been acquired since 1881.

Northern Greece has a semi-continental climate with hot summers and bitterly cold winters. Winters are severe in all the mountain areas. Southern Greece has a typical Mediterranean climate.

Modern Greece is the descendant of the greatest maritime power of the ancient world. Yet today it is an economically backward country with the majority of its people simple peasant farmers. The modern state was created in 1830 after almost 400 years of tyrannical and inefficient Turkish rule. The country is still overwhelmingly agricultural, despite only 28 per cent of the land being cultivable. Everywhere a combination

of rock type (limestone), poor soils and climate make farming difficult.

Grain crops, cotton, tobacco, currants and citrus fruits are grown in the fertile lowland basins, while Mediterranean tree crops – almonds, chestnuts, olives and figs – are found in the uplands. Vines manage to survive everywhere, even in the poorest soil, and sheep and goats graze the barren mountains. Most farms are small, less than five hectares in area each, and often fragmented in scattered holdings. There is a great deal of hand cultivation.

Agricultural products make up 40 per cent of Greek exports. In recent years the government has

made great efforts to improve farming. Irrigation and reclamation schemes, particularly in New Greece, have helped increase the cultivable area. Consolidation of the scattered holdings is being encouraged as is the formation of farming cooperatives. These will lead to greater efficiency and make possible increased mechanization. It is also anticipated that the farmers will grow more fodder crops and so increase meat production.

Greek mineral production is limited. Lignite, bauxite, nickel and iron ore are the most important. This lack of raw materials coupled with the small home

Below: There are many fishing villages along the coasts of Greece.

Much of the fishing is done at night and lights are used to attract the fish.

Above: Urban Greece. Work is difficult to find in Greece and wages low. Tens of thousands of Greeks emigrate to more prosperous countries every year.

Left: Rural Greece. These three old peasant men still wear their traditional dress. The beliefs and attitudes of the country people change slowly.

market has long hampered the development of industry. Only 25 per cent of the working population are in industrial jobs. Traditional craft industries such as pottery, lace and glove-making still exist, helped to a certain extent by tourism. Apart from these the major Greek industries are food processing, metallurgy, petrochemicals, engineering and textiles. The major industrial centres are the Athens–Piraeus area and Salonika.

Eleusis to the north of Piraeus is the country's only iron and steel centre. Both coke and ore are imported. Imported oil is refined at Megara and provides the basic materials for the petrochemical industry and also man-made textiles. Wool is imported for the textile industry but home-produced cotton is used. Piraeus is a major shipbuilding and marine engineering centre and the home of the large Greek merchant navy. The Greek merchant marine is one of the largest in the world.

Right: A typical Greek village with its whitewashed, flat-roofed houses. The narrow twisting streets are not very suitable for modern traffic.

Inevitably, the value of Greek imports far exceeds that of its exports. The resulting trade gap is filled by earnings from the merchant navy and the tourist industry.

Modern Greece has been plagued by political unrest but at present there is an elected government. The prospects of finding oil in the Aegean and the future of Cyprus with its Greek and Turkish communities in a state of uneasy peace has led to a certain amount of friction between Greece and Turkey. Greece is a member of NATO and an associate member of the EEC. There are plans for it to become a full member in the near future.

Arctic Ocean

Scandinavia

Europe

Mediterranean
Sea

Black Sea

Persian
Gulf

India

Minsk

Leningrad

Moscow

Gorki

Dnieper

Kiev

Kharkov

Ukraine

Don

Volgograd

Volga

Caspian
Sea

Kuybyshev

Ural

Aral
Sea

Tashkent

Karaganda

Lake Balkhash

Ob

Irtysh

Tobol

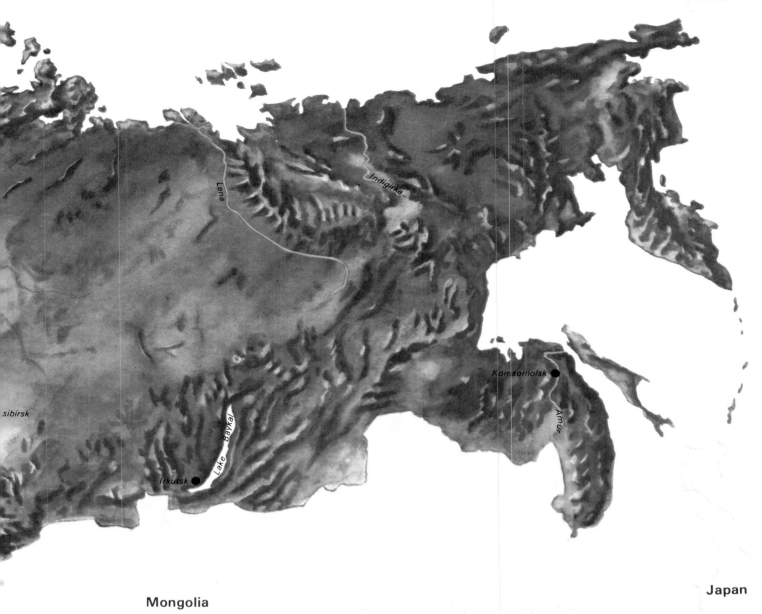

Alaska

Lena

Indigirka

sibirsk

Komsomolsk ●

Lake Baykal

Amur

Irkutsk ●

Mongolia

Japan

Pacific Ocean

China

The U.S.S.R., often called Russia, though correctly referred to as the Soviet Union, is the world's largest country, covering 22,274,900 square kilometres. Seventy-five per cent of its land area lies in Asia and the rest in Europe.

Population: approximately 255,520,000.

Fifteen republics make up the U.S.S.R. Russia occupies about 75 per cent of the country and is by far the largest one.

The **highest peak** is Communism Peak in the Pamirs which is 7,495 metres high.

The **longest river** in European Russia is the Volga which flows for 3,690 kilometres, and the longest in Asian Russia is the Amur which is 4,350 kilometres long.

The world's **deepest lake,** Lake Baikal, is in Siberia.

The **coldest place** in the U.S.S.R. is Verkhoyansk where the average January temperature is −50° centigrade. The coldest temperature ever recorded there was −70° centigrade.

The world's **longest railway line,** the Trans-Siberian, crosses the Soviet Union with 9,334 kilometres of track.

The **largest cities** are Moscow with 7,632,000 people, Leningrad with 4,311,000 and Kiev with 1,947,000.

U.S.S.R.

The U.S.S.R.
Area: 22,274,900 square kilometres
Population: 255,520,000
Capital city: Moscow
Language: Russian, though over 100 other languages are spoken
Currency: Rouble

The U.S.S.R. is the world's largest country covering almost 16 per cent of the total land area, yet it has only the third largest population of any country, adding up to just over six per cent of the world's total. It is entirely in the northern hemisphere and stretches across two continents – Europe and Asia. Only 25 per cent of its area is in Europe, yet 75 per cent of its people live there.

From Moscow, the capital city, it is 640 kilometres as the crow flies to Leningrad, 770 kilometres to Kiev and 1,950 kilometres to Baku, all in the west. Distances to cities in central Siberia and the far east are much greater: 4,200 kilometres to Irkutsk and 6,500 kilometres to Vladivostok.

West to east the Soviet Union extends from its Baltic Sea coast at about 20° East to the Bering Strait at 170° West, which means that it stretches almost half the way around the globe. From north to south it extends from the islands well beyond 80° North to its boundary with Afghanistan and Iran at about 36° North.

The Union of Soviet Socialist Republics was officially set up in

Above: The modern city of Moscow stands on the banks of the Moskva River. Wide roads run along the embankments and there are impressive public buildings.

Large areas in Siberia and Soviet Central Asia, shown in the palest green, are hardly settled at all. In the rest of the country many different national groups are found. Over 50 per cent of the population are Russians, living mainly in the west. The Ukrainians, most of whom live in the south-west, are the next largest group with nearly 50 million people. About ten million White Russians also live in the west. These three groups, who make up about 75 per cent of the Soviet population, are all Slavonic peoples. Of the other national groups, the Turkic peoples include nine million Uzbeks, five million Tatars and nearly five million Kazakhs. No other national group has more than five million people.

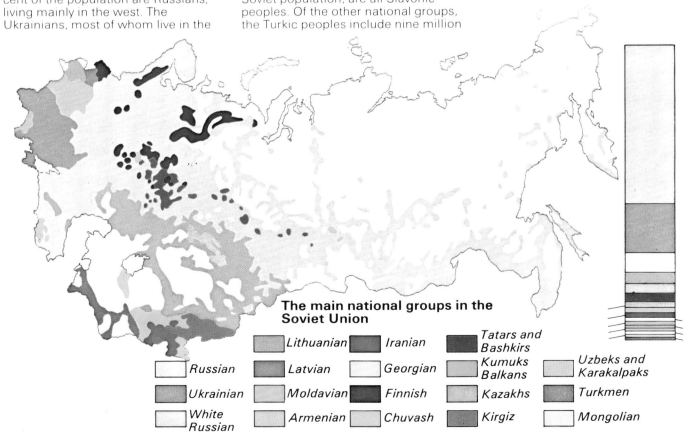

The main national groups in the Soviet Union

Lithuanian	Iranian	Tatars and Bashkirs
Russian	Latvian	Georgian	Kumuks Balkans
Ukrainian	Moldavian	Finnish	Kazakhs	Uzbeks and Karakalpaks
White Russian	Armenian	Chuvash	Kirgiz	Turkmen
				Mongolian

Some national costumes

The Soviet Union is a land of many peoples, cultures and a wide range of climates, from the cold wastes of the Arctic to the dry heat of the south. Heavy woollen clothes are vital in the north whilst cottons are more usual in the south. As well as everyday clothes, a range of national costumes may be worn for special events.

Nijni Novgorod Province

Cossack the Urals

Voronezh Province

Tambov Province

Vereya Moscow Province

Central Russian travelling costumes

1922. Politically it is made up of 15 republics, each of which has equal status, though they are very different in size. The Russian Republic is the largest, extending for over 17 million square kilometres, which is more than 75 per cent of the whole country.

Bordering Iran, Afghanistan and China are the five republics of Soviet Central Asia, Kazakhstan, the second largest in the union, Kirghizia, Tadzhikistan, Turkmenistan and Uzbekistan. Between the Caspian and Black Seas are three more, Armenia, the smallest of all, Azerbaidzhan and Georgia. On the Baltic Sea coast are three more, Estonia, Latvia and Lithuania. Finally, bordering the east European countries are Byelorussia, the Ukraine and Moldavia.

Left: In the centre of Moscow stands the well known State Universal Store (G.U.M.). It is really a shopping arcade on two floors, with lots of shops selling all kinds of merchandise. It is a great attraction for Muscovites as well as visitors to the capital.

U.S.S.R.

Most of western and central U.S.S.R. is lowland. In the west, the North European Plain extends to the Ural Mountains at about 60° East. East of the Urals, which lie north to south and rise to over 1,600 metres, the West Siberian Plain extends for 2·5 million square kilometres and is the largest single area of plain in the world. Smaller lowland areas are found in Soviet Central Asia. Farther east the Central Siberian Plateau is less flat and slightly higher above sea level.

The long southern borders of the country are mainly mountainous. The Caucasus Mountains east of the Black Sea rise to over 5,000 metres. Farther east, the Pamirs and Tien Shan rise to above 7,000 metres. Communism Peak, the highest mountain in the country, reaches 7,495 metres. The rest of the borders with China and Mongolia, though mountainous, are lower. Within the eastern U.S.S.R. are more mountains rising in places to over 3,000 metres.

The U.S.S.R. is a land of long rivers. Some of these, like the Ob, Yenisey and Lena, flow northwards to the Arctic. Others flow into the large inland seas and lakes which have no outlets to the sea. A few shorter rivers flow into the Baltic and Black Seas in the west and the Pacific in the east. Most of the rivers freeze for part of the winter.

The climate and natural plant life of the Soviet Union is very varied. Much of the extreme north has a polar climate where only lichens, mosses and small trees grow. South of this, where the temperatures and rainfall are slightly higher, coniferous forests stretch from Finland to the Pacific. In the warmer areas still farther south, you find first mixed coniferous and deciduous woodland succeeded by natural grasslands. Lastly, much of the area east of the Caspian Sea and south of the fiftieth parallel is desert land.

Huge areas of the country are a long way from the moderating influences of large oceans. Thus winter temperatures are very low and summer ones surprisingly high.

Rain and snowfall in much of the country are surprisingly low. Some places in the north-east and Central Soviet Asia have less than 250 millimetres in a year. Few places, even in the mountains, have more than 1,500 millimetres whilst most places in the great plain lands have between 250 and 750 millimetres.

Above: The spring thaw comes to a tributary of the River Ob near Novosibirsk. The river ice breaks up and local people take a dangerous but enjoyable ride downstream on the ice floes.

Below: Much of the Soviet Union is a long way from the nearest sea coast and beaches. However, there are many riverside beaches, where people can go for a day's outing with swimming and sun bathing. The beach shown here is on the River Dnepr near to the great city of Kiev in the Ukraine.

The historical background

Late in the ninth century the state of Kiev Rus was established with two main towns, Novgorod and Kiev. This was the beginning of Russia and her empire. In A.D. 988 the country became Christian. By this time it had gained lands on all sides and extended from the Baltic to the Black Seas. There was then a period of over 400 years when the country was engaged in wars with neighbouring countries and, in particular, was overrun from the east by the Mongols.

After the Mongols were finally beaten, Moscow and the state of Muscovy were the focus of Russian expansion. Tsar Ivan III (the Great) (1462–1505), his son Vasili (1505–33) and then Ivan IV (the Terrible) (1533–84) all reigned during periods of rapid territorial growth.

Ivan the Terrible pushed the eastern frontiers way beyond the Volga and the Urals, he created a new class of gentry and introduced serfdom. He developed trade with the rest of Europe, but is remembered most for his brutality.

Following a short period of wars with other European powers, a new dynasty was established in 1613 with Michael as the first Romanov Tsar. This family ruled Russia for the next 304 years. Peter the Great (1682–1725) and Catherine the Great (1762–96) were two famed rulers in this line.

Peter the Great was aware that Russia was lagging behind the times. He introduced new ideas from the west, regained some lands bordering the Baltic and established the great city of Leningrad, which was known at the time as St Petersburg. Catherine the Great was anxious that Russia should advance with the rest of western Europe. She was concerned for the state of the peasants, but could do little to improve their conditions. During her reign Russia extended its territory southwards to the Black Sea and westwards into the area of modern Poland.

Revolutionary ideas grew in Russia during the 19th century. Karl Marx published the communist manifesto in 1848, Tsar Alexander II (the Liberator) abolished serfdom in 1861, Lenin, the father of the eventual revolution, was born in 1870 and the Marxist Party was founded in 1898.

Early in the 20th century costly and unsuccessful wars against Japan and Germany enraged many Russians. In 1917 the communist revolution started five and a half years of strife and civil war. Only in December 1922 was the U.S.S.R. officially set up.

The greatest figure behind the Russian revolution was Lenin. He was an inspiring orator and a great tireless worker in the setting up of the Socialist state. He died soon after the new country was born.

Since 1923 the Soviet Union has developed into one of the world's greatest political and economic powers. Another costly war against Germany was fought from 1941 to 1945 but in the last 35 years it has emerged as the leading country in the European communist bloc. Major Russian communist leaders have included Lenin, Stalin, Khruschev and Brezhnev.

Above: Catherine the Great was one of the late 18th-century Romanov rulers who showed a deep concern for the welfare of the Russian peasants.

Below: Lenin was the greatest figure behind the Russian revolution. After the revolution, the Russians were hopeful for their future, but the new regime faced enormous problems. Civil war broke out, and in the countryside, millions died of starvation.

Although it is a large country, much of the U.S.S.R. is of little use for farming. About 50 per cent of the country is woodland and another 25 per cent is tundra, desert or mountains. That leaves about 25 per cent of the area as farmed land. Of this, just over 50 per cent is grazing land and the remainder, about ten per cent of the whole country, is used for growing crops. The area used for arable farming is increasing slowly as new lands are opened up. This is being done by clearing the forests, by introducing schemes of irrigation in dry areas and by using new strains of seed which will grow in the harsher climates of the north and east.

Before the revolution, far more Russians lived by farming the land than in any other way. However, agriculture in the late 19th and early 20th centuries was badly organized. After the revolution all land was taken over by the state and organized in state farms (*sovzhoz*) and collective farms (*kolkhoz*). State farms are owned and controlled nationally and the farm workers are paid wages by the state. Most state farms are large and are well organized.

Collective farms are controlled by an elected committee of the farm workers and are usually smaller than state farms. The land is rented from the state but the animals, machines and buildings are owned by the workers. There are far more collectives than state farms, though it often happens that collectives band together and are then transformed into state farms.

Many farm workers have a small plot of land on which to grow vegetables and keep animals for their family use. Potatoes, root crops, meat, milk and eggs are produced in large amounts on these small holdings.

In a broad area from the Ukraine and western Russia to the new lands of southern and south-eastern Russia beyond the Urals, more cereals are grown than in any other single country. The open,

treeless steppes of the Ukraine and southern Russia are well suited for the growing of wheat, barley and other crops on large farms. Modern mechanical methods of sowing and harvesting can be used.

There are sometimes great differences in the amounts grown from one year to the next, but normally the Soviet Union grows between 20 and 25 per cent of the world's wheat, about 33 per cent of its barley and 40 per cent of its rye.

Livestock farming has developed rapidly since World War Two. There are now over 110 million cattle, 140 million sheep and 60 million pigs in the country. These are mainly south of latitude 60° North. While animal and crop farming are well mixed in the European parts of the U.S.S.R., farther east animal farming is most important in many areas.

A number of other important crops are grown in certain areas. For example, in the irrigated areas of Soviet Central Asia, cotton is a leading crop; the Soviet Union grows more than 20 per cent of the world total. Tea growing is concentrated in Georgia where other irrigation schemes have been introduced. Tobacco is an important crop in both these areas as well as in parts of the Ukraine and south-west Russia.

Forestry and fishing

There are over 7·5 million square kilometres of forests in the U.S.S.R. About twice as many of these are in Asia, east of the Urals, as in Europe. Coniferous trees, which can be felled for soft wood, pulp and paper making, are far more numerous than deciduous trees, which can be felled for hard wood. Each year the Soviet Union produces about 16 per cent of the world's total timber and timber products. 85 per cent of the country's production comes from coniferous trees and only 15 per cent from deciduous trees. In all, nearly 400 million cubic metres of sawn timber, both soft and hard wood, are felled and four million

Above: Cereal growing is important both on the great treeless areas of the steppes and in the new developing lands farther east. Modern machines are used to obtain high yields and reduce the manpower needed.

Above right: Cotton growing is a major activity in the irrigated lands between the Black and Caspian Seas and in Soviet Central Asia. A wide range of machines harvest the cotton.

Right: The seemingly endless coniferous forests of the north are a source of great wealth both for sawn timber and for a range of wood, pulp and paper products.

tonnes of paper produced.

Within European Russia, forest industries are scattered throughout the whole area from Moscow northwards to the White Sea. In Asiatic parts, where forestry is less well developed, the industry is based close to the line of the Trans-Siberian Railway.

Soviet fishing fleets tend to travel great distances from both the Pacific and European coastal ports. Using the ports of the Barents Sea which remain open all year, the Baltic and Black Seas, as well as the far eastern ports, Soviet fishermen account for nearly 15 per cent of the world's total catch. This makes the country the world's second most important fishing nation. In addition, Soviet whalers gather 50 per cent of the world's annual catch of whales.

U.S.S.R.

At the time of the revolution there was only a limited amount of industry in the Soviet Union and this was mainly in the old towns and cities of the west. Since that time, the country has grown into one of the world's industrial giants.

By the time of World War Two, industrial developments in the western U.S.S.R., especially of heavy basic industries like iron and steelmaking and engineering, had achieved uneven results in a series of five-year plans. When Germany invaded the country, many of these developments were destroyed, but the Soviet people set about establishing their industries farther east, out of the way of land invaders.

Soviet industry is based on the production of coal, oil, natural gas, iron ore and a number of other minerals. The country has good reserves of all these minerals. It is the world's leading producer of bituminous (hard) coal. Between 600 and 700 million tonnes are mined each year. This comes mostly from four areas: the Donbass coalfield north of the Black Sea, the Kuzbass and Karaganda fields east of the Urals and the Pechora field in northern Russia. Other large coalfields are known, particularly in Siberia, but as long as the fields nearer to the main centres of population and industry still have reserves, there is little need to develop the others. The Soviet Union also produces more lignite (soft coal) than any other country except East Germany.

In the last 20 years Soviet crude oil production has increased dramatically so that it is now a more important source of energy than coal. Annual output is now about 500 million tonnes. In earlier times the oilfields of the Caspian Sea, particularly around Baku, were most important, but now the southern and central Ural oilfields have taken the lead. The oilfields in Kazakhstan and central Siberia have yet to be developed. The transport of crude oil is mainly through a network of pipelines linking the fields with the main industrial areas.

Above: The Soviet Union has many large oilfields. A wide range of petrochemical products are made in chemical plants such as this one.

Below: Most people in the Soviet Union use public transport to travel. There are far fewer car owners than in Western Europe, but car production is rising slowly. In Soviet factories there are often as many women as men. Women certainly play a vital part on car assembly lines.

Natural gas outputs have also increased rapidly since the mid-1950s. The U.S.S.R. is believed to have the largest reserves in the world, but each year she produces little more than half that of the U.S.A., the world leader. Similarly, the U.S.S.R. has more potential hydro-electric power than any other country.

Above: This poster shows some of the main sources of fuel and power in the U.S.S.R. In particular it shows two important sources of electricity – coal-fired and hydro-electric power stations.

After fuel and power, most industry depends in some way on iron and steel. Over 25 per cent of the world's iron ore is mined from the Krivoy Rog district in the Ukraine, the central Urals area and the Kuznetsk region farther east. Iron and steel production is concentrated in the first two districts, though new developments are taking place in the third. The country also produces a wide range of other minerals and precious metals, including 40 per cent of the world's manganese and gold, 25 per cent of its chrome and about 20 per cent of its nickel, tungsten and vanadium.

Until the death of Stalin in 1953, most effort went into the building up of heavy industries, like iron and steel, engineering and petro-chemicals. Since that time greater emphasis has been placed on manufacturing goods for individuals to buy, so-called consumer goods industries. In this way the standard of living of the Soviet peoples, which was so much lower than so many others, is being improved.

Much of this new industry is centred in the European parts, in Soviet Central Asia and the new areas developing along the line of the Trans-Siberian Railway. The processing of foodstuffs is widespread, mainly to meet the demands of the people where they live.

For a long period of time the

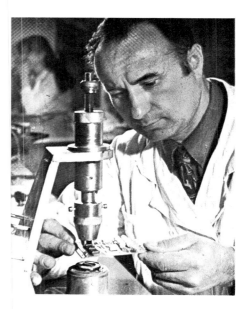

Above: Skilled technicians, like this engineer in an electronics factory, are needed in many Soviet industries.

Soviet peoples had to go without personal possessions whilst the country built up its industries. Now they are allowed to have more luxuries as the country is gradually becoming more and more geared to increasing the material standards of its people.

Left: Steel making, and other heavy industries like shipbuilding are important industries in the U.S.S.R.

Below: Soviet experience and technical knowledge of the building of great dams and power stations has been used to help overseas countries. The Aswan Dam in Egypt was built with the help of the Soviet Union.

U.S.S.R.

The Soviet Union has a population of over 255 million today which includes more than 150 nationalities. Many of the national groups are small, though over 20 of them have more than one million people each. The Slavonic peoples make up 75 per cent of the total population; the 135 million Russians are the largest group; then the 50 million Ukrainians and the 10 million White Russians. The Turkic peoples who live mainly in Soviet Central Asia, the Volga–Ural area and parts of Siberia are the second largest. Other groups include the 9 million Uzbeks, over 5 million Tatars and 4·5 million Kazakhs.

Each nationality has its own language and customs which it is encouraged to keep. Over a hundred different languages are spoken in Soviet schools but every child has to learn Russian as well as its own. This helps peoples to see themselves as part of the large country. Not all languages use the same script, so that children may have to learn to use more than one.

As well as language, each nationality may have its own costumes, temperament and ways of life. For example, when Russians first meet someone they

Above: Housing shortages in the Soviet Union have been reduced by the building of tall blocks of flats.

Above: Farm workers sell fresh fruit and vegetables at an open-air market.

seem to be shy and reserved but they become friendly and warm as they get to know them. They also have a sense of humour which is similar to that of the British people. Many families in the Soviet Union are more united than in other countries. Often, more than two generations live in the same house or flat. Many women go out to work and then the young children may be looked after by the grandmother, the *babushka*.

Old houses, often made of wood, are found in many Soviet towns and villages. More recently, houses and flats have often been built in prefabricated sections. Families may share a large house or live in a compact modern flat where they have less space than they would have in other countries. Their day begins at about 7 a.m., by 8 a.m. they have eaten a quick breakfast and by 9 a.m. they are all at work or school. They may eat a mid-morning snack and then a modest lunch at about midday. Following afternoon work and school most people go home by 5 p.m. and, after supper, the biggest meal of the day at about 6 p.m., they relax in the evening.

There are many famous dishes from the different regions of the Soviet Union. For example, a beetroot soup (*borshch*) or cabbage

Above: A cakes and pastries stall at an open-air market.

Above: National costumes are worn on special occasions. Here, two Ukrainian children are wearing hand-embroidered garments. The little girl has a headdress of fresh flowers. The children are probably on their way to a family party.

Above: May Day is the most important national holiday. Military and civilian parades are held to mark the founding of the Communist state.

Above: New Year's Day is a family festival. Grandfather Frost is the equivalent of the West's Father Christmas. He traditionally brings presents for young children.

soup (*shchi*) are both very elaborate and filling starters to a meal. Beef stroganov or chicken Kiev are two famous main dishes. Kebabs, a traditional dish in the Caucasus republics and Soviet Central Asia are now eaten in many parts of the country. Sweets, like the rest of the traditional meal, tend to be filling and may include pastry and fruit.

Shopping in the country is now easier than it was. Shops are owned by the state and the workers are paid a weekly wage. Many shops just sell one thing like shoes or clothes or furniture, but there are now a growing number of food supermarkets and department stores in the large cities and towns. Working women find it difficult to shop except in their lunch hours or at the weekends.

Some festivals are keenly observed in the country. The state has tried to discourage religion but the Christian calendar is still important to many people. While Christmas is not a state holiday, the New Year is. This is the time when presents are given and a Santa Claus-like figure called Grandfather Frost amuses and greets young children. But the great modern festivals relate to the creation of the communist country and are headed by the May Day

celebrations. Great parades and displays by the armed forces and the workers are held in many towns and cities.

Music and ballet, as well as opera, are great art forms to the Soviet peoples. Even before the revolution, composers like Tchaikovsky, Rimsky-Korsakov and Moussorgsky were world famous. Today their music and that of later composers like Prokofiev, Khachaturian and Shostakovich is widely enjoyed and played. The Bolshoi and Kirov ballet companies as well as dance companies from many regions flourish at home and make highly successful overseas tours. The Georgian State Ballet Company has its own theatre in Tbilisi. Georgia has many fine traditional dances which have been handed down through the centuries when this region was ruled first by one strong power and then another.

Young people in the Soviet Union are aware of physical fitness. Many of them take part in some game or sport in their spare time. The most devoted and skilled may be given state support and coaching and the best will represent their country against others. The Soviet Union is very successful in events like the European and Olympic Games.

Above: Valeri Borzov, the double Olympic sprint champion in 1972, has been a great name in international athletics in recent years. He is a national hero to the Soviet people.

U.S.S.R.

Left: In many Soviet towns and cities, trams are the easiest way of travelling. Services are good and a system of flat fares makes travel fairly cheap.

For such a large country as the U.S.S.R., good communications are essential. Most railways and roads are in the west where the majority of the people live. From other parts, good contact with the west is necessary. Since all communications are run by the state best use should be made of each means of transport – road, rail, water and air.

After the revolution road improvement lagged behind general progress and there is still a pressing need for more roads. In towns they are often good and are used by state-owned buses and trams as well as lorries. There are comparatively few private cars in the U.S.S.R. In country areas, the best roads lead to and from the large towns and rail centres. Bus routes between towns are becoming increasingly important. There is still no major road right across the country though there is a pressing need for a modern road linking Europe with Siberia and eventually the Far East coast. Already, a start has been made.

Railways are the chief means of transport in the Soviet Union. Although the proportion of goods and passengers using trains are both falling slowly, over 60 per cent of all freight and 40 per cent of all passengers are carried by rail. The rail network is densest in the west. Farther east the Trans-Siberian Railway, built between 1891 and 1917, is a vital lifeline in the development of Siberia and the far east. Only part of this line has been electrified. Now the Baikal–Amur line is being built north of this across the Siberian Plateau to the Pacific. This should open soon and will help in developing the areas north and east of Lake Baikal.

Many rivers in the U.S.S.R. flow from south to north whilst most traffic is moving along a west–east line. For this reason the rivers are not of great transport use. Most freeze up for part of the winter. In some places canals have been built to link major rivers together, particularly to connect the River Volga to others in the west. Large amounts of freight are now moved along these inland waterways.

Since it was started in 1923, Aeroflot, the state airline, has grown into the world's largest. In many parts of the country, such as along the Arctic coast, in parts of Siberia and in Soviet Central Asia, air is the most suitable way to travel. Aircraft of various sizes and speeds, from large sub-sonic jets and Concordski to smaller turbo-prop aircraft and helicopters, serve towns throughout the country.

After the revolution the national plan was to try to be self-sufficient and so trading with the outside world fell dramatically.

Since the death of Stalin in 1953 there has been a complete reversal of this policy. Records show that foreign trade had dropped by over 66 per cent between 1913 and 1938; but by 1975 the trade figures were over 20 times higher than in 1913.

All foreign trade today is controlled by the state which only issue

Right: More and more freight is being carried by road in juggernauts like this. However, road haulage is still far less important than in most of Europe.

export and import licences for those goods which fit within the current state plan. Exports and imports are each valued at about 25,000 million roubles each year and just over 50 per cent of this trade is with other countries in communist Eastern Europe.

It is not easy to forecast what the Soviet Union of the year 2000 will be like nor what policies she will pursue in international affairs. The next few years are likely to see changes in the leadership of the country and the ideas of the new men are not yet known. It seems likely that the country will continue to work for peaceful co-existence with the democratic western countries. At the same time she will try to exert her influence in the developing countries of the Third World. Her attitude towards communist China is even more difficult to predict, especially as the new leaders there are only just beginning to show a desire for better overseas relationships.

At home, the U.S.S.R. has a steadily growing population which understandably seeks a higher living standard. More undeveloped areas in the east can be opened up, new cities established and resources used. Though it may mean devoting less money and resources to such things as defence and space research, the government is likely to expand the production of consumer goods and attempt to make the life of the Soviet people a happier one.

Above: A modern electric train on the Trans-Siberian railway between Moscow and Vladivostok. It takes nine days to complete the whole journey.

IL-76 jumbo jet (cargo carrier)

V-12 helicopter (freight carrier)

TU-144 "Concordski" (supersonic passenger jet)

Above: Because the Soviet Union is so vast, air transport is of enormous importance. Passengers can travel rapidly over large distances in jet aircraft including "Concordski", the TU-144. Cargo is sometimes moved in small quantities by helicopter, like the V-12, but larger amounts can be carried great distances in freight liners like the IL-76.

Left: This Soviet ship, which can patrol the world's oceans, is equipped with radar and other devices for tracking spacecraft as they orbit the earth.

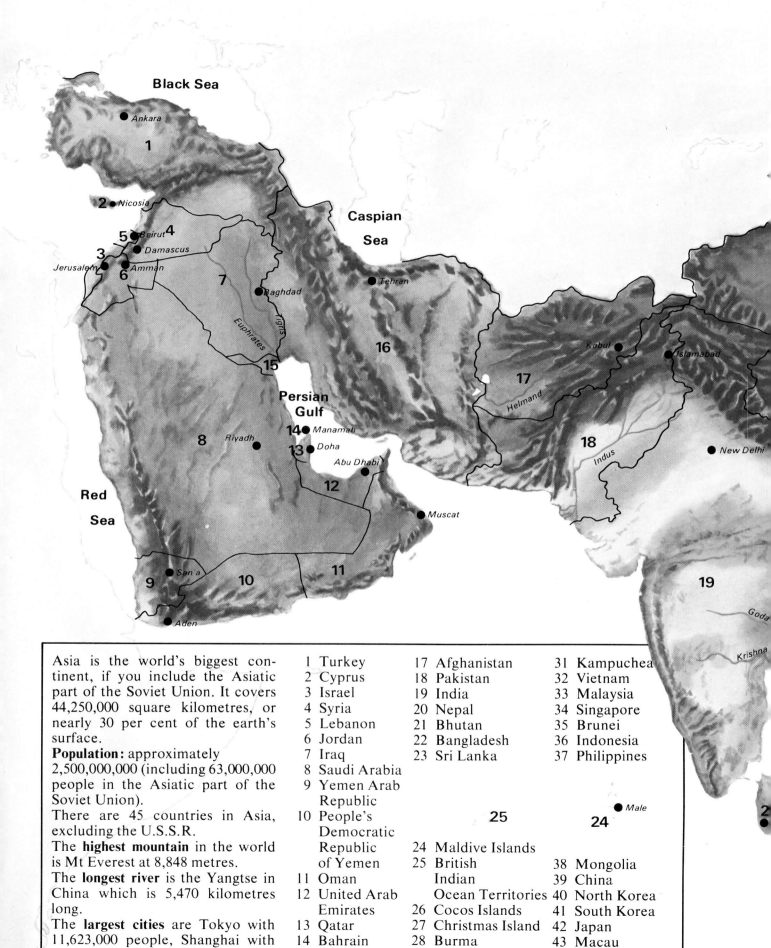

Black Sea

Ankara

1

2 • Nicosia

Caspian Sea

5 Beirut 4
Damascus
3
Jerusalem
6 Amman
7
Baghdad

Tehran

16

Euphrates

Tigris

15

17

Kabul

Islamabad

Helmand

Persian Gulf

14 Manamah

8 Riyadh

13 Doha

Abu Dhabi

12

18

Indus

New Delhi

Muscat

Red Sea

11

19

San'a

9

10

Goda

Aden

Krishna

Asia is the world's biggest continent, if you include the Asiatic part of the Soviet Union. It covers 44,250,000 square kilometres, or nearly 30 per cent of the earth's surface.

Population: approximately 2,500,000,000 (including 63,000,000 people in the Asiatic part of the Soviet Union).

There are 45 countries in Asia, excluding the U.S.S.R.

The **highest mountain** in the world is Mt Everest at 8,848 metres.

The **longest river** is the Yangtse in China which is 5,470 kilometres long.

The **largest cities** are Tokyo with 11,623,000 people, Shanghai with 10,820,000 and Peking with 7,570,000.

1	Turkey
2	Cyprus
3	Israel
4	Syria
5	Lebanon
6	Jordan
7	Iraq
8	Saudi Arabia
9	Yemen Arab Republic
10	People's Democratic Republic of Yemen
11	Oman
12	United Arab Emirates
13	Qatar
14	Bahrain
15	Kuwait
16	Iran

17	Afghanistan
18	Pakistan
19	India
20	Nepal
21	Bhutan
22	Bangladesh
23	Sri Lanka

25

24

• Male

24	Maldive Islands
25	British Indian Ocean Territories
26	Cocos Islands
27	Christmas Island
28	Burma
29	Thailand
30	Laos

31	Kampuchea
32	Vietnam
33	Malaysia
34	Singapore
35	Brunei
36	Indonesia
37	Philippines

38	Mongolia
39	China
40	North Korea
41	South Korea
42	Japan
43	Macau
44	Hong Kong
45	Taiwan

Indian Oce

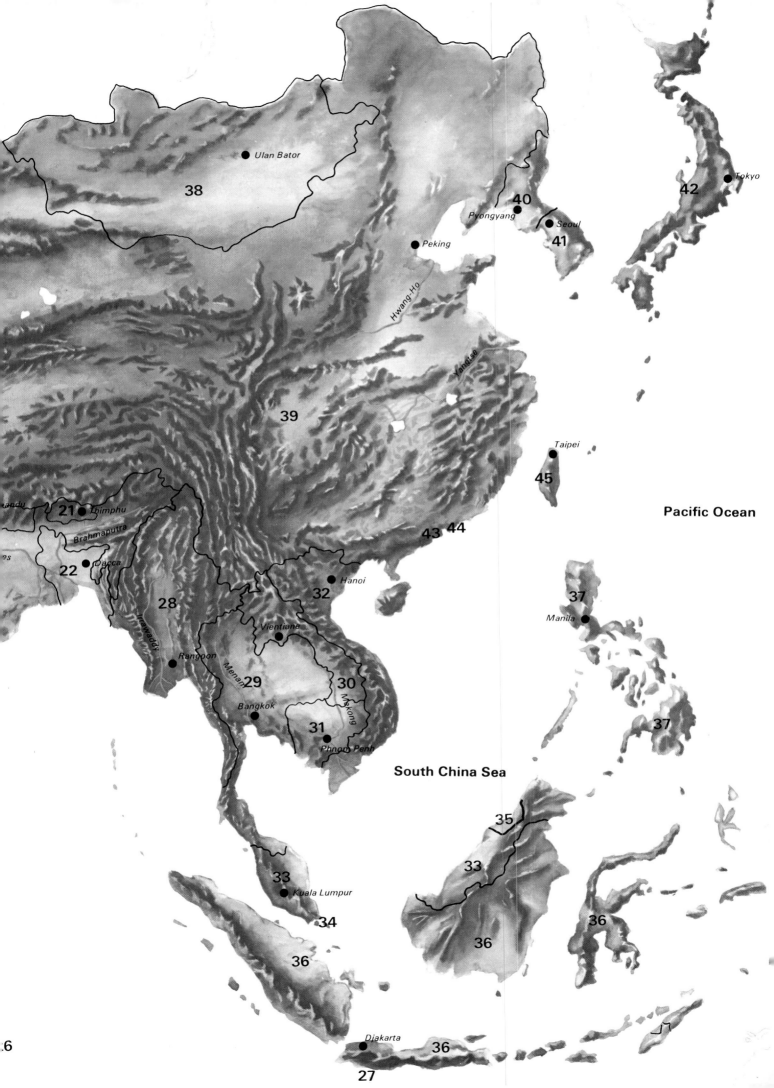

Ulan Bator

38

Pyongyang 40

Peking

Hwang-Ho

Yangtse

Seoul 41

Tokyo

42

39

Taipei

45

Pacific Ocean

21 Thimphu

andu

Brahmaputra

43 44

es

22 Dacca

28

Irrawaddy

Hanoi

32

37

Manila

Vientiane

Menam

Rangoon

29

30

Mekong

37

Bangkok

31

Phnom Penh

South China Sea

35

33

33

Kuala Lumpur

34

36

36

36

Djakarta

36

27

Asia

Asia spreads across over 30 per cent of the world's land mass, making it by far the largest of all the continents. It covers over 44 million square kilometres and consists of 45 separate countries.

This vast region ranges from icy wastes to scorching deserts and from steaming, tropical jungles to snow-capped mountains. It contains approximately 2,256 million people. This staggering figure represents more than 50 per cent of the world's total population.

Asia is a continent of extremes. Its mountains are the highest in the world while the lands around the Dead Sea, between Israel and Jordan, are farther below sea level than anywhere else. The rainfall in southern Asia is the world's heaviest. The western deserts are among the world's hottest and driest regions.

Some of Asia's people, notably those who live in the oil-rich Arab states, enjoy the highest per capita

Above: The Japanese *Noh* drama is performed as slow dance or mime to the accompaniment of music.

to a square kilometre than anywhere else in the world.

Asia contains China, the world's most populous country and over 60 per cent of the U.S.S.R., the world's largest. This great, sprawling continent extends from the warm waters of the Indian Ocean in the south to the Arctic Ocean in the north; and from the Pacific Ocean in the east to Turkey and the limits of Asia Minor in the west. Between Asia and Europe

Above: The Thar desert of Rajasthan is one of the most inhospitable areas of the Indian sub-continent.

income in the world. Others in the mountainous barren lands of Nepal, Bhutan and Mongolia, as well as parts of India, Pakistan and Bangladesh, have the lowest.

There are parts of Asia, such as the Maldive Islands in the Indian Ocean, where the population is small and thinly spread. There are also places like Macau and Hong Kong where there are more people

Below: This cloth market stall in Turkey shows the striking contrast between the brightly-dressed peasant women and the more sombre males.

desert plateaus. Its countries include Tibet (now part of China) and Mongolia.

Eastern Asia is perhaps better known as the Far East and includes Japan, North and South Korea and the major part of China. It is a region of fertile farmlands, and its climate is characterized by hot summers and cool winters.

Southern Asia consists of India, Afghanistan, Pakistan, Bangladesh, Sri Lanka, Nepal and Bhutan. This region lies south of the Himalayan Mountains. It is rich in natural resources that are as yet mainly unexploited.

South-East Asia is mainly rain forest with a hot and humid climate. The area includes countries such as the Philippines, Indonesia, Vietnam and Burma.

The last region is south-west Asia, or the Middle East. The climate is largely hot and dry. Countries in the area include Saudi Arabia, Turkey, Israel, Jordan, Iraq and Iran. Oil and natural gas are the vitally-important resources which dominate the economies of the area.

Below: These Kathakali dancers from India act out legends of the past using only their eyes and hands to bring alive the characters. Green men are heroes, red ones are villains.

Above: Jews gather to pray at the Western Wall in Jerusalem. This is the most sacred site of their faith. The city is dominated by religion.

lies the mighty 3,200-kilometre-long Ural Mountain chain.

Asia is geographically divided into six major land regions, separated from one another by mountains.

Northern Asia consists almost entirely of Siberia, a part of the U.S.S.R. It is, in the main, a bleak, inhospitable land where, in the far north, temperatures can fall below −60° centigrade. Siberia covers over 30 per cent of the entire continent.

Central Asia is an isolated, barren area consisting of great mountain ranges, deep valleys and

Asia

Turkey

Area:	780,576 square kilometres
Population:	40,200,000
Capital city:	Ankara
Languages:	Turkish and others including Arabic, Kurdish, Greek and Yiddish
Currency:	Turkish lira

Most of Turkey lies in south-western Asia. A small part, however, around 23,698 square kilometres, extends into south-east Europe.

Turkey is situated between the

Left: Women harvesting wheat in the Black Sea area. Women do as much work in the fields as men.

Below: Istanbul has a unique situation, lying at the meeting point of east and west cultures. It gives the city a character all its own.

Black Sea to the north and the Mediterranean Sea to the south. Her position gives her control over the sea lane from the Mediterranean to the Black Sea. This narrow stretch of water which separates Asian from European Turkey is called the Straits. It consists of the Bosphorus, the Sea of Marmara and the Dardanelles.

Asian Turkey centres on a vast saucer-shaped plateau, surrounded by rugged mountains which rise in places to over 3,000 metres. The northern edge of the plateau is dominated by the Pontus Mountains; the southern edge by the Taurus range. They converge eastwards in the "Armenian Knot", an inhospitable area of earthquakes, isolated volcanoes and dry, steep-sided valleys. It contains Turkey's highest mountain, Mt Ararat (5,185 metres).

The climate of the Turkish plateau is harsh. There is less than 200 millimetres rainfall a year and winter monthly average temperatures fall below −20° centigrade.

Along the coast the climate is less severe. The north, south and west enjoy hot, dry summers and mild, wet winters.

Agriculture is still Turkey's most important activity and the government has done much to help farmers increase their output. The chief crop is wheat followed by sugar beet, barley and grapes. Other crops include cotton, sultanas, figs and nuts. Turkey is the world's second-largest exporter of tobacco after the United States.

The wheat is mainly grown in the central plateau. Most of the other crops are raised in the fertile coastal regions.

Much of Turkey's considerable mineral wealth has yet to be fully exploited. Coal, iron ore and crude oil are the leading minerals extracted. A few medium-sized iron and steel works have been built.

Tourism is an important new industry. Centres are developing along the picturesque Mediterranean and Black Sea coasts,

Above: The view from the Suleymaniye Mosque shows the Galata bridge and the meeting point of the Golden Horn, Bosphorus and the Sea of Marmara.

where visitors are attracted to the large expanses of as-yet uncrowded beaches.

Istanbul is Turkey's largest city and the heart of industry and commerce. It is situated on the Straits, straddling Asia and Europe. In 1923 Ankara was made the capital in place of Istanbul, and grew quickly from a small provincial town to a thriving administrative centre.

The country has been a republic since 1923 when Mustafa Kemal Ataturk became its first president, and began the long, hard process of westernizing a nation whose economy and culture was still firmly entrenched in the past.

Right: Donkeys are a very common form of transport in the Turkish countryside. This picture was taken in Cappadocia, a region of the Anatolian plateau.

Asia

Cyprus

Area:	9,251 square kilometres
Population:	639,000
Capital city:	Nicosia
Languages:	Greek, Turkish and English
Currency:	Cyprus pound

At its greatest length Cyprus is 235 kilometres, its greatest width, 96 kilometres. This makes Cyprus the third largest island in the Mediterranean after Sicily and Sardinia. It is an independent republic within the Commonwealth.

Cyprus is situated in the north-east corner of the Mediterranean. Turkey is about 70 kilometres to the north and Syria about 100 kilometres to the east.

The island consists of two high mountain ranges, the Kyrenia chain in the north and the Troodos in the south-west. Both chains lie from east to west and are separated by a wide, flat plain open to the sea at both ends. The Troodos chain covers almost half of Cyprus and has the island's highest peak, the 1,951-metre Mt Olympus.

The central plain is called the Mesaoria and is the most fertile and densely populated part of Cyprus. The island's main crops of wheat and barley are grown here.

Around 40 per cent of the workforce are engaged in agriculture, still the predominant industry. There is an expanding export trade in citrus fruits, potatoes, carrots and other vegetables.

Vines are grown on the lower slopes of the Troodos Mountains. The resulting wine, sherry and brandy provide valuable exports.

The mineral wealth of Cyprus is fairly limited. The dwindling deposits include asbestos, iron pyrites and copper concentrates.

Cyprus enjoys a hot, dry summer and warm, wet winters. Average monthly temperatures in summer reach the high 20° centigrade. Rainfall averages 380 millimetres a year in the central lowlands to over 500 millimetres in the uplands.

The island's reliable climate has helped build a valuable tourist trade. Over 200,000 people visit the island each year and this figure is expected to increase as more hotels are built.

In 1974 continuing tension between the Turkish and Greek communities brought civil war to Cyprus for the second time in ten years. Following a Turkish invasion of the north, thousands of Greeks fled to the south.

Israel

Area:	20,700 square kilometres
Population:	3,000,000
Capital city:	Jerusalem
Languages:	Hebrew and Arabic; others include English, French and Yiddish
Currency:	Israeli pound

Above: These members of a kibbutz in the Negev Desert are harvesting melons from beneath their plastic covering.

Israel consists of a narrow strip of land lying between the eastern Mediterranean Sea to the west and the Jordan Valley to the east. Syria and Lebanon border Israel to the north, Jordan to the east and Egypt to the south-west.

Apart from the Galilee Highlands which rise to 1,208 metres in the north, Israel is very low-lying.

The climate is Mediterranean – hot summers and cool winters – in the north and along the coast. In the barren Negev Desert, which forms about half of Israel's southern region, there is little rain and summer average temperatures soar to above 40° centigrade.

Israel's principal river is the Jordan. This rises beyond the country's northern border and

Above: Tel Aviv is Israel's largest city. It is also the country's chief commercial, industrial and communications centre.

flows through the Sea of Galilee (Lake Tiberias). The river finally flows into the Dead Sea after crossing through Jordan.

The Dead Sea, which lies in both Israel and Jordan, is 395 metres below sea level. The saline (salt-rich) waters of the Dead Sea enable Israel to produce more than one million tonnes of potash salts through evaporation every year.

Although Israel still imports far more goods than she exports, the country's industry is highly developed, and Israel is the most advanced country in western Asia.

Israel is second only to Belgium as the world's largest exporter of polished diamonds.

Agriculture too plays an important part in Israel's economy. Citrus fruits, including the famous "Jaffa" oranges, are major exports.

Israel is surrounded by hostile Arab nations and has been on an almost constant state of alert since it was formed in 1948. The country is a democracy and is currently governed by the right-wing *Likud* party.

Syria	
Area:	185,680 square kilometres
Population:	8,300,000
Capital city:	Damascus
Languages:	Arabic and others including Aramaic, Armenian and Assyrian
Currency:	Syrian pound

Syria lies at the eastern end of the Mediterranean and stretches inland for nearly 600 kilometres. Jordan lies to the south, Turkey to the north, and Iraq to the east. Syria's Mediterranean coastline extends only 128 kilometres between Turkey and the Lebanon. There is a 72-kilometre border with Israel in the south-west.

Geographically, Syria can be divided into five main areas: rolling plains in the north; the Jazirah Plains beyond the Euphrates in the east; the Syrian Desert; the Plains of Hauran and the Anti-Lebanon mountains in the south-west.

Syria's coastal climate is mild all year round. Rainfall averages 940 millimetres and summer average temperatures in the west are around 26° centigrade. However, inland, particularly in the desert regions, summer average temperatures are over 32° centigrade and the rainfall is less than 100 millimetres.

Agriculture is the main industry and this occupies over 60 per cent of the population. Many are Bedouins and the desert pastures provide grazing for some five million sheep and 700,000 goats.

Syria's most fertile area is in the river valleys of the Euphrates and Orontes. The main crops are barley, cotton, fruit, potatoes and wheat.

Oil production is growing in importance and now accounts for 12 per cent of Syria's exports.

Syria is governed by a People's Council but the army exerts the most influence.

Lebanon	
Area:	10,400 square kilometres
Population:	2,780,000
Capital city:	Beirut
Languages:	Arabic, French and English
Currency:	Lebanese pound

Lebanon is a comparatively small country, situated in south-west Asia. It is bordered on the north and east by Syria and by Israel on

Asia

Above: Methods of farming in the Middle East remain quite primitive. This wooden plough is Lebanese.

the south. The Mediterranean lies to the west.

The country is divided into four main geographic areas. These are: the narrow coastal strip; the Lebanon mountains which run the full length of the coast; the inland, fertile Bekaa plain and the Anti-Lebanon mountains on the border with Syria in the east. The highest peak is Mount Hermon, some 2,814 metres high.

There are two major rivers which rise in the Bekaa. These are the Litani and the Orontes. The Litani is 145 kilometres long and flows south then west into the Mediterranean. The Orontes is 396 kilometres long but it flows northwards into Syria.

Lebanese summers are hot and dry, the winters cool and moist. In Beirut the average monthly temperature range is between 21° and 27° centigrade. The city's annual rainfall is 920 millimetres.

Nearly 40 per cent of the total land area is cultivable. Fifty per cent of the workforce are farmers. Fruit is the most important crop, particularly citrus fruits, apples, grapes, bananas and olives.

Lebanon was once world-renowned for its cedar trees. Now only a few carefully tended groves remain.

There are few mineral reserves and nearly all the country's industrial material has to be imported. Manufacturing is still on a fairly limited scale. Food, tobacco and textiles are the main products.

Lebanon has long been one of the most important trading and business centres in the Middle East, but 19 months of civil war between Muslims and Christians, which ended in 1976 when an Arab Deterrent Force (mainly Syrians) imposed a ceasefire, has diminished the country's commercial activity. The elegant capital has been almost reduced to rubble.

Jordan	
Area:	97,740 square kilometres
Population:	2,750,000
Capital city:	Amman
Language:	Arabic
Currency:	Jordanian dinar

Jordan, an Arab kingdom in south-west Asia, occupies part of what was once ancient Palestine. Since 1952 it has been ruled by King Hussein.

Israel lies to the west, Saudi Arabia to the east and south, Syria is to the north and Iraq to the north-east. Jordan has a few kilometres of coastline on the Red Sea, at the port of Aqaba.

The country can be divided into three main geographic regions: the western uplands; the rift valley and the great eastern desert plateau.

Below: Prayers being said at the al-Hussein Mosque in Jordan during Ramadan (a period of fasting).

The western uplands have been occupied by Israel since 1967. The area is known as West Jordan and extends westwards from the River Jordan and the Dead Sea. The uplands rise to more than 1,000 metres and the northern half – known as Samaria – is reasonably fertile.

The rift valley, the northern extreme of the great crustal fault system which extends into East Africa, stretches south from the Sea of Galilee in Israel to the Gulf of Aqaba.

To the east of the rift valley lies a great desert plateau. This covers an area of over 90,000 square kilometres. This slopes eastwards towards Syria and contains Jebel Ram (1,754 metres), Jordan's highest mountain.

Jordan's climate varies between Mediterranean and desert. Summer average temperatures in the rift valley rise well above 30° centigrade. Winter temperatures in Amman average only 8° centigrade. Annual rainfall in the west is 300 millimetres but is below 100 millimetres in the eastern desert.

Agriculture is the country's main economic activity. But as only 12 per cent of the land is cultivated it is not enough to meet the total food requirements. The chief crops are barley, wheat, citrus fruits, olives and water melons. Sheep and goats are also reared.

Jordan's main important industrial product is phosphate. This accounts for 40 per cent of exports. Otherwise there is little development and Jordan leans heavily on foreign aid.

Iraq	
Area:	438,446 square kilometres
Population:	11,500,000
Capital city:	Baghdad
Languages:	Arabic and Kurdish
Currency:	Iraqi dinar

Iraq is situated in south-west Asia at the head of the Persian Gulf. It

Above: Water is scarce in the Arabian peninsula. Its use is regulated.

is bordered on the east by Iran, on the south by Saudi Arabia and Kuwait, on the west by Syria and Jordan, and by Turkey to the north.

The country is divided into three distinct and different physical regions: mountains in the north-east; inhospitable desert in the south and west; and extensive lowlands which are crossed by the rivers Tigris and Euphrates. This is often referred to as the delta lowlands, and is Iraq's most fertile area. It runs about 560 kilometres inland from the Persian Gulf. This lower plain was known in ancient times as Mesopotamia. It was here that some of the world's greatest early civilizations were founded. These include those of the Sumerians and Babylonians.

Iraq's climate varies between the river valleys, mountains and desert regions. The lowlands experience dry and very hot summers. Winter is relatively humid and cool. In the mountains the winter is usually severe. During the month of July strong winds result in fierce sandstorms, particularly around Baghdad.

In 1927 oil was discovered in the hills of the north-east around Kirkuk. Oil now accounts for 90

per cent of Iraq's export trade and much of the large oil income is now being spent on irrigation projects to improve the country's agricultural output. Crops grown include wheat, barley, rice, maize and dates. Iraq provides 80 per cent of the world's total date supply.

Since 1958, Iraq has been an Arab republic. Before that time it was a monarchy. The country is now ruled by the military Revolutionary Command Council.

Saudi Arabia	
Area:	2,400,000 square kilometres
Population:	9,160,000
Capital city:	Riyadh
Language:	Arabic
Currency:	Rial

Saudi Arabia occupies a large part of the desert peninsula between the Persian Gulf to the east, the Red Sea to the west and the Arabian Sea to the south. Jordan, Iraq and Kuwait lie to the north; the two Yemen states, the United Arab Emirates, Qatar and Oman lie to the south and east. There is a neutral zone of approximately

6,000 square kilometres between Saudi Arabia and Iraq. This was created for the benefit of nomadic tribesmen who wander the Arabian peninsula in search of grazing.

There are four distinct regions: the narrow plain which runs along the Red Sea coast; the western mountains which rise from the plain and then slope gently east; the interior plateau which covers 90 per cent of Saudi Arabia and is mainly desert and, finally, the eastern coastal plain.

The interior is marked by two great deserts: the Nafud in the north and the Rub al Khali in the south-east. The latter is known as the "Empty Quarter" and is thought to be the world's most arid stretch of land.

Saudi Arabia is one of the most inhospitable desert lands in the world and possesses no lakes or rivers. Recorded day temperatures in the interior can reach 55° centigrade in July and August, monthly averages being well over 30°. Rainfall varies from around 250 millimetres a year in the western oases to less than 50 millimetres elsewhere.

Whilst money is invested in drilling more water wells and building irrigation schemes, few crops are yet grown. Dates, some fruit and cereals are the leading products.

Below: The skylines of major Muslim cities are nearly always dominated by mosques. This one is in Baghdad.

Yet less than one per cent of the land is cultivable. Keeping sheep and camels is still more important than growing crops.

Saudi Arabia is the second largest producer of oil in the world after the U.S.S.R. Since oil was discovered in 1938 the economy has been transformed and Saudi Arabia is one of the world's richest countries. Its oil reserves are estimated at 23 per cent of the world's total. Oil accounts for 85 per cent of the country's income. The government has plans to improve and diversify the economy to guard against the day when the oil wells finally run dry.

Yemen Arab Republic	
Area:	195,000 square kilometres
Population:	5,240,000
Capital city:	San'a
Language:	Arabic
Currency:	Riyal

Yemen Arab Republic is situated in south-west Arabia. Saudi Arabia lies to the north and east, the People's Democratic Republic of Yemen to the south and the Red Sea to the west.

On the Red Sea coast is a low plain varying in width from 30 to 80 kilometres. Towards the east the land rises steeply towards the Yemen Highlands.

The highlands give way to the central plateau which is the most fertile tract of land in the whole of the Arabian peninsula, supporting a large peasant community.

Yemen's lowland areas are hot and, along the Red Sea coast, arid. Rainfall averages only 120 millimetres a year. However, in the mountains this rises to more than 1,000 millimetres.

Ninety per cent of Yemen's population are farmers. They grow millet, wheat, barley, citrus fruits, apricots, onions, and qat (the leaves of which have a narcotic effect when chewed). Coffee is grown but is declining in importance.

Cattle and sheep play a significant part in the economy. Hides and skins are major exports as is cotton grown in the coastal plain.

There is little mineral wealth, except salt. Traces of oil have been found but there has yet to be a major discovery.

Turkish rule ended in 1918 but until 1962 Yemen was governed by corrupt Imams. A republic was then formed, but civil war followed until 1967. In 1974 there was a coup and Yemen is now governed by a military junta.

Below: This Yemeni woman is in purdah, the traditional Arab way of secluding women.

Above: This small mosque lies in Hadramaut valley, one of the few fertile areas of South Yemen.

The People's Democratic Republic of Yemen	
Area:	290,000 square kilometres
Population:	1,660,000
Capital city:	Aden
Language:	Arabic
Currency:	South Yemen dinar

As well as Aden which in itself covers 194 square kilometres, the country embraces 17 former sultanates and emirates. The country is now divided into six governorates. Collectively they are situated in southern Arabia. Yemen lies to the west, Oman to the east. The Arabian Sea runs along the south coast and the huge country of Saudi Arabia lies to the north.

The coastal plain is narrow and arid. It rises inland to a mountain plateau, parts of which are more than 2,000 metres above sea level.

This is cut into by a number of deep valleys, some of which contain the most fertile land in this largely arid country. Beyond the mountains lies the great arid heart of the Arabian peninsula.

Rainfall is sparse throughout the country. The exceptions are some of the valleys where the annual total may reach 600 millimetres. In Aden the average is 120 milli-

Above: The sheikh's palace in Sharjah in the United Arab Emirates. Oil revenues help them to fill their homes with the comforts of Western civilization.

metres but in the east, towards Oman, it may rain only once in ten years.

Agriculture occupies 70 per cent of the population. Much of it is at a subsistence level only. Crops include barley, millet and wheat. Cotton is the most important cash crop and provides a valuable export trade.

With the closure of the Suez Canal in 1967 the country declined as a trading nation. This has yet to be reversed even though the canal was re-opened in 1975.

In 1967 the last British troops withdrew from what had been Aden. This ended 129 years of British rule. In 1969 South Yemen was created, a one-party republic under the government of the Marxist National Liberation Front.

Oman

Oman	
Area:	212,450 square kilometres
Population:	750,000
Capital city:	Muscat
Language:	Arabic
Currency:	Rial Oman

Oman is an independent sultanate

in the south-east corner of Arabia. The Gulf of Oman lies to the north-east and the Arabian Sea to the south-east.

The country's interior is desert but there is a limestone mountain chain in the north-east. The coastal plain of Dhofar in the south is watered by the south-east monsoon.

Oil has been exported since 1967 and has brought Oman many benefits. The state is rich in natural gas and has large copper reserves.

Dates, sugar cane and other fruits are grown at some oases and on the coastal lowlands. Incense trees grow in Dhofar and incense is

a major export. As with most of the oil-rich states, it is a big banking and commercial centre.

United Arab Emirates

United Arab Emirates	
Area:	83,600 square kilometres
Population:	655,000
Capital city:	Abu Dhabi
Language:	Arabic
Currency:	Dirham

The U.A.E. is a federation of seven oil-rich emirates which joined economic forces as an independent state in 1971 when Britain withdrew from the Persian Gulf.

The seven emirates are: Abu Dhabi, Dubai, Sharjah, Ras al Khaimah, Ajman, Fujairah and Umm al Quawain.

The federation lies in south-eastern Arabia along the coasts of the Persian and Oman Gulfs. The Persian Gulf coast extends for nearly 650 kilometres east from Qatar. That of the Gulf of Oman runs for a further 112 kilometres. Saudi Arabia lies beyond the U.A.E.'s landward boundaries.

Abu Dhabi is the largest and by far the most prosperous of the seven. Oil production began in 1962. During the intervening years Abu Dhabi grew from a poor fish-

Below: The oil-rich emirate of Dubai is now a banking and commercial centre.

Asia

Above: The ruler's palace in Doha is ultra-modern in design.

ing village into a state whose people enjoy a per capita income twice that of the U.S.A.

Dubai is the second largest of the emirates and is the U.A.E.'s main port. Once a gold smuggling centre, Dubai now boasts a fine harbour, supertanker dry docks and an international airport.

Fujairah is the poorest and most remote. It lies on the Gulf of Oman and has been connected by road to the rest of the U.A.E. since 1975.

The smallest of the emirates are Ajman and Umm al Quawain on the Persian Gulf coast.

Most of the U.A.E. is barren, desert country. The only cultivable areas are the coastal plains at Fujairah and Ras al Khaimah. Crops include dates, vegetables, fruit and tobacco.

Summer monthly temperatures exceed 36° centigrade. In winter they fall to around 18° centigrade. The rainfall rarely exceeds 130 millimetres a year.

There is a tiny export trade in dried fish but the only current export of any importance is oil. There is, however, a developing natural gas industry.

Eighty per cent of the population live in the towns. There is a large expatriate community, many of whom are involved in the U.A.E.'s civil engineering projects.

The U.A.E. is ruled by a council of ministers with the Sheikh of Abu Dhabi as president.

Qatar

Area:	10,750 square kilometres
Population:	202,000
Capital city:	Doha
Language:	Arabic
Currency:	Riyal

Thanks to the discovery of oil in 1939 the once poor people of Qatar now enjoy a high standard of living. Almost all the business carried on in the towns is associated with oil production and export.

Very few Qataris now follow the traditional industries of fishing, pearl diving and camel raising. Sixty-six per cent of the population live in the capital, helping to diversify the economy.

Qatar is situated on the Persian Gulf. Abu Dhabi lies to the southeast, Saudi Arabia to the west.

The land is mainly desert. Summer monthly average temperatures exceed 34° centigrade and there is virtually no rain.

Bahrain

Area:	600 square kilometres
Population:	276,000
Capital city:	Manamah
Language:	Arabic
Currency:	Bahrain dinar

In 1932 Bahrain became the first Arab country to strike oil. The discovery transformed the tiny sheikhdom's economy. The traditional way of life—pearl diving, fishing and growing dates—soon gave way to oil technology.

Bahrain consists of 33 coral islands in the Persian Gulf between Qatar to the east and Saudi Arabia to the west.

Bahrain's climate is oppressively hot. Summer temperatures average 32° centigrade, rainfall less than 80 millimetres a year.

Kuwait

Area:	24,280 square kilometres
Population:	1,070,000
Capital city:	Kuwait
Languages:	Arabic and English
Currency:	Kuwait dinar

Although Kuwait is mainly desert, the fact that it sits on a huge reservoir of oil gives the people the highest per capita income in the world. In 1974 this was estimated at around £5,500 per head.

Oil riches have attracted a very large immigrant population. Millions of pounds are being spent on major civil engineering projects, hospitals, schools and housing.

Kuwait lies at the north-west head of the Persian Gulf. It is bounded on the north and west by Iraq and by Saudi Arabia on the south. The country enjoys a subtropical climate.

Below: Most Arab cities possess a bazaar or market. This one is in Bahrain in the Persian Gulf.

Above: The development of the oil-producers in the Middle East is evidenced by this city centre in Kuwait. The country even has its own airline.

Iran

Area:	1,648,000 square kilometres
Population:	34,000,000
Capital city:	Tehran
Languages:	Farsi, Kurdish and Arabic
Currency:	Rial

Iran is bounded on the north by the U.S.S.R. and the Caspian Sea. Afghanistan lies to the east, Iraq and Turkey to the west. The southern coast stretches along the Persian and Oman Gulfs.

Iran is mainly a land of mountains and deserts. Much of its mass is made up of a central plateau with an average height of 1,200 metres above sea level. This is a bleak, desolate area where daytime temperatures can exceed 50° centigrade. However, in the Zagros Mountains to the west, the temperature can fall to below freezing. Rainfall is just as extreme. It varies from 1,500 milli-metres on the Caspian coast to 20 millimetres in the arid interior. This is one of the most inhospit-able regions on earth. It has yet to be fully explored.

Over 50 per cent of Iran's population make a living from agriculture. Wheat is the principal crop, followed by barley and rice. Most of the farming community live in small villages. Nomads roam the mountain pastures with their herds of sheep and goats.

Land reform in the 1960s went some way to improving the conditions of the peasant farmer. But agriculture is still extremely backward despite the country's huge revenues. Oil accounts for 90 per cent of Iran's exports.

Until early 1979 Iran was ruled by the Shah, a constitutional but autocratic monarch. His "white revolution", financed by oil revenues, attempted to reform Iran along western lines, and make it the strongest military power in the Middle East. But religious leaders, guided by the Ayatollah Khomeini, and opposition groups revolted against the Shah and he was forced to leave the country. Its political future is at present uncertain.

Afghanistan

Area:	657,500 square kilometres
Population:	19,580,000
Capital city:	Kabul
Languages:	Pushtu and Persian
Currency:	Afghani

Mountain ranges cover more than 75 per cent of Afghanistan. The peaks in the Hindu Kush rise to over 7,000 metres.

This rugged land-locked country is situated in one of the most impenetrable parts of Asia. It is bounded on the north by the U.S.S.R. and by Pakistan to the south and east. Iran lies to the west.

The only cultivable areas are in the mountain valleys and river basins. This represents a mere 10 per cent of the total land. Yet farming is the main occupation of around 80 per cent of the people. Others are nomads, roaming the mountain pastures with their camels, cattle, sheep and goats.

Most of the population grow only enough food and raise enough livestock to meet their own needs. Afghanistan is one of the poorest

Above: The Salang Pass is 3,000 metres high in the Hindu Kush.

Asia

countries in the world; the average annual income is approximately £50 per head.

The climate varies considerably between different parts of the country. In the south lie deserts where the annual rainfall is less than 60 millimetres and summer average monthly temperatures reach 35° centigrade. In the mountains the winter average temperatures are well below freezing.

Afghanistan leads the world in the production of lapis lazuli, a deep blue semi-precious stone. Other resources include copper, oil, gold, silver, mica, iron, lead and coal, mostly unexploited.

A series of five-year development plans have been introduced by the government to improve the country's agricultural and industrial output. At the moment Afghanistan's major exports are dried fruit, natural gas, lamb-skins, carpets and cotton.

Afghanistan was a monarchy until 1973 when it was declared a republic following a *coup d'état*.

Above: The ancient city of Mohenjo-Daro has now been excavated. It was a river port of the Indus valley civilization.

Pakistan	
Area:	796,095 square kilometres
Population:	74,900,000
Capital city:	Islamabad
Languages:	Urdu, Punjabi and English
Currency:	Pakistan rupee

Pakistan is one of the world's poorest nations and at the same time has one of the fastest growing populations.

Iran lies to the west and India to the east. Pakistan's coast in the south faces the Arabian Sea. Afghanistan is to the north-west and China to the north-east.

Pakistan consists of three main regions: a great, flat eastern plain which covers 500,000 square kilometres; the hills and mountain ranges in the north and west; and a desert plateau in the south.

The lowland plain is called the Punjab. It is the country's most fertile area and is watered by the Indus and five of its tributaries.

The chief mountains in the north are the Himalayas, the Hindu Kush and the Karakoram. The average height of these peaks is more than 6,000 metres.

Pakistan's climate ranges from the heat of the deserts to the sub-zero temperatures of the snow-capped mountain ranges. Rainfall is generally low but increases towards the mountain regions.

The Punjab is cool from November to February, extremely hot from March to May and progressively cooler and rainy between June and October. However, even during the wet monsoon season, rainfall is slight, the annual average in the Punjab being only 150 millimetres.

Fifty per cent of Pakistan's population work on the land, but crop yields are very low. The main crops are cotton, wheat, maize, sugar cane, rice and barley. Cotton and cotton goods are important export commodities.

Pakistan's mineral resources have yet to be fully exploited. The country does have, however, reserves of natural gas that are among the highest in the world.

Until a civil war in 1971, Pakistan was divided into two, East and West, with 1,500 kilometres of Indian territory in-between.

India	
Area:	3,166,828 square kilometres
Population:	605,000,000
Capital city:	New Delhi
Languages:	Hindi and English (official) and a total of 854 separate languages and dialects
Currency:	Indian rupee

India is a land of extremes and paradoxes. It is the second most populous country in the world and also one of the poorest. Despite the attempts of various governments to introduce birth control on a large scale, the population is still increasing at the rate of over ten million a year.

The country is shaped like an enormous triangle. The base of the triangle, in the north, runs along the mighty Himalayan mountain chain. The apex is more than 3,000 kilometres to the south where Cape Comorin meets the Indian Ocean. India's western coastline runs along the Arabian Sea. To the east lies the Bay of Bengal.

In the north India shares her borders with China, Bhutan and Nepal. Bangladesh and Burma lie to the east, Pakistan to the north-west.

The country has three main physical regions: the Himalayas in the north; the northern plains; and the Deccan, or southern plateau.

The Himalayas is the world's highest mountain range. Many of the peaks along its 2,500-kilo-metre curve exceed 7,000 metres. India's highest mountain, Nanda Devi, stands 7,817 metres above sea level.

India's northern plains stretch from Bengal in the east to the Punjab in the west. The area is drained by the Indus, Ganges and Brahmaputra rivers and is one of the world's most fertile regions. The northern plains cover about 30 per cent of India.

The northern plains are cut off from the Deccan by the Vindhya and Satpura mountain ranges. South of these, the terrain is very different. The Deccan is a vast plateau of farmland and forest which spreads across most of India's southern peninsula.

Climatically, India has three seasons. These are the cold season, the hot season (pre-monsoon) and the rainy season (south-west monsoon). The cold season lasts from the beginning of November to

Above: This temple at Madurai is typical of southern Indian architecture. It looks like a stepped pyramid.

Below: Bathing in the River Ganges at Varanasi is believed to wash away all one's sins.

Asia

February. There is snow in the northern mountains and the temperatures can fall below freezing as far south as New Delhi. During the hot season (March to June), the hottest part of India is the northern plains area. Here the day temperatures often rise to above 40° centigrade and cyclones (storms) are frequent. The rainy season affects India from June to October. The people of India depend on the south-west monsoon for their agricultural livelihood. Too little rain means a crop failure; too much and the crops are ruined through widespread flooding.

India's north-east receives the most rain. The average annual rainfall in Assam is over 2,500 millimetres. The world's highest average annual rainfall occurs at Cherrapunji—10,800 millimetres. The northern plains and Deccan average 1,000 millimetres of rain a

Above: The transplanting of rice is very hard work and is done in very wet conditions.

year. However, in the western deserts of Rajasthan, rainfall averages only 250 millimetres or less.

Below: The plough pulled by a bullock is common throughout India. The pace of agricultural mechanization is slow.

More than 70 per cent of India's vast population live by farming, but for many of them this is mere subsistence. The average per capita income is only £60 a year.

Most of India's farms are about five acres and concentrated mainly in the northern plains. Primitive methods and poor irrigation mean that the average farm yield is very low. However, India still leads the world in the production of tea, peanuts and sugar cane. She is second only to China in rice and to Brazil in bananas, third in tobacco and fourth in wheat.

India has nearly 200 million cattle, more than any other country. They are protected by religious belief and allowed to wander at will, eating the country's sorely needed grain crops.

A series of five-year plans introduced in 1951 have improved India's industrial output. There is a heavy concentration on iron and

Right: This festival at Madurai is highlighted by an elaborate temple car being drawn through the city's streets.

steel and the country supplies about 30 per cent of the world's mica.

Off-shore oil was discovered near Bombay in 1974. By 1986 India hopes that her drilling activities will make her self-sufficient. India's largest traditional industry is textile spinning and weaving. Her fine fabrics and carpets are exported world-wide.

The United Kingdom, from whom she gained independence in 1947, is India's biggest customer followed by the U.S.A. and U.S.S.R. Her leading exports in 1976–77 were iron and steel; her leading import, oil.

There are 86 universities in India, but only 30 per cent of the population are able to read and write. The country has a highly developed religious caste system. This helps divide the people even further.

Since 1947 India has been a democratic republic. She is a member of the Commonwealth.

Nepal

Area:	141,400 square kilometres
Population:	12,705,000
Capital city:	Kathmandu
Language:	Nepali
Currency:	Nepalese rupee

The kingdom of Nepal is an isolated country set high in the mighty mountains of the Himalayas. It is totally land-locked. China lies to the north and India to the west, south and south-east.

Nepal comprises three distinct zones. These are: a narrow humid lowland strip in the south called the Terai; the Valley of Kath-

Right: This festival at Madurai is highlighted by an elaborate temple car being drawn through the city's streets.

Right: The white splendour of the Taj Mahal at Agra in India. It was built by Shah Jehan in memory of his wife.

Asia

mandu in the centre and the rugged Himalayan mountain area known as the Pahar, to the north.

The Terai is mainly tropical rain forest. Parts are cultivated and the Nepalis grow rice, wheat, sugar cane and jute. The rest is jungle, inhabited by some of the world's few remaining tigers and Indian rhinos.

The Valley of Kathmandu contains most of Nepal's population, centred on the cities of Kathmandu, Patan and Bhadgaon. The valley is an area of hills, fertile valleys and intensive rice cultivation. Rainfall averages 1,400 millimetres a year and summer temperatures can reach 30° centigrade. January temperatures average 18° centigrade.

Kathmandu is the great stepping-off point for expeditions climbing in the Himalayas, the "roof of the world". Mountains include Everest, which at 8,848 metres is the world's highest; Kanchenjunga, 8,598 metres; Makalu, 8,480 metres; Dhaulagiri, 8,172 metres and Annapurna, 8,078 metres.

There are also three great river systems. They rise within and beyond the Himalayas and flow south to join the Ganges in India.

The vast majority of the population is illiterate and most make a living through farming. Productivity is low and Nepal relies heavily on foreign aid.

Roads are still scarce and there are only two short railway lines.

Nepal is ruled by an absolute monarch, King Birendra, and his council of ministers.

Above: A rice field near Kandy in Sri Lanka. Rice is the main food crop on the island, whereas tea is grown mainly for export.

north and India to the south and east. The land is entirely mountains and deep valleys. Some of the peaks exceed 7,000 metres.

Most of the population live in the valleys of the central region. They are virtually all farmers or foresters. The main crops are maize, wheat and barley. Tourism and the sale of postage stamps provide the main sources of foreign currency.

Bangladesh

Area:	142,775 square kilometres
Population:	77,650,000
Capital city:	Dacca
Languages:	Bengali and English
Currency:	Taka

Until 1971 Bangladesh was the eastern province of Pakistan. The country then declared itself an independent republic, following a nine-month civil war with West Pakistan.

Bangladesh is bounded by the Bay of Bengal to the south and by her giant neighbour, India, on the north, west and east. A small stretch of the south-eastern border is shared with Burma. Pakistan lies more than 1,500 kilometres to the west.

Much of Bangladesh is near sea level. It consists mainly of a vast alluvial plain and the delta systems of the Ganges and Brahmaputra rivers.

These mighty rivers rise in the Himalayas and spread out across Bangladesh before flowing into the Bay of Bengal. Flooding is prevalent, caused by rains which, in some districts, can average more than 3,400 millimetres a year.

Virtually the whole of Bangladesh rises no higher than 30 metres, except in the south-eastern hills of Chittagong. Here the land reaches over 900 metres.

The climate generally is hot and humid during the summer and hot and dry in the winter. Summer temperatures average 30° centigrade. In January they fall to 20° centigrade. Rainfall varies but is never less than 1,700 millimetres a year.

Around 80 per cent of the people are farmers. Most are illiterate and manage only a subsistence living. Rice accounts for 80 per cent of the crops grown. Others include jute – the country's main export – sugar cane and tea.

There are few roads or railways.

Bhutan

Area:	47,000 square kilometres
Population:	1,185,000
Capital city:	Thimphu
Language:	Dzongkha
Currency:	Ngultrum

Bhutan is a remote, isolated kingdom set high in the Himalayas. Chinese Tibet bounds it to the

Above: Fishing is an important industry in the Maldives. These islands rely heavily on the money they get for their fish to be able to buy in food.

The Maldives

Area:	298 square kilometres
Population:	140,000
Capital city:	Male
Language:	Divehi
Currency:	Rupee

The Maldives are a chain of som 2,000 coral islands stretching kilometres down throug Indian Ocean, starting metres south-west of Sr

Only 220 island They are all tin the height of metres.

This poor th

And, apart from coal and natural gas, mineral resources are poor.

Bangladesh is one of the world's poorest countries. The birth rate is high and life expectancy low.

Since 1975 Bangladesh has been ruled by martial law.

Sri Lanka

Area:	65,609 square kilometres
Population:	14,270,000
Capital city:	Colombo
Languages:	Sinhalese and English
Currency:	Ceylon rupee

Until 1972 this tropical island in the Indian Ocean was known as Ceylon. Then the former British Crown Colony, which had been independent since 1947, changed its name to Sri Lanka, the translation of which means "resplendent island".

Sri Lanka lies about 30 kilo metres off the south-east tip o India. It is separated from th mainland by the Gulf of Mannar the north-west and the Palk Str to the north.

The country comprises two m geographic zones: the coastal l

land plain which broadens out ir the north and the central u and mountain area.

The mountains rise metres and includ highest, the 2,518-r agala. However, country is lowe

Sri Lanka' Mahaweli (rises on th central mc into the se

Tempe all year lowland the a Rain 5,00 w m

...on pagoda in
...ost highly
...t in the

...n).

1609 by an Englishman, Captain William Keeling. They became a British Protectorate in 1857 and were ceded to Australia in 1955.

Christmas Island

Area:	135 square kilometres
Population:	3,300
Capital city:	The Settlement
Languages:	Chinese and Malay
Currency:	Australian dollar

Christmas Island lies in the Indian Ocean about 360 kilometres south of Java.

The island, which is densely wooded, has only one industry to occupy its inhabitants. This is the export of phosphates of lime from guano deposits (bird droppings). Most of it is sent to Australia and ...Zealand.

...957 Christmas Island was ...apore. It was then ad- ...a separate British ...tober 1958 when it ...n territory.

...uare

...English

...ld's
...ay,

however, even though rice occupies 70 per cent of the cultivated land, there is barely enough to meet home consumption.

The Bay of Bengal and the Andaman Sea lie to the west of Burma's swampy coastal region. India and Bangladesh are to the north-west; China to the north and north-east; and Thailand and Laos to the east.

Burma divides into four natural areas: eastern Burma is largely plateau country; the Arakan mountains lie parallel to the north-west coast; between these two lies an extensive central lowland area occupied by the Irrawaddy and Sittang rivers; and the Pegu Yoma mountains which lie between the two rivers.

The climate is dominated by the hot south-west summer monsoon. From May to October parts of Burma suffer heavy rainfall. In the coastal regions of Arakan and Tenasserim this can mean over 5,000 millimetres. The lower valleys of the Irrawaddy delta in the south receive less, around 2,500 millimetres. Temperatures in the delta, where most of Burma's rice is grown, average 28° centigrade all year.

More than 75 per cent of the population depend on agriculture for a living. Rice is still the country's main crop but adverse monsoon weather, poor farming methods and political uncertainty have drastically reduced the output.

Other crops include oilseeds,

maize, millet, cotton, wheat, jute, sugar cane and rubber. There is a flourishing trade in teak wood.

Burma has a healthy mineral industry. The country is virtually self-sufficient in oil as well as natural gas. Other valuable minerals include silver, lead, zinc, tin and coal.

In 1974 Burma became a one-party state – the Socialist Republic of the Union of Burma.

Thailand

Area:	514,000 square kilometres
Population:	44,200,000
Capital city:	Bangkok
Language:	Thai
Currency:	Baht

The northern part of Thailand lies on the Asian mainland. The southern region extends through the Malayan peninsula. Burma is to

Above: This huge, reclining Buddha is found in a temple in Thailand. Note the monks' saffron robes.

the west and north-west; Laos is to the north-east and Kampuchea lies to the south-east.

Thailand is easily divided into four main geographic areas: north, south, east and central.

The north consists of high mountains and deep valleys. It lies between the Mekong and Salween rivers. The tallest peak is Doi Inthanon (2,595 metres).

In the south the land is long and narrow, sometimes as little as 17 kilometres wide. This is the Isthmus of Kra, an area of tropical

rain forests and mountains.

East Thailand consists mainly of the Korat plateau, a flat and dry basin drained by the Mekong River and some 100 to 200 metres above sea level.

Thailand's central region is its heartland. It is a flat alluvial plain covering an area of about 176,000 square kilometres. It is drained by the Chao Phraya River. This is the country's most fertile area, a vast rice field producing about 14 million tonnes a year.

Thailand is subject to the southwest monsoons. Rainfall averages 1,500 millimetres in the central plain and up to 3,300 millimetres

Above: A floating shop at Donburi. The most famous floating market is in Bangkok. Peasants bring their produce in from the surrounding area.

Above: Buddhist monks form a large unproductive element in many Indochinese countries. Nevertheless, people are happy to give them food and money.

along the Isthmus of Kra.

Rice is Thailand's most important crop and the biggest export earner. Seventy per cent of the working population work on the land. As well as rice they grow cassava, maize, sugar cane, coconuts and rubber. Thailand is the world's third largest producer of rubber.

Thailand accounts for around 12 per cent of the world output of tin, although reserves are declining. Other minerals include antimony, tungsten and gypsum.

Thailand is the only country in South-East Asia not to have been occupied and ruled by a European power.

Laos

Area:	235,700 square kilometres
Population:	3,900,000
Capital city:	Vientiane
Languages:	Lao and French
Currency:	Kip

Laos is an underdeveloped, unexploited country that has been torn apart by war and civil unrest since the end of World War Two. It is the poorest state in Indo-China and there seems no way in which this situation will change.

Laos is bounded on the north by China, on the east by Vietnam, on the south by Kampuchea, and on the west by Thailand and Burma. It lies in the Mekong basin between the Mekong River and the Annam mountains.

Apart from the Mekong valley in the south-west, where 75 per cent of the population live, Laos is mountainous and covered in dense, tropical rain forest. The mountains are highest in the north-central region, rising to Mt Bia (2,619 metres).

Average monthly temperatures in the valley area range from 10°–36° centigrade throughout the year. During the rainy season, May to October, the monsoons bring up to 2,000 millimetres of rain.

More than 90 per cent of the largely peasant population are subsistence farmers. Rice is the staple crop, grown along the banks of the Mekong. Maize and sweet potatoes are raised in the hills, as is opium. The drug is smuggled out into the neighbouring countries.

Below: Rice is the staple crop grown in Indochina.

Laos's mineral potential has yet to be properly tapped. Tin is currently the only mineral of any consequence. Together with small amounts of coffee and teak it provides the country's tiny export trade.

The teak is floated down the Mekong, the country's main means of transportation. There are no railways and what few kilometres of road exist, occur only in the north, in and around the capital, Vientiane.

Laos is ruled by the *Pathet Lao,* an austere communist government which assumed control in 1975.

Kampuchea (Cambodia)	
Area:	181,000 square kilometres
Population:	7,800,000
Capital city:	Phnom Penh
Languages:	Khmer and French
Currency:	Riel (although officially abolished)

Kampuchea is situated in South-East Asia between Thailand on the north and west and Vietnam in the south. Laos lies to the north-east.

Geographically the country is dominated by the great Mekong River. The Mekong rises in the Tibetan plateau and flows south

Above: This Malaysian is selling brushes—a typical handicraft industry of South-East Asia.

through Laos and then into Kampuchea. It flows through Kampuchea for 500 kilometres of its total 4,184-kilometre length before entering Vietnam.

Kampuchea's climate is tropical. The south-west mountain fringes receive up to 5,000 millimetres of rain a year. In the lowland plain this falls to around 1,300 millimetres. Average annual temperatures range between 27°–32° centigrade.

The floodwaters and tributaries of the Mekong have created a central alluvial plain which covers about 75 per cent of Cambodia's total area. In the middle of this vast lowland area is a huge lake, the Tonlé Sap, 160 kilometres long by 17 kilometres wide.

During the rainy season, water from the Mekong River flows into the Tonlé Sap causing it to spread over the surrounding fields and forest. The lake is well stocked with fish, providing valuable protein for a generally under-nourished people.

The majority of the population are subsistence farmers. Rice is the main crop. Kampuchea is also an important rubber-producing country although the almost continual fighting has reduced the output considerably.

In 1975 Cambodia, or the Khmer republic, was overrun by communist forces after six years of war. The country was renamed Kampuchea and a period of austerity was initiated. Thousands of people were forced out of the towns and cities and made to earn their living from the land or starve.

Vietnam

Area:	329,466 square kilometres
Population:	47,160,000
Capital city:	Hanoi
Languages:	Vietnamese, French and Chinese
Currency:	Dong

Vietnam is a long, narrow and mountainous country in South-East Asia. Kampuchea and Laos are to the west, the South China Sea to the east.

The main mountains are the Annam range. These run through the centre of the country and rise to more than 2,500 metres. They slope gently to the west but fall away steeply to the east coast.

Vietnam's most important rivers are the Song Hoi in the north and the Mekong in the south. Each has created fertile deltas.

In the south the annual rainfall averages 2,000 millimetres and temperatures range between 21°–35° centigrade. In the north there are 1,700 millimetres of rain a year and a temperature range of 17°–42° centigrade.

In the north the majority of the population is concentrated in the

Below: Ho Chi Minh City, formerly Saigon, is overcrowded. Many people live in boats on the River Mekong.

delta region around Hanoi. About 80 per cent of them are farmers. The population centre in the south is the Mekong delta. Rice is the most important crop but sugar cane is increasing in importance. So too are maize, cotton, tea and vegetables. Rubber is the most valuable forest product.

The north is rich in minerals including coal, anthracite, iron ore, chrome and tin. Much of it is used in developing the country's industrial programme.

Vietnam has suffered more from the effects of modern warfare than any other country in the world.

In 1976, after a war between the north and south which had gone on intermittently since 1940, Vietnam was reunited as a socialist republic.

During the fighting, which escalated violently from 1960, involving both America and the U.S.S.R., Vietnam's economy was wrecked. The land was devastated by large-scale bombing.

Malaysia

Area:	332,633 square kilometres
Population:	12,600,000
Capital city:	Kuala Lumpur
Languages:	Malay, English, Chinese and Tamil
Currency:	Malaysian dollar (Ringit)

The Federation of Malaysia comprises Malaya, Sarawak and Sabah.

Malaya, or West Malaysia, occupies the southern part of the Malayan Peninsula, extending south from 6° North latitude to the Singapore Strait. It is bounded by Thailand to the north, the Malacca Strait on the west, and the South China Sea on the east.

Sarawak and Sabah, or East Malaysia, occupy the north-west area of the great island of Borneo. At its closest point, this is some 650 kilometres east of Malaya across the South China Sea.

The Malayan Peninsula is

Above: Rubber is still one of Malaysia's major industries. Tapping a tree is a very specialized craft.

dominated by a chain of mountains lying north-north-west to south-south-east. The tallest peak is Gunong Tahan (2,189 metres). The mountains are flanked by swampy, low-lying coastal areas.

Malaysia is the world's largest producer of natural rubber, tin and palm oil.

Rubber is Malaysia's most important single crop and covers 60 per cent of the country's cultivated land. The biggest food crop is rice, grown largely in the north-west and north-east. However, there is not enough to satisfy home consumption and about 30 per cent of the demand has to be imported.

East Malaysia is much poorer than the west. Sabah, on the northern tip of Borneo, is covered in tropical rain forest. Hardwoods and palm oil account for over 95 per cent of her exports.

Sarawak lies in the centre of north-west Borneo. It is a densely

forested region with a swampy coastland. Both Sabah and Sarawak are mountainous. Kinabalu on Sabah is, at 4,101 metres, one of the highest peaks in South-East Asia.

The whole of Malaysia is rich in exotic flowers and vegetation. This is helped by the climate with its all-year-round high rainfall and high temperatures.

Singapore

Area:	602 square kilometres
Population:	2,280,000
Capital city:	Singapore
Languages:	English, Chinese, Malay and Tamil
Currency:	Singapore dollar

In physical terms the island of Singapore is tiny, 42 kilometres long by 22 kilometres wide. Yet commercially it is a centre of world importance.

Singapore lies off the southern tip of the Malayan Peninsula in South-East Asia. There is a causeway 1·5 kilometres long which connects the island to the mainland over the Johore Strait. The causeway was built in 1918 and carries both rail, road, and the main water pipeline.

Above: Singapore is a major port and commercial centre.

The highest point on the island is 177 metres. The climate is hot, humid and equatorial; Singapore is just over one degree north of the equator.

Monthly average temperatures are consistently around 28° centigrade and annual rainfall averages 2,440 millimetres.

Singapore was established as a trading post of the East India Company in 1819 by an Englishman, Sir Stamford Raffles. It was then nothing more than a fishing village with a population of 150. Five years later this had grown to 10,000 and by 1918 it had increased to 250,000.

The island had few natural resources but soon established its importance as a trading port. This was based on the sale and distribution of raw materials from neighbouring countries and the importing and re-exporting of finished goods. Singapore is now one of the world's largest seaports.

During the 19th century most of Singapore was a vast mangrove swamp. Today, however, most of this has been reclaimed for the building of huge government high-density housing projects and factories.

Manufacturing industries include chemicals, textiles, electrical goods and glassware.

There are about 54 other islands in the Singapore republic. Most of them are small and uninhabited.

Brunei

Area:	5,765 square kilometres
Population:	177,000
Capital city:	Bandar Seri Begawan
Languages:	Malay, English, Chinese and Iban
Currency:	Brunei dollar

The sultanate of Brunei is a former protectorate on the northern coast of Borneo. It is bounded on three sides by Sarawak. To the north lies the South China Sea. Today, the sultanate has internal self-government and enjoys British control of its foreign affairs and defence.

Brunei is a rugged and densely forested country. The climate is equatorial. Crops include rice, sugar cane and fruit. Rubber trees cover 80 per cent of the agricultural land. Crude oil from an offshore field accounts for 95 per cent of the export trade.

Below: These boat-shaped houses are found on the Sulawesi Islands of Indonesia. Rice terraces can be seen in the distance.

Indonesia

Area:	1,903,650 square kilometres
Population:	133,350,000
Capital city:	Djakarta (on Java)
Languages:	Bahasa Indonesian
Currency:	Rupiah

Indonesia is an independent republic which has historical associations with the Netherlands. It consists of more than 3,000 islands stretched along the equator between Australia and South-East Asia. Many of the islands are small and sparsely populated. Others are large and densely populated, e.g. New Guinea (western part only); Borneo (except for the northern area); Sumatra; Java and Timor.

With the exception of Java most of the islands are underdeveloped and poorly exploited. Some areas, notably Borneo and New Guinea, have yet to be fully explored.

Indonesia's climate is hot and wet. The average annual temperature is 28° centigrade. Rainfall averages 2,500 millimetres a year but can go as high as 4,000 millimetres.

There are 140 volcanoes in Indonesia. Many are extinct but others remain active.

More than 70 per cent of Indonesia is tropical rain forest. The timber industry includes teak, ebony and sandalwood and provides the country with an important export.

Eighty per cent of the population inhabit villages and live by subsistence farming. Rice is the staple diet and about 40 per cent of the cultivable land is given over to its production. Other crops include maize, sugar cane, tea, coffee and copra.

Indonesia was described by early explorers as the "spice islands". Today, however, even though large quantities of pepper, nutmeg and cloves are produced, the economy is more dependent on rubber, oil and timber. Indonesia is South-East Asia's major producer of ʼde oil.

Philippines

Area:	297,419 square kilometres
Population:	43,940,000
Capital city:	Manila
Languages:	Pilipino, English, Spanish and other local languages
Currency:	Philippine peso

The Philippines are a scattered archipelago in South-East Asia containing more than 7,000 islands. Of these, however, more than 4,000 are unnamed; only 463 are larger than 1·5 square kilometres, fewer still are actually inhabited. They lie about 660 kilometres south-east of mainland Asia.

Ninety-three per cent of the total land mass consists of eleven islands. The largest is Luzon. It has an area of 104,692 square kilometres. The present capital city of Manila, with a population of 1.5 million, and the old capital of Quezon City, with a population of almost one million, are both on this island. Luzon is still the main commercial centre.

Most of the population live on the lower coastal areas. The islands are all very mountainous, some rising above 2,500 metres. The highest peak in the Philippines is Mt Apo (2,954 metres) on Mindanao.

There are at least 25 active volcanoes in the Philippines. Mt Taal on Luzon erupted violently in 1911, killing 1,400 people. Earthquakes are also prevalent. In 1976, 8,000 people were killed by the floods which followed a major tremor off Mindanao.

The climate varies considerably. In the south the annual rainfall is 2,000 millimetres and the temperature is fairly constant between 25°–28° centigrade. In the north the temperature range is much larger and rainfall can exceed 3,000 millimetres.

The economy of the Philippines is mainly agricultural. Major products include rice, coconuts, hemp, maize, tobacco and sugar cane. Fishing is also important as are minerals, but these have yet to be fully exploited. At the moment copper, gold, chrome ore and iron are mined.

Below: The system of rice terracing has been practised in the Philippines for 2,000 years. It is a way of using very hilly ground and making it highly productive.

Asia

Mongolia

Area:	1,565,000 square kilometres
Population:	1,500,000
Capital city:	Ulan Bator
Language:	Mongolian
Currency:	Tugrik

Mongolia is a vast, sparsely populated land-locked country situated between China and the U.S.S.R.

Much of it is a bleak plateau lying above 1,500 metres. The summers are short, the winters long and severe. Almost 30 per cent of Mongolia consists of the Gobi Desert, where the annual rainfall is less than 100 millimetres.

The people are mainly nomadic herdsmen; 80 per cent of the land is poor-quality pasture. Some wheat, barley and millet are grown.

The People's Republic of China

Area:	9,597,000 square kilometres
Population:	900,000,000
Capital city:	Peking
Languages:	Chinese (official dialect: Mandarin) and various minority languages and dialects
Currency:	Renmimbi Yuan

China has the highest population of any country in the world. Esti-

Above: Political slogans are even found in the Chinese fields, urging the maximum effort from workers.

mates vary considerably as to the actual number. The figure above is that most widely quoted by the Chinese themselves. However, some western experts are of the opinion that it is much higher.

China is situated in central and eastern Asia. It extends approximately 3,600 kilometres from north to south and 4,400 kilometres from east to west.

Obviously a country as vast as China consists of many different land regions. These include fertile plains, deserts and mountain ranges. China may be divided into three main areas: northern China, southern China and western China.

Northern China includes the vast, flat North China Plain, the Hwang Ho river valley and the Manchurian Plain in the north-

Left: Tsingtao in Shantung province is a leading Chinese seaside resort.

east. This is China's best agricultural land and consequently one of the country's most populated regions.

Southern China is separated from the north by the Tsinling Mountains. These are part of the central mountain belt and some peaks exceed 4,500 metres.

Farther south lies the Yangtze Plain, a huge fertile area watered by the Yangtze Kiang. The Yangtze is one of the world's five longest rivers. It rises in the west and flows 5,550 kilometres before entering the Yellow Sea. The Yangtze flows through the Szechwan Basin which, with a population density of around 800 people per square kilometre, is China's most densely peopled area.

Western or Outer China consists of endless areas of forbidding desert, high plateaus and snow-capped mountain ranges. Among these are the Takla Makan (desert), Tibet (high plateau) and the Himalayas, isolating China from the of southern Asia. On the bo with Nepal is Mt Everest which, at 8,848 metres, is the highest mountain in the world.

Tibet was, until 1950, virtually independent. It is now, however, part of China. Most of this bleak, barren country is above 4,500 metres. The population is sparse, around 1,600,000 people living in about 1,222,000 square kilometres.

Because of its vast area China experiences many types of climate. The greatest single climatic influence is the seasonal monsoon. During the winter the monsoons from Siberia carry cold, dry airstreams across China towards the Pacific. In the summer the monsoons blow in the opposite direction, bringing warm, wet air (typhoons) in from the Pacific.

Rainfall can vary from more than 2,000 millimetres a year in the south and along the coast, to as little as 100 millimetres a year in the western desert regions.

Temperatures are just as varied. The average winter temperature in northern Manchuria is −9° centi-

Right: Workers in China spend on average about ten hours a day, six days a week, cultivating the fields. In winter there is much less to do.

grade; in Canton on the South China Sea coast it is 13° centigrade. Summer temperatures average 25° centigrade in Canton. In Manchuria they are around 20° centigrade.

With such a huge population, China's main concern is producing enough food for everybody. Agriculture is by far the country's biggest industry and 80 per cent of the total workforce are peasant farmers.

In 1958 a series of radical reforms resulted in almost all China's agricultural land being re-organized into people's communes. There are now 50,000 such communes throughout the country, each divided into production brigades and teams.

Rice is the main crop. China grows – and consumes – about 116 million tonnes of rice a year. This is over 30 per cent of the world

total. Other major crops include wheat, barley, maize, soya beans, kaoliang and sweet potatoes.

China raises more livestock than any other country. It is estimated that there are over 260 million pigs.

Fishing is very important to China's economy. The country stands third to Japan and the U.S.S.R. in the catch size. One of China's oldest industries is rearing silkworms.

China's mineral wealth is vast and as yet largely unexploited. Oil, coal and iron are of major importance, as are wolfram, tin, antimony and bismuth.

In the 20th century, China was frequently involved in Far Eastern and civil wars until, in 1949, the Communist People's Republic was established. Its leader was Mao Tse-tung, who was the first chairman until his death in 1976.

Left: These volcanic hills in Kwangsi province form the subject of many ancient Chinese paintings. They provide a striking contrast with the paddy fields.

Asia

North Korea

Area:	122,370 square kilometres
Population:	16,035,000
Capital city:	Pyongyang
Language:	Korean
Currency:	Won

North Korea is a land of high mountains, deep valleys and dense forests. It is situated on a peninsula in north-east Asia. Korea Bay lies to the west, the Sea of Japan to the east and South Korea to the south. China and the U.S.S.R. are beyond the northern borders.

The north-central area is extremely mountainous, the highest peak being Mt Paektu at 2,744 metres on the Chinese border. The mountains form part of a chain which extends along the east coast into South Korea.

Only about 20 per cent of the land is cultivable. These fertile lowland areas are found mainly along the west coast.

The lowlands are watered by large navigable rivers including the Taedong and Chonchon.

North Korea's climate is characterized by severe winters, particularly in the mountains of the north. Summers tend to be fairly short but hot and humid.

The rain is brought by the wet monsoon between May and September. It varies from 1,500 millimetres a year in the south to only 500 millimetres near the northern border with China.

About 50 per cent of North Korea's working population are involved in agriculture. Rice is by far the main crop. There is also a heavy dependence on maize and, to a lesser extent, on millet, sweet potatoes and soya beans. The land is organized into state farms and collectives.

The country's mineral wealth is concentrated in the north. Deposits include iron ore, coal, copper and lead. Steel production has reached around four million tonnes a year.

North Korea has been separ-

ated from South Korea since 1948. The country is now a communist people's republic and is economically supported by both the U.S.S.R. and China. Her trade with the U.S.S.R. and other communist countries is double that with Japan and the west.

South Korea

Area:	98,447 square kilometres
Population:	35,900,000
Capital city:	Seoul
Language:	Korean
Currency:	Won

The Republic of South Korea has been politically separated from North Korea (the Democratic People's Republic) since 1948.

Below: This street is in Seoul, South Korea. The city has many features that reveal the American influence on the people's life-styles.

Above: These Japanese children show the typical Mongoloid features: high cheekbones and almond-shaped eyes.

Physically, the two countries remain similar. South Korea is mountainous and, in parts, densely forested. The mountains are less rugged than those in the north, rising to a maximum height of 1,915 metres.

The border between north and south is drawn along latitude 38° North, referred to as the 38th parallel. The Sea of Japan lies to the east, the Yellow Sea to the west and the East China Sea to the south. Japan lies 180 kilometres to the south-east.

There are around 3,000 small islands off the southern and western coasts. They are mostly rocky and uninhabited, apart from Chin Do which has a population of 255,000 and an area of 1,839 square kilometres.

Winter temperatures average between −7° and 2° centigrade. In summer these range from 23° to 27° centigrade. Rainfall is heaviest in the south and over the whole country ranges between 1,270 and 1,500 millimetres a year.

Most of the people live in the south-west. This is an area of cultivated plains watered by the Han, Kum and Yongsan rivers. Rice is the main crop, followed by barley, wheat and soya beans.

Fishing is important to the South Korean economy and includes some whaling.

South Korea's mineral resources are limited, with the exception of coal and tungsten. Manufacturing is growing steadily and exports include textiles, automobiles, fertilizers, footwear, electrical goods and ships.

Since the end of the Korean War in 1953, South Korea has received economic and technical aid from the U.S.A. and Japan.

Above: Japan's farmland is extremely restricted in area. Mechanization helps to boost the harvest. Rice is Japan's staple food and her chief agricultural product.

the world put together.

Japan's astonishing growth rate has been helped in part by massive American investment. But above all, the country's revival is due to the energy and character of the Japanese people themselves.

Japan consists of four main islands and hundreds of smaller ones. In order of size the four are: Honshu, Hokkaido, Kyushu and Shikoku. The largest group of small islands is the Ryukyu chain. These extend for 560 kilometres from the southern tip of Kyushu,

towards the north-east coast of Taiwan.

Japan is separated from the mainland of Asia by the Sea of Japan to the west. The Pacific Ocean lies to the east.

Japan's physical geography is dominated by mountains. They cover more than 75 per cent of the total land area. Little more than 15 per cent is suitable for agriculture. The great majority of the population live in towns and cities. Tokyo, the capital, with nearly 11,700,000 inhabitants, is the most populous city in the world.

The highest and most rugged mountains in Japan are the so-called Japanese Alps in central Honshu. Many exceed 3,000 metres. There are also more than 200 volcanoes in Japan. Most of them are inactive, including Mt Fujiyama which, at 3,776 metres, is the country's highest mountain.

Although Japan may no longer be troubled by volcanoes, the country is subject to earthquakes and tremors. As many as 1,500 can occur in any one year.

In 1923, however, an earthquake struck Tokyo and the nearby port of Yokohama with such force that it left 143,000 people dead. Japan also suffers from *tsunami*, or tidal waves, caused by tremors on the ocean floors.

The climate in Japan varies considerably from north to south. Hokkaido, the northernmost of the main islands, has cool summers and cold winters when temperatures fall well below freezing.

Honshu, the central and by far the largest island, enjoys mild winters in the south and severe ones in the north. Summers are generally warm and humid. The southern islands of Shikoku and Kyushu have long, hot summers and mild winters.

Rainfall is plentiful over the

Japan	
Area:	372,197 square kilometres
Population:	113,100,000
Capital city:	Tokyo
Language:	Japanese
Currency:	Yen

Following Japan's defeat in 1945, thus signalling an end to World War Two, the country lay in ruins. Intensive air attacks, ending in the dropping of two atomic bombs, one on Hiroshima and the other on Nagasaki, had left the land devastated, industry in ruins and the people demoralized.

Today, however, Japan is one of the world's top three industrial giants. Japan leads the world in shipbuilding, producing almost as much annual tonnage as the rest of

Left: Osaka Castle was a medieval stronghold of the Toyotomi family. Castles were built as the seats of *daimyo* (lords).

Asia

Above: Japan's inland areas are a mixture of unspoilt forest and mountains.

whole country. It ranges from 1,000 millimetres a year on Hokkaido to more than 2,000 millimetres on Kyushu.

The south-west of Japan is prone to typhoons which sweep in from the Pacific in the summer and autumn. The resultant violent winds and torrential rainfall cause a great deal of damage, especially in the agricultural areas.

Fewer than 12 per cent of the working population are employed on the land. Most of them live in the south and west where the climate and terrain is more conducive to farming. Rice, being the staple diet, is the chief crop. Others include wheat, barley, fruit and vegetables.

The Japanese are the world's highest consumers of fish. Japanese fishermen make the world's largest annual catches: over 15 per cent of the world total. In spite of worldwide opposition Japan is still a major whaling nation.

Japan's natural resources are limited. There are supplies of lead, zinc, chrome, copper and iron ore but none in sufficient quantity to meet home requirements. Oil and natural gas have been discovered off the west coast of Honshu, but

Above: Advertising signs abound in this shopping precinct. Most day-to-day shopping is done at small local shops or street markets.

Above: The world-famous "bullet train" runs from Tokyo to Osaka. The 500-kilometre trip takes just one hour.

again only in small amounts.

Virtually all of Japan's raw material and fuel has to be imported. Japan imports more crude oil than any other country in the world, some 95 per cent of its total requirements. This makes the economy very vulnerable to shifting patterns in world trade, particularly the price of oil.

Nevertheless, Japan is now by far the most advanced nation in the Far East and the world's third largest exporter of manufactured goods after America and West Germany. Major industries include electrical goods, vehicles, textiles and machinery. Japan's ability over the last 20 years to increase her exports at a very rapid rate has given the Japanese an extremely high standard of living.

The country is a democracy with an hereditary emperor as head of state.

Macau

Area:	16 square kilometres
Population:	260,000
Capital city:	Macau
Languages:	Chinese and Portuguese
Currency:	Pataça

Macau is a tiny outpost of Portugal, situated on the south-east coast of China at the mouth of the Pearl River, on the opposite bank to Hong Kong.

It comprises the tip of the Macau peninsula and the islands of Taipa and Colôane.

Macau is the most densely populated country in the world. All food and water has to be imported from China. The port mainly handles goods in transit to and from China.

Hong Kong

Area:	1,046 square kilometres
Population:	4,750,000
Capital city:	Victoria
Languages:	Chinese (Cantonese dialect), English and various Chinese dialects
Currency:	Hong Kong dollar

The British Crown Colony of Hong Kong is one of the most densely populated places in the world. There are approximately 4,300 people to every square kilometre.

Hong Kong consists of the island of Hong Kong itself, the Kowloon Peninsula and the New Territories on the mainland of China. There are, in addition, more than 230 scattered tiny islands.

Hong Kong is situated at the mouth of the Pearl River on the south-east coast of China. It is about 145 kilometres south-east of Canton and 65 kilometres east of the Portuguese colony of Macau on the opposite river bank.

Only 13 per cent of the total land area is cultivable and less than ten per cent of the population live in the rural regions. Rice and vegetables are the main crops. The climate is monsoonal. Rainfall averages 2,000 millimetres a year, mostly falling between May and September. Temperatures average over 25° centigrade in the summer and 16° in the winter.

Hong Kong and Kowloon are separated by nearly two kilometres of sea. This is one of the finest deepwater harbours in the world and can accommodate the largest ships.

Hong Kong has virtually no natural resources and the colony's prosperity depends on the export of its manufactured goods, such as textiles, electrical equipment, cameras, watches and toys. For these it has to import large quantities of raw materials. Thirty per cent of all exports go to the U.S.A. West Germany, Britain and Japan are also big customers.

Taiwan

Area:	35,981 square kilometres
Population:	16,290,000
Capital city:	Taipei
Languages:	Chinese (Amoy dialect) and Japanese
Currency:	New Taiwan dollar

Taiwan is an island 145 kilometres off the south-east coast of China, separated from the mainland by the Formosa Strait.

About 25 per cent of this mountainous island is cultivated. Rice and other crops are grown in the western lowlands. Mineral resources include coal, natural gas and copper.

There is an average rainfall of 2,500 millimetres a year. Summers are long and hot and winters short and mild.

Taiwan, formerly called Formosa, is the home of the Chinese nationalists who were expelled from mainland China by the communists in 1949. The island is largely supported economically by the U.S.A.

The continent of Africa occupies approximately 30,000,000 square kilometres.
Population: approximately 423,000,000.
There are 55 countries in Africa, including offshore islands.
The **smallest country** is the French island of Mayotte whose 38,000 people occupy 374 square kilometres.
The **largest country** is the Sudan—2,496,800 square kilometres with a population of 17,000,000.
The **highest peak** is Mt Kilimanjaro in Tanzania which is 5,895 metres high.
The **longest river** is the Nile which at 6,680 kilometres is the longest in the world.
The **largest lake,** covering 69,484 square kilometres, is Lake Victoria. It lies within the boundaries of three countries, Uganda, Kenya and Tanzania.
The world's **largest desert,** the Sahara, covers 9,065,000 square kilometres. Most of Algeria, Niger, Libya, Egypt and Mauritania lie within it and parts of Morocco, Tunisia, Senegal, Mali, Chad and the Sudan.
The **largest cities** in Africa are Cairo with 5,715,000 people, Alexandria with 2,259,000 and Kinshasa with 2,008,000.

1 Morocco
2 Algeria
3 Tunisia
4 Libya
5 Egypt
6 Cape Verde Islands
7 Mauritania
8 Mali
9 Niger
10 Chad
11 Sudan
12 Ethiopia
13 Djibouti
14 Somali Republic
15 Senegal
16 Gambia
17 Guinea Bissau
18 Guinea
19 Sierra Leone
20 Liberia
21 Ivory Coast
22 Ghana
23 Togo
24 Upper Volta
25 Benin
26 Nigeria
27 Cameroon
28 Sao Tome and Principe
29 Equatorial Guinea
30 Central African Empire
31 Gabon
32 Congo
33 Zaire
34 Rwanda
35 Burundi
36 Uganda
37 Kenya
38 Tanzania
39 Seychelles
40 St Helena
41 Angola
42 Zambia
43 Malawi
44 Mozambique
45 Comoros
46 Mayotte
47 Madagascar
48 Reunion
49 Mauritius
50 Namibia
51 Botswana
52 Zimbabwe Rhodesia
53 South Africa
54 Swaziland
55 Lesotho

Mediterranean Sea

Rabat
Algiers
Tunis
Tripoli
Cairo

1
2
3
4
5

Nile
Lake Nasser

Red Sea

7
Nouakchott

8
Niger
Bamako

9

10
Lake Chad

Khartoum

12

13
Djibouti

14

Niamey
15
16
ssau 17
Conakry
18
Freetown 19
Monrovia 20
Abidjan
Accra
21
22
23
24
Ouagadougou
25
26
Porto Novo
Lome Lagos

N'Djamena
Benue

11

Addis Ababa

27
Yaoundé
28
29
São Tomé
Libreville
31
Brazzaville
Kinshasa
32
30
Bangui
Zaire

33

36
Kampala
Lake Victoria
Nairobi

37

Mogadiscio

Bar

35
Bujumbura

38
Lake Tanganyika

Dar es Salaam

39

Atlantic Ocean

Luanda

41

40 Jamestown

50

Windhoek

Gaborone

Orange

51

53

Lake Malawi
Lilongwe
42
Lusaka
Lake Kariba
Salisbury
52
44
Zambezi
43

Limpopo
Maputo

Mbabane
Pretoria 54
Maseru 55

Moroni
45
46

47 Antananarivo

49

48

Indian Ocean

Africa

Africa is a large continent, three times the size of Europe and the second largest after Asia. The many geographical barriers such as tropical rain forests, deserts, mountains, rivers and lakes have tended to isolate groups of African peoples so that they developed their own languages, religions, social customs, and ways of life. There are more than 1,000 different ethnic groups in Africa today.

There was no detailed map of Africa until about 200 years ago. European sailors began to discover the continent beyond the desert coast, south of the Sahara, in the 15th century. Gold was the major incentive for opening up the continent. The slave trade started in a small way but soon caught on. From the 15th century Portugal and Spain, followed by the Dutch, British and French, began to ship thousands of black Africans to the Americas to work on the cotton plantations. This trading continued until the 19th century.

Slave-trading was confined mainly to the coasts of Africa, and it was not until the 19th century that the "Dark Continent" began to be explored thoroughly. Missionaries were the first explorers. Their aim was to civilize the Africans. After them came the traders and the colonial administrators. In the 1880s the scramble for African colonies led to the continent being divided up among the Western European nations.

The period since World War

Two has seen one after another of the colonial nations fighting for and gaining independence. South of the Sahara, Ghana led the way in 1957. The rest followed and the colonial empires collapsed like a house of cards.

Living in Africa

Africa is essentially a farming continent. Its 400 million people are distributed unevenly over the continent and the majority work on the land. Vast areas, such as the Sahara Desert, are almost uninhabited. Other areas have a high population density, for example in Nigeria, South Africa, and along the River Nile in Egypt.

Above: The temple at Karnak in Egypt. Karnak was extended and embellished by the Pharaohs over 2,000 years.

Where the land is reasonably fertile the people live in villages and grow their own crops, such as maize and cassava. The peoples that live by the coast, large lakes or rivers also live by fishing. The peasants of Egypt called *fellahin* carry on the same traditional methods of farming along the banks of the River Nile that were used in the time of the Pharaohs. This is shown by wall paintings in ancient Egyptian tombs. The Nkundo of the forests of central Zaire live by hunting. Other peoples live nomadic lives, travelling with their herds of cattle, sheep, goats and, in some areas, camels. The people that live in the semi-arid open lands of the Sudan depend on their herds for their livelihood.

Left: Most Bedouin are nomads who move from place to place in the desert. They live in simple huts or tents.

Right: Market day in Ibadan, Nigeria. There is a thriving business here in everything from love potions to hot peppers.

Africa

Morocco

Area:	659,970 square kilometres
Population:	17,800,000
Capital city:	Rabat
Languages:	Arabic, Berber, French and Spanish
Currency:	Dirham

Morocco has the largest population in north-west Africa, and it is increasing at a rate of 3·2 per cent a year. It has been an independent kingdom since 1956.

Mountain chains dominate the landscape and geography of Morocco. The Rif Mountains are separated from the Atlas ranges by the Sebou and Innaouen plains. The Atlas Mountains run from the Algerian border in the north-east almost to the Atlantic coast in the south-west. At their highest, these mountains rise above 4,000 metres. Farther west lies a large plateau. The interior plains border on the Sahara Desert.

West and north Morocco have a warm Mediterranean climate of winter rainfall associated with cyclones (tropical storms), and hot, sunny, rainless summers. The south and east of the country is arid and daytime temperatures often rise above 50° centigrade in the summer.

Agriculture is important throughout Morocco. The coastal

Left: Tetouan, capital of the north. This mountainous area of Morocco is called the Rif. Good roads for access have only recently been constructed.

lowlands produce wheat, beans and peas. Vines are grown for fruit and in recent years improved varieties have been used to make wine, much of which is exported. Citrus fruits and vegetables are grown for the European market. The Berbers in the mountain regions raise goats, camels and sheep.

The cool Atlantic waters off the north-west coast are valuable fishing grounds for sardines, anchovies and tunny.

Algeria

Area:	2,381,745 square kilometres
Population:	17,000,000
Capital city:	Algiers
Languages:	Arabic and French
Currency:	Algerian dinar

The independent republic of Algeria is the second largest country in Africa. It divides clearly into two distinct regions. In the south is the dry expanse of the Sahara Desert and the Hoggar Mountains. In the north are the Atlas Mountains and the coastal

Left: The Medina in Marrakech. This market is the main one of southern Morocco, with farmers bringing their produce from the surrounding area.

Right: The interior of the Sidi bu Medien Mosque at Tlemcen in Algeria. The Arab and Berber population are almost entirely Muslim.

plains. Most of the population live in the north, on about 12 per cent of the total land area.

Arabs and Berbers make up most of the population. The Berber tribes of the Tuaregs and Kabyles are found in the arid Sahara.

Good agricultural land is limited to the Mediterranean coastal zone. In the fertile valleys and basins, cereals, citrus fruits and vines are the most important crops. In the hills, Berber peasants grow wheat, olives and figs for their own consumption, as well as tending flocks of sheep.

Oil and gas were discovered in the Sahara in 1962. This was also the year the country gained its independence from French rule, which led to more than 1,000,000 French settlers returning to their native country. The oil boom offset the economic disaster resulting from the French departing. Oil now accounts for over 90 per cent of the country's exports. Other minerals mined include iron ore, lead, zinc and copper.

Since its independence, the country has been a one-party state, the FLN nominating the president who is then elected by the people.

Tunisia

Area:	164,150 square kilometres
Population:	5,770,000
Capital city:	Tunis
Languages:	Arabic and French
Currency:	Tunisian dinar

Tunisia is an independent republic on the Mediterranean coast. Arabs make up the majority of the population and Arabic is the main lan-

Above: Qayrawan Mosque, Tunisia, is one of the finest mosques in Africa. It is a centre of pilgrimage for Muslims.

guage spoken, although French is widely used and taught in schools. The French governed Tunisia until its independence in 1956. The original inhabitants, the Berbers, on the whole live in the less fertile interior.

The country lies at the eastern end of the Atlas Mountains, which separate the area of best agricultural land to the north from the desert regions to the south.

The Mediterranean climate of the north brings between 400 and 600 millimetres of rain a year, mostly during the winter months. The development of dams, flood control and irrigation channels in

this region means that vines for fruit, dried fruit and wine, and citrus fruits, vegetables and wheat can all grow well. The major agricultural export is olive oil and this comes from the drier areas along the coast of central Tunisia. Dates come from the more arid south, especially around the Djerid oasis.

The mining of phosphates and iron ore were once the leading sources of foreign earnings. They have become less important since the discovery of oil at the Al Borma and Douled fields which are linked to the refinery at Bizerta. Refined products are exported. The most important industry at the moment is food processing, including wine production. However, the tourist trade is a rapidly expanding business.

Libya

Area:	1,759,540 square kilometres
Population:	2,630,000
Capital city:	Tripoli
Language:	Arabic
Currency:	Libyan dinar

Libya is a republic on the Mediterranean coast of North Africa. It is often called a Saharan state because nearly 90 per cent of its land area is the Sahara Desert or semi-desert. It was from these large barren tracts that oil was discovered in 1955. Exports of this valuable new source of foreign

earnings began in 1962. From being a country of universal poverty in an extreme form, today it is one of the richest African states.

The majority of Libyans are Muslim Arabs. The original inhabitants, the Berbers, now live only in the remote north-west of the country.

The main centres of populations are concentrated in the coastal lowlands where all the best agricultural land lies, and the oases which occur in belts to the south of this area. Citrus fruits, figs, cereals, groundnuts and olives are grown mainly for home consumption. Between the coastal cultivated lands and the arid desert are regions of steppe and scrub that are used for pasture to raise cattle, sheep, goats and camels. About 30 per cent of the population work the land.

The climate of Libya is very hot and dry. Tripoli in the north-west receives 350 millimetres a year, but the rest of the country receives much less.

Libya was a constitutional monarchy until 1969 when a group of army officers under Colonel Gaddafi staged a *coup*. The country is run by a Revolutionary Command Council.

Egypt

Area:	1,000,250 square kilometres
Population:	39,000,000
Capital city:	Cairo
Language:	Arabic
Currency:	Egyptian pound

Egypt, called *Masr* in Arabic, occupies the northeastern corner of Africa. It is the home of one of the oldest civilizations and has a marvellous history that spans more than 6,000 years. It is connected to Asia by the Sinai peninsula, a large

Left: Water carriers in Egypt. Although Egypt is a prosperous country, many people live simply, in a similar way to their ancestors.

Africa

Above: The Great Pyramid of Cheops. The largest of some 80 pyramids in Egypt, it took 20 years to build using shifts of 100,000 men.

Above: The Cairo Tower is a modern landmark in this ancient city. Its design is based on an old lotus flower motif.

portion of which has been occupied by Israel since the war of 1967. After the Six Day War of 1967 the land border with Israel was marked by the Suez Canal, which was then closed to shipping until June 1975.

Less than four per cent of the land area is inhabited, cultivated land. The rest is desert. Egypt has a Mediterranean coastline and also borders the Red Sea for 1,360 kilometres.

Most of the Egyptian people are of Arab and Turkish descent and they mainly inhabit the lands along the banks of the River Nile. The Nile is like an elongated oasis which cuts through the country from south to north for a distance of almost 1,100 kilometres from Wadi Halfa on the Sudan border to Cairo. Along most of its length the Nile Valley is between 16 and 24 kilometres wide but it enlarges towards its seaward end into a great delta. Cairo stands at the apex of the delta. The Nile is the basis of Egypt's prosperity. Ninety-

five per cent of the population live in the fertile valley of the Nile. The average population density here is 1,700 per square kilometre, one of the highest in the world.

There are four main groups of people. The peasant farmers, who are called *fellahin*, live in the villages along the Nile and in the delta. The Copts are a group of people who claim to be direct descendants of the Ancient Egyptians. The Bedouin are nomadic Arabs and probably account for less than two per cent of the population. Before the 1952 revolution, Europeans, Turks and Levantines dominated the commerce and politics of Egypt. Today they are small minorities.

In the last 30 years there has been a shift in population from the countryside to towns and cities. Today, only 75 per cent of the

Right: A traditional Arab boat passes a modern block of flats. Throughout Africa there are contrasts between the traditional and the modern.

Above: The Colossi of Memnon were guardians of the mortuary temple of Amenophis III at Thebes, Upper Nile, Egypt.

Below: Midan al Tahrir (Liberation Square) is the centre of modern Cairo, surrounded by major business and shopping streets.

population live in the countryside with the rest in towns and cities.

The main religion in Egypt is Islam. Approximately 85 per cent of the population are orthodox or Sunni Muslims.

For thousands of years, the large population along the Nile has been sustained on an agriculture based on natural irrigation by the river's waters. Annually the river used to overflow its banks and flood the valley. Rich and fertile, reddish-grey silts were deposited as the water level fell. The silt is very rich in mineral salts. Today, the Aswan High Dam controls the seasonal flow of the river. The flood waters from the upper reaches of the Nile are held back and gradually released for irrigation. Flooding is thus avoided.

The main crop grown along the Nile is cotton, Egypt's principal export. Rice is also grown for export, but other crops such as wheat, maize, sugar, vegetables and fruit are grown mainly for domestic use.

Oil in the western desert provides enough for home use and export. In Cairo, Alexandria, and Suez there are oil-refining and steel manufacturing industries.

Cape Verde Islands	
Area:	4,033 square kilometres
Population:	360,000
Capital city:	Praia
Language:	Portuguese
Currency:	Conto

The Cape Verde Islands consist of ten islands and five islets which were formerly a Portuguese colony. The islands lie in the Atlantic Ocean some 650 kilometres west of Cape Verde in Senegal. Africans, Creoles and Europeans are the main groups living there.

The islands are mountainous and volcanic, lying in the belt of trade winds. The rainfall is between 125 and 250 millimetres a year.

Africa

Sisal, a vegetable oil called purgeira (rather like castor oil), oranges, and a little coffee are agricultural products that are produced in excess of local requirements.

The islands gained their independence from Portugal in July 1976. The country hopes to unite with Guinea-Bissau on the mainland.

Mauritania

Area:	1,097,200 square kilometres
Population:	1,480,000
Capital city:	Nouakchott
Languages:	French, Arabic
Currency:	Ougiya

Mauritania is an Islamic republic in West Africa. The capital is the only large settlement. It has a population of over 70,000. Over 80 per cent of the people are Moors, descended from Berber/Arabs. The remainder are Black Africans.

Over most of the land less than 200 millimetres of rain falls each year. Even Nouakchott has to have water supplied from a large desalination plant.

The cultivation of crops is limited to the valley of the Senegal River and a few oases. Maize, millet, sorghum, rice, tobacco and vegetables are grown. The oases produce dates.

The Arab population generally follows a nomadic life raising sheep and camels. The cold offshore waters are good fishing grounds. Large deposits of iron ore and copper are mined.

Mali

Area:	1,204,021 square kilometres
Population:	6,300,000
Capital city:	Bamako
Languages:	Tribal languages and French
Currency:	Malian franc

Above: The mosque at Mopti, Mali. Traditional Islamic mosque design has been adapted by the Muslims living in West Africa.

This land-locked country is situated in West Africa. The main tribal groups are the Malinke, Bambara, Dioula, Sarakole, and Bozo. The majority of the people are Muslims, with a few Christians.

French is still the official language, a throwback to the era of colonial rule from 1893 to 1958. The capital is situated on the Niger River which flows through the south of the country.

The northern part of the country is desert; the south is savanna. The climate is hot and dry with the majority of agriculture being carried out along the Niger River, which is used for irrigation. Crops include rice, cotton and groundnuts which are exported, and maize, millet and sorghum for home consumption. Cattle, sheep and goats are also reared – some are exported, as are leather and hides.

Below: A village in Mali. The country's economy depends mainly on the livestock kept by these villagers.

Below: Market life, Agades, Niger. Home-grown produce is bartered for, with other items from tyres to shirts being on sale.

Niger

Area:	1,187,000 square kilometres
Population:	4,240,000
Capital city:	Niamey
Languages:	Tribal languages and French
Currency:	Central African franc

Formerly a part of French West Africa, Niger has been an independent republic since 1960. Fifty per cent of the population is made up of Hausa peoples. Other peoples include the Tuaregs, Peulh and Jerma peoples as well as some 3,000 Europeans. Less than two per cent of the people live in towns.

The north of this extensive country is desert. The south, however, is open savanna that has enough vegetation to support large numbers of cattle, goats and sheep as well as smaller numbers of asses, camels and horses. It is watered by the Niger River in the south-west. Certain parts of the south are also a favourite for "big game hunters" as lions, elephants, buffaloes and various antelopes abound.

Most of the country's people are engaged in agriculture. The Hausa cultivate millet, peanuts, beans, and cassava, with rice and cotton being grown near rivers. Little is exported except small amounts of peanuts and cotton together with hides, leather and livestock. Exports are mainly to France and Nigeria.

Uranium has been discovered near Arlit and production began at the beginning of 1970.

Chad

Area:	1,284,000 square kilometres
Population:	3,870,000
Capital city:	N' Djamena
Languages:	French and tribal languages
Currency:	Central African franc

Formerly a territory of French Equatorial Africa, Chad became an independent republic in August 1960. It is a land-locked country which contains the towering Tibesti Mountains in the north.

In its geography, Chad has much in common with Niger, Upper Volta and Mali. In the south is a belt of savanna land that receives more rainfall than the rest of the country. The northern parts stretch into the Sahara Desert where the rainfall is less than 25 millimetres a year. Overall, Chad has a very low population density.

Cotton is the principal export, although cattle are driven into neighbouring countries to be sold there.

Chad is to a great extent isolated, with only one railway.

Below: A Faluni cattleboy in the Sahel savanna. Cattle-herding is a way of life for African nomads.

The nearest ports are over 1,600 kilometres away, and this affects the economy of the country. The only mined mineral of importance is natron.

Sudan

Area:	2,496,800 square kilometres
Population:	17,000,000
Capital city:	Khartoum
Languages:	Arabic in north; tribal languages in south
Currency:	Sudan pound

Sudan has been an independent republic since 1956 and is the largest country on the African continent. It has 640 kilometres of coastline bordering on the Red Sea in the north-east. The word Sudan comes from the Arabic word *suda* which means black.

The northern desert lands of the Sudan are inhabited by Arabs and Nubians, who live mainly along the banks of the Nile. Black African tribes live in the savanna lands and tropical rain forests of the south. The official language of the Sudan is Arabic.

Through the Sudan flow both the White Nile and the Blue Nile which meet at Khartoum and continue north as the Nile. The source of the waters of the Blue Nile is in Ethiopia, while that of the White Nile is in East Africa.

In the savanna belt the people cultivate millet, peanuts, rice and sweet potatoes. In the dry months they collect gum arabic from acacia trees. This gum arabic is exported and supplies 80 per cent of the world's needs. In the region where the White and Blue Niles meet a great irrigation scheme controlled by the Sennar Dam, and called the Gezira, enables cotton to be produced. This is the chief export of Sudan.

There is a wide variety of minerals in the Sudan including iron ore, copper, manganese ore, gold and chromite.

Africa

Ethiopia

Area:	1,221,900 square kilometres
Population:	29,416,000
Capital city:	Addis Ababa
Language:	Amharic
Currency:	Ethiopian dollar

Formerly known as Abyssinia, this ancient Christian kingdom, hidden and protected in its fortress of mountains, has many buildings to remind us of its past history. It has castles and churches that most African countries lack. The country's last monarch, Emperor Haile Selassie, was forced to surrender in 1974 to a military junta.

Christianity was introduced to the country in the fourth century and about 50 per cent of the population practise Coptic Christianity. The rest are mainly Muslims.

In the north and east are arid plains, the area being amongst the hottest places in the world. However, the western half of the country contains extensive mountains, many of which reach over 3,000 metres. This area is bounded by a great fault scarp overlooking part of the rift valley which extends from East Africa north into the Levant. The mountains receive abundant rainfall (over 2,000 millimetres a year) and have swiftly running mountain streams carving their way through deep gorges. In the mountains, cattle, sheep and goats are reared. In the wetter regions, sugar cane, bananas, and coffee are grown. Maize, sorghum and millet are grown in drier areas. In the arid regions gum arabic, frankincense and myrrh (gum resins) are collected. Beeswax is obtained from wild bees' honeycomb. The chief exports are coffee, hides and skins, pulses and oilseeds.

Mineral production is negligible. Salt is produced and there are deposits of potash salts. Oil prospecting is in progress and natural gas occurs near Massawa.

Djibouti

Area:	23,000 square kilometres
Population:	125,000
Capital city:	Djibouti
Languages:	Afar, Arabic and French
Currency:	Djibouti franc

Djibouti is a small country in north-east Africa. It was formerly called French Somaliland and then after 1967 The Afars and Issas (an overseas territory of France). It gained its independence in 1977.

The two main groups of people are Somalis of the Issas clan and the Afar. A few thousand Arabs and Europeans also live in this desert country, which consists mainly of dry plains broken by inland mountain ranges. The country's economy depends on the nomadic livestock industry. Hides and cattle are exported. There is also fishing for pearls, sponges and shellfish along the coast.

There is no mineral production. Reserves of gypsum, mica, amethyst and sulphur have not been exploited as yet.

Below: Lalibela church, central Ethiopia. This town has a dozen churches all carved from solid rock

Below: A valley in the Balé mountains of Ethiopia. The large spiky-leaved plants in the picture are giant lobelias.

Somali Republic

Area:	630,000 square kilometres
Population:	3,200,000
Capital city:	Mogadiscio
Languages:	Somali and English
Currency:	Somali shilling

Somalia became an independent republic in 1960 when the British Somaliland and Italian Somalia merged. The country is situated on the horn of north-east Africa.

Many of the Somali people in the south of the country are descended from the original Bantu-speaking population.

Somalia is a very arid land. Only in the south and the northern plateau does the annual rainfall exceed 500 millimetres. The dryness and lack of water over most of the country means that a nomadic herding life is followed by the people. Livestock and skins and hides are major exports.

In the more fertile, irrigated southern region, bananas, sugar cane and fruits are grown as cash crops. Sorghum, maize and beans are also grown as food crops.

Senegal

Area:	197,722 square kilometres
Population:	5,090,000
Capital city:	Dakar
Language:	French
Currency:	Central African franc

Senegal is the most westerly country of Africa. The country of Gambia cuts into Senegal along the Gambia River in the south. About 30 per cent of the peoples of Senegal are Wollof and most are Muslims.

Although well within the tropics, the climate from Dakar northwards is affected by the cool Canaries offshore current, giving pleasant sea breezes from November to February.

Floods of the Senegal River permit the growing of millet and guinea corn. Elsewhere people settle only where water is available and the soil is fertile enough to cultivate crops such as peanuts, which are a leading export. About 75 per cent of the population is engaged in agriculture. Phosphates and cement are supplied to neighbouring countries.

Gambia

Area:	10,601 square kilometres
Population:	493,000
Capital city:	Banjul
Language:	English
Currency:	Dalasi

Gambia is the West African country that projects like a finger into Senegal, following the Gambia River for 480 kilometres inland. It is the smallest state on the African mainland. It has been independent since 1970.

The valley floor of the Gambia River is often swampy but has rich soil due to flood deposits. The valley rises to a plateau which

Above: Stalls in Banjul, Gambia's capital. The men wear cotton clothes produced by Gambia's textile industry.

extends into Senegal and is covered with poor sandstone soils. Apart from tropical forest along the river most of the rest of the vegetation is savanna. The tropical climate gives a dry season from November to April.

Most agriculture takes place along the fertile river valley, with crops such as maize, millet and rice being grown for local consumption. Groundnuts are the most important crop and are shipped down the Gambia River to Banjul for export.

Guinea Bissau

Area:	36,125 square kilometres
Population:	800,000
Capital city:	Bissau
Languages:	Portuguese and Cape Verde Creole
Currency:	Escudo

Guinea Bissau was formerly called Portuguese Guinea and lies on the Atlantic coast between Senegal and Guinea. It includes many islands off its coast such as Bolama and Bijagoz.

Most of the population are Muslims but there are many ethnic groups. The peoples of the interior herd cattle, goats, sheep and pigs as well as growing crops such as groundnuts and millet. On the coastal strip the land is swampy and where the mangrove forests have been cleared rice is grown. Palm oil and kernels and coconuts are commercial crops. Most of its trading is done with Portugal which conceded Guinea Bissau its independence in 1974.

Guinea

Area:	245,857 square kilometres
Population:	5,140,000
Capital city:	Conakry
Languages:	French and ethnic languages
Currency:	Sylis

Guinea was formerly a territory of French West Africa, and became an independent republic in 1958.

Africa

Most of the people are Muslims.

The coast of Guinea is mangrove swamp, dotted with islands. The capital stands on Tombo Island. Inland from the coastal plain the country becomes mountainous. About 50 kilometres inland, the volcanic Kakoulima massif rises to more than 1,000 metres. Middle Guinea is dominated by the uplands of the Fouta Djallon massif. The cattle-raising Fulani people live here. The northeast is grassy plain.

In the tropical, humid climate of Guinea, the rainy season comes from May to October. Cattle rearing, tropical fruit growing and rice cultivation are very important. Coffee, pineapples and bananas are exported.

Rich mineral deposits include diamonds, bauxite and iron ore. Since independence mineral production has increased.

Above: Festivities in Guinea. Dancers make their way to Kindia, one of the main towns of the country. The main ethnic groups are Peuls, Malinke and Soussous.

work the land as subsistence farmers. Rice, maize, cassava, palm kernels and oil, coffee and cocoa beans are grown. Chief exports are diamonds, iron ore and other minerals. Industries include oil refining and diamond cutting and polishing.

similar to that of Sierra Leone.

Rice is grown in the swamps and cassava on the uplands. Vegetables, cotton, tobacco, rubber, palm oil and kernels, and coffee are also grown.

The chief exports are iron ore, rubber, industrial diamonds, coffee, and palm oil and kernels. Extra foreign income is gained from the foreign ships that register under the Liberian flag. Thus the country appears to have a very large merchant fleet.

Sierra Leone	
Area:	73,326 square kilometres
Population:	3,000,000
Capital city:	Freetown
Languages:	English and several ethnic languages
Currency:	Leone

Sierra Leone on the west coast of Africa has been an independent republic within the Commonwealth since 1961. It was founded in 1787 as a settlement for free slaves.

The coastline is broken by a series of rivers draining direct from the interior highlands to the coast. At the mouth of the Rokel is a fine natural harbour on which Freetown stands. The coastal plain rises to broad lowlands with some hills. Inland a plateau rises to over 600 metres.

In the wet season (May to October) over 1,400 millimetres of rain fall. About 400 millimetres fall in July alone. This decreases inland and orchard bush and savanna areas are reached.

About 80 per cent of the people

Liberia	
Area:	112,600 square kilometres
Population:	1,500,000
Capital city:	Monrovia
Languages:	English, Kru, Mandinka and other ethnic languages
Currency:	Liberian and U.S. dollar

Liberia is the oldest republic in West Africa, gaining its independence in 1847. About one per cent of the population is descended from free Afro-American slaves. These Americo-Liberians control the political and economic life of the country. Ethnic peoples include Mandingos who are Muslims.

Inland from the flat coastal plain, the land rises to a grassy plateau about 900 metres above sea level. The climate is equatorial and

Ivory Coast	
Area:	322,463 square kilometres
Population:	6,673,013
Capital city:	Abidjan
Languages:	French and many ethnic languages
Currency:	Central African franc

This square-shaped country gained its independence from France in 1970. The coastal region of swamps, and lagoons and tropical rain forest extends inland for about 290 kilometres. In the centre of the country is drier, wooded scenery, succeeded by open savanna lands in the north. In the west of the country are the forested Guinea highlands that rise to over 1,500 metres. The climate is tropical with high temperatures and rainfall over most of the country.

About 70 per cent of the people are peasant farmers. They grow cotton, peanuts, maize and rice for local consumption. The main exports are cotton and coffee, plus cocoa and pineapples. The extensive forests yield a plentiful timber supply.

Ghana	
Area:	238,305 square kilometres
Population:	9,600,000
Capital city:	Accra
Languages:	English and ethnic languages
Currency:	Cedi

Ghana has been an independent republic within the Commonwealth since 1957, being formerly known as the Gold Coast. About 45 per cent of the population is made up of the Akan group who live in the southern forested region. Central Ghana is inhabited by the Guang and the Brong. The Ewe live in the east.

Ghana is much drier than its western neighbour the Ivory Coast. The dusty Harmattan wind blows from the Sahara from January to March and monsoon winds blow from the Atlantic from May to September. The average temperature is 27° centigrade with between 1,000 to 1,800 millimetres of rain falling each year.

Cocoa has made Ghana rich. It normally accounts for 50 per cent of the value of the country's exports. A single crop as the basis of the country's economy is dangerous, so attempts are being made to produce and export other crops, including cotton, oil palm, sugar, tobacco and rubber.

Timber, such as mahogany and sapele, is exported as well as veneers and plywoods. Depending on world demand, either timber or

Africa

gold is second in value to cocoa among exports. Gold is both panned from streams and mined. Diamonds, manganese ore and bauxite are also mined.

Fishing provides an income along the coast but now oil and gas have been found offshore. This will alter the economy when their importance is established.

Above: The fortress at Elmina, Ghana. The Portuguese started to build this in 1841, with the Dutch, British, Danes and Germans playing their part in the town's history.

Left: The Post Office in Accra, capital of Ghana. This modern city used to be the chief outlet of all goods from the "Gold Coast".

Togo

Area:	56,000 square kilometres
Population:	2,200,000
Capital city:	Lomé
Languages:	French and Ewe
Currency:	Central African franc

This small West African country has a coastal strip of only 65 kilometres along the Gulf of Guinea. The southern half of Togo is inhabited by the Ewe people. The Kabre and various other ethnic groups live in the north.

Behind the well-watered coastal plain are grasslands. The climate is hot and humid.

Oil palms, maize, bananas and cocoa are grown on the grasslands. Cotton is grown farther north. Small amounts of cocoa, coffee, cotton, peanuts and cassava are exported to neighbouring Ghana. The country has phosphate mines and some light engineering factories.

Upper Volta

Area:	274,200 square kilometres
Population:	6,100,000
Capital city:	Ouagadougou
Languages:	French and ethnic languages
Currency:	Central African franc

Upper Volta is a land-locked country of West Africa, north of Ghana. It was formerly a French colony but gained its independence in 1960. About 50 per cent of the population are Mossi peoples.

Most of the country receives an average of 900 to 1,100 milli-

metres of rain annually. In the north, however, lies the edge of the Sahara and rain is very infrequent. Average monthly temperatures here rise above 32° centigrade in the hot season.

The majority of the people are involved with agriculture. Cattle and other livestock are reared on the savanna lands. Food crops such as maize, millet, rice and sorghum are grown. Recently cotton and groundnuts have been produced and exported.

Benin

Area:	112,600 square kilometres
Population:	3,200,000
Capital city:	Porto Novo
Languages:	French and tribal languages
Currency:	Central African franc

168

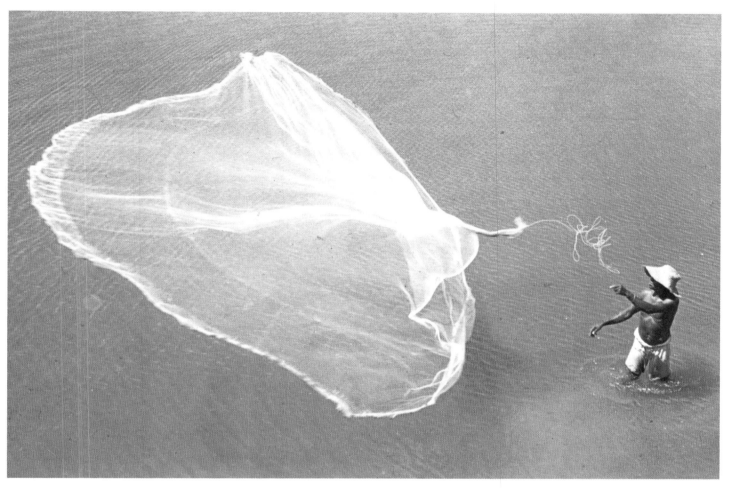

Above: A Togo fisherman casts his net into a coastal lagoon. The net is weighted with lead around the edges so that it sinks, trapping the fish.

Benin is a people's republic formerly called Dahomey. It is a narrow country of West Africa with a coastline of 110 kilometres on the Gulf of Guinea. There are over 50 different ethnic groups in the country which include the Fon, Fula, Somba, Bariba, Adja and Yoruba peoples. The majority follow their own native religions although about 30 per cent are either Muslims or Christians.

A wet tropical climate is found along the tropical forests of the coast but towards the north of the country the climate becomes much drier. The majority of the people

Right: Camels in Nigeria. In many African countries camels are used for transport because they can travel for long periods without needing water.

Africa

are farmers. The forests of the south provide palm oil and kernels, with coffee and cotton being commercial crops in the north. Food crops grown include cassava, maize, millet, rice, sweet potatoes and yams.

Nigeria	
Area:	923,773 square kilometres
Population:	73,000,000
Capital city:	Lagos
Languages:	English, Hausa, Igbo and Yoruba
Currency:	Naira

Nigeria is comparable in size to Texas and Arizona combined and its large population is about 16 per cent of the total population of Africa. Less than 20 per cent live in towns. The country became independent of Britain in 1960 and is a member of the Commonwealth.

There are some 250 ethnic groups each with its own language. Just under 50 per cent of the population are Muslims, and 35 per cent practise Christianity. The people enjoy a comparatively high living standard.

The 760-kilometre-long coastline is much indented with lagoons and the river deltas including the Niger and Cross. Much of it is dense mangrove swamp. These low coastlands rise to the high plains in the Yoruba country and to the Udi plateau which reaches 300 metres above sea level. Tropical forests give way to savanna country in the centre. This area is well watered by the Niger and Benue rivers.

Between the valleys of the Niger and Benue is the Bauchi plateau, rising to over 900 metres. In the north of Nigeria is a belt of open savanna land merging into scrub. The north-east corner of the country borders part of Lake Chad and this area is swampy in the rainy season.

Climatically the almost equatorial tropical belt in the south receives in places over 2,500 milli-

Above: Lagos, federal capital of Nigeria, is partly situated on an island in a lagoon. Mainland Apapa, on the right of the picture, handles most of the country's trade.

metres of rain a year and high temperatures averaging 27° centigrade all year round. The dry season lasts for nine months in the north. The annual rainfall here averages about 500 millimetres although it is very variable.

During the '70s the economy of Nigeria expanded rapidly. Agriculture is very important, involving 80 per cent of the population. The agriculture zones follow the natural vegetation belts. In the coastal and wet belts, common crops in forest clearings include yams, cassava, maize, sugar cane, bananas and oil palms. Cocoa grown in the west is important.

Over the savanna or plateau areas the Hausa tribes practise shifting cultivation. They cultivate millet, peanuts, cassava, tobacco and cotton. In irrigated areas rice and sugar cane are grown. The Hausas are the crop growers of this area while the Fulani who share the lands are the pastoral tribe, tending over 10 million cattle plus many sheep and goats. In the north of the country the great cash crop is the peanut. About 51,000 tonnes of fish are caught annually along the coast and from inland waters.

Crude oil has revolutionized the Nigerian economy and made it an important economic power. Over 50 per cent of the country's foreign earnings come from oil exports. Oilfields occur offshore, within 100 kilometres of the coast. There are extensive coal deposits at Enugu on the eastern railway to Port Harcourt. There are also extensive sources of natural gas and iron ore.

Nigeria's industry is mainly concerned with processing agricultural products. Although a wealthy country when compared to other African states, the average wage per person is less than £35 per year. This is because of the country's enormous population.

Above: Market selling in Nigeria. Over 80 per cent of the population are involved with agriculture, and many foods are exported.

Cameroon

Area:	474,000 square kilometres
Population:	7,500,000
Capital city:	Yaoundé
Languages:	French, English and ethnic languages
Currency:	Central African franc

Cameroon is an independent republic in central West Africa with a coastline facing the Atlantic on the Gulf of Guinea. Mount Cameroon is a prominent landmark on the west coast rising to 4,070 metres. In the north-west lies a chain of mountains that reach 1,800 metres. These fall away to the lowlands that surround Lake Chad in the extreme north of the country.

In the north of Cameroon the climate is tropical while in the south it is equatorial. The rainfall on the slopes of Mount Cameroon is very high, averaging 10,000 millimetres a year.

About 85 per cent of the population work in agriculture. Many practise the system of rotation or shifting cultivation. Others live nomadic lives with their herds of cattle, sheep and goats.

Bauxite is the only mineral which is mined extensively and exported. Other minerals include gold and tin which are mined in small quantities.

The main agricultural exports are cocoa beans and coffee, as well as raw cotton, bananas and peanuts.

São Tomé and Principe Islands

Area:	964 square kilometres
Population:	76,000
Capital city:	São Tomé
Language:	Portuguese
Currency:	Escudo

These islands are volcanic in origin and were discovered by the Portuguese in 1470. They lie in the Gulf of Guinea some 200 kilometres off the West African coast. They gained their independence from Portugal in 1975. São Tomé has good roads and numerous well-equipped plantations. Exports include cocoa, coffee, copra, palm oil and cinchona. The fertile volcanic soils and hot humid climate with a long rainy season provide good yields. Principe is also called Princes Island, its chief town being San Antonio.

Equatorial Guinea

Area:	28,051 square kilometres
Population:	290,000
Capital city:	Bata
Languages:	Spanish and Bantu
Currency:	Guinean peseta

This small independent republic in West Africa consists of a mainland area, Rio Muni, and the island of Macias Nguema Biyoga (formerly Fernando Póo) plus smaller offshore islands.

The Bubi are the most numerous people on the island of Macias Nguema Biyoga, while on mainland Rio Muni the Fang people make up the majority. Both groups speak Bantu.

The coastal plain rises to over 1,200 metres inland in the form of the Cristal Mountains. This is a forested plateau which provides timber for export.

On the island of Macias Nguema Biyoga there are many volcanic peaks and rich lava plains. In this area there are extensive plantations growing coffee and cocoa for export.

Central African Empire

Area:	625,000 square kilometres
Population:	1,640,000
Capital city:	Bangui
Languages:	French and several ethnic languages
Currency:	Central African franc

The country lies just north of the equator in the centre of the continent. The central area is a large plateau of savanna grasslands, mainly above 400 metres. This tropical country receives a total annual rainfall of over 1,500 millimetres. There is a marked dry season, December being the driest month.

The country is poor, most people surviving by subsistence farming. Cassava is grown and is the staple diet. Coffee, cotton, rubber and tobacco are the main cash crops. Cattle are kept, but can only be reared in areas free from the tsetse fly. Diamonds used to be the main mineral resource of the country, until uranium was discovered.

The country gained its independence from France in 1960.

Africa

Gabon

Area:	267,667 square kilometres
Population:	950,000
Capital city:	Libreville
Languages:	French and Bantu
Currency:	Central African franc

Gabon is an independent republic on the west coast of Africa situated on the equator. Its capital, Libreville, was founded for resettled slaves.

About 30 per cent of the population are the Bantu-speaking Fang people, with other groups including the Echira, Adouma and Okande.

The small population of the country is mainly involved in agricultural work although only about five per cent of the country is under cultivation. About 85 per cent of the country is still covered with equatorial forest which yields over one million tonnes of hardwood timber each year. The climate over this forested hilly country is tropical and wet, receiving up to 2,500 millimetres of rain annually.

Timber used to be the mainstay of Gabon's economy but rich mineral resources of uranium, manganese and iron ore are now the leading exports. Crude petroleum is also exported and natural gas is being exploited. Inland communications are poor.

Congo

Area:	342,000 square kilometres
Population:	1,320,000
Capital city:	Brazzaville
Languages:	French and Bantu
Currency:	Central African franc

Formerly a territory of French Equatorial Africa, the Congo became an independent republic in 1960 and was known as Congo Brazzaville until 1971. Brazzaville

Left: Camels carrying equipment for locust control scientists in East Africa. Plagues of locusts still attack the crops in tropical Africa.

is situated on the north shore of Stanley Pool on the Zaire River. Here it receives river traffic from upstream and ships goods by rail to the Atlantic port of Pointe Noire.

The Zaire River and its tributary the Ubangi form the greater part of the country's eastern border. The Bateke plateau and the Mayombe escarpment in the south are separated by a wide valley through which the Niara River flows. The tropical climate provides between 1,000 and 1,200 millimetres of rain annually and an average temperature of 24° centigrade. About 60 per cent of the workforce cultivate the land, mainly on small holdings. Bananas and cassava are the main food crops, with coffee, cocoa, peanuts, sugar cane and tobacco as cash crops. Timber is a major export. Others include diamonds and potash.

Zaire

Area:	2,345,409 square kilometres
Population:	25,600,000
Capital city:	Kinshasa
Languages:	French and Bantu
Currency:	Zaire

Zaire became a republic in 1960 but was known as the Democratic Republic of the Congo until 1972. It is the second largest country in the African continent, after Sudan. The whole vast area has a tiny but very important coastline on the Atlantic. This coastal area north of the Zaire River forms the boundary with Angola.

Below: African Pygmies in Zaire's equatorial forest. They live by hunting and gathering wild fruits, insects and roots, although they have been influenced by Western ways.

The Pygmies live in the central equatorial rain forests of Zaire. These tiny people grow to a height of between 1.2 and 1.5 metres and survive by hunting and gathering wild fruits, insects and roots.

Zaire occupies much of the drainage area of the Zaire River and its tributaries. Much of the country is a dissected tableland with a general level of about 400 metres in the west and 600 metres in the south and east. Mountains rise in the east to a height of about 5,000 metres and form the eastern border of the country. Tropical rain forest covers the centre of the country, with savanna to the north and south. The tropical climate gives between 1,500 and 2,000 millimetres of rain each year; average temperatures reach as high as 30° centigrade.

About 75 per cent of the population work the land. Cash crops include cocoa, coffee, cotton, palm oil, rubber, sugar and tea. Crops grown for local consumption are mainly cassava, maize and millet as well as bananas and peanuts. Ebony trees cut from the extensive forest are exported.

Minerals are the country's biggest money-maker. Copper, zinc, gold, cobalt and diamonds are all mined and exported.

Manufactured goods include beer, cigarettes, textiles and fuel oils, all for the home market.

The Zaire River and its tributaries provide hydro-electric power for electricity.

Rwanda

Area:	26,330 square kilometres
Population:	5,500,000
Capital city:	Kigali
Languages:	French and Kinyarwanda
Currency:	Rwanda franc

Rwanda is a tiny land-locked country with a high population density. Most of the people are descended from Hutu peoples who

Above: A steamy jungle in Zaire. Few people, apart from Pygmies, inhabit these forests of the congo basin which cover ten per cent of the country.

came to the area over 1,000 years ago. The Tutsi group are tall while the Twa are pygmies.

In the west of the country are high mountains rising to over 4,000 metres. Farther east lies a high plateau cut into by many rivers. Part of the western border lies on the shores of Lake Kivu, 1,460 metres up in the Great Rift Valley of East Africa. This is the hottest area of the country. The mountains of the east are the wettest with an annual rainfall of over 1,500 millimetres. The eastern plateau, once forested, is now cleared for farming. Over 90 per cent of the population work the land growing bananas, peas, beans, sorghum and sweet potatoes for home consumption. Coffee, cotton, pyrethrum and tea are grown as cash crops. Tin and tungsten ores are mined.

Burundi

Area:	27,834 square kilometres
Population:	3,900,000
Capital city:	Bujumbura
Languages:	French and Kirundi
Currency:	Burundi franc

This small independent republic is very densely populated. It was formerly linked with Rwanda but gained its independence in 1962 and became a republic four years later. Two ethnic groups live in Burundi —the Tutsi and the Hutu.

The eastern part of the country is a fertile plateau with highlands to the north-west and south. In the west the land slopes down to Lake Tanganyika. Most of the population grow bananas, beans, cassava and maize. Coffee and cotton are the cash crops. Hides from the numerous cattle are also exported. The long-horned cattle are much valued by their owners.

Mineral reserves are few; tin ores, kaolin and gold are mined.

Africa

Right: Agricultural landscape outside Kigali, the capital of Rwanda. The economy of the country is based on farming. Coffee is the most important export crop.

Uganda

Area:	236,860 square kilometres
Population:	11,250,000
Capital city:	Kampala
Languages:	English, Swahili and Bantu
Currency:	Ugandan shilling

Uganda became an independent country in 1962. At one time it was part of a British colony called Kenya, Uganda and Tanganyika.

Most of the country lies between 900 and 1,500 metres above sea level. Flat-topped hills with broad valleys are a feature of the Buganda region north-west of Lake Victoria. Central and northern Uganda is a large savanna plain. On the south-west border are the Ruwenzori Mountains that reach 5,000 metres. Lake Victoria is situated in the south-east of the country, and about 30 per cent of this huge lake lies within the boundary of Uganda. The overflow from this lake passes through the Owen Falls Dam at Jinja to form the Victoria Nile River.

The climate is of a modified equatorial type due to the generally high altitude. The average annual rainfall is between 1,000 and 1,500 millimetres. In southern Uganda cultivation is possible all year round.

The main export crops are cotton, coffee, sugar, tea and tobacco. Livestock rearing is also important, especially in the drier north. Valuable timber such as mahogany is cut from the tropical forests. The lakes and rivers provide good fishing. Copper and tin ore are mined, and cement is manufactured.

Right: Zebras grazing on the Serengeti grasslands of East Africa. This area is famous for its huge herds of plains animals, such as gnu, gazelle and zebra.

Kenya

Area:	582,600 square kilometres
Population:	13,800,000
Capital city:	Nairobi
Languages:	Swahili and English
Currency:	Kenyan shilling

Kenya, an independent republic within the Commonwealth since 1964, is the size of Texas with lots of wildlife and spectacular landscapes. About 40 different ethnic peoples live in the country including the Kikuyu, Kamba, Luo and the Luhya. There are small numbers of Asians, Europeans and Arabs. About 50 per cent of the population practise ethnic religions, Christians and Muslims make up the rest.

A dry semi-desert area is found over the north and north-east of the country. Eighty per cent of the population are found living in the

174

well-watered lands of the south-west which consist of highlands and the Kenyan portion of the Lake Victoria basin.

The coastal zone has a greater rainfall, higher temperatures and lower altitudes than the plateau. The Great Rift Valley bisects the highlands from north to south.

Farming is the basis of the country's economy. However, in recent years tourism, especially safaris to see the great variety of wildlife, has brought added wealth to the country. About 90 per cent of the population farm the land, growing maize, wheat, cotton, sugar cane, sisal, coffee and tea.

Above: Tourists watch a Masai display in Kenya. These tall warriors are a living symbol of Kenya's past and have resisted the changes of the 20th century.

Below: Muslim mosque at Malindi, a beach-resort in Kenya. About 20 per cent of the population are Muslims, 35 per cent Christians and the rest practise ethnic religions.

Above: A typical Kenyan landscape with an elephant browsing on the savanna vegetation near a road. In the background is snow-capped Mount Kenya, which is situated on the equator.

Africa

Pyrethrum, grown for insecticide, is an important commercial crop of the highlands. Coconuts and cashew nuts on the lower lands are important export crops. In recent years fresh fruits have been increasingly grown for export. Mangroves that grow along the coastline supply tanning bark. Hardy cattle and camels and other livestock are raised in the semi-desert of the north.

There is little mineral wealth in the country. Although gold has been produced in western Kenya, the only large mineral production is soda ash dug out of the alkaline Lake Magadi on the floor of the Rift Valley.

Many secondary industries have developed that process local raw materials to make, for example, soap, paint, margarine and blankets. Imported raw materials are processed into products such as plastics and cement.

The Mombasa–Uganda railway runs from Mombasa on the coast through Nairobi and on to Kampala in Uganda. There are several branch lines linking up with other towns along its length. There are over 1,600 kilometres of metalled roads throughout the country.

The first leader and prime minister of the independent country was Jomo Kenyatta. He was a leading figure in African

Left: Flamingos on Lake Nakuru in Kenya. This soda lake is famous for the million or so flamingos that breed here. The birds feed on algae.

nationalist movements before independence. He ruled from 1963 until his death in 1978.

Tanzania	
Area:	945,087 square kilometres
Population:	15,000,000
Capital city:	Dar es Salaam
Languages:	English and Swahili
Currency:	Tanzanian shilling

The United Republic of Tanzania is the largest country in East Africa, smaller than Alaska in size but bigger than Texas. It is the union of mainland Tanganyika with the island of Zanzibar. Lying just south of the equator, it has 800 kilometres of coastline.

There are many ethnic groups in this country including the Sakuma, Nyamwezi, Makonde and Ha. There are small groups of Asians, Arabs and Europeans.

The climate ranges from hot and humid on the coast to that of the cold, thin mountain air on the heights of Mount Kilimanjaro. This is the highest mountain in Africa at 5,895 metres. Parts of the large Lake Tanganyika and Lake Victoria are also within the country. The centre of the country is mainly dry and hot. The dry season is from June to September

and mid-December to February. The heaviest rains come between mid-March and May.

Most people are subsistence farmers. Sisal, cotton, coffee and cashew nuts are the main crops grown for export. Zanzibar and Pemba Islands are the world's largest suppliers of cloves and clove oil. Cattle and sheep are numerous.

Although gold was an important mineral in the past, most mines are now closed. Diamonds are now far more important exports. The textile, fishing, leather and hide industries are quite well developed. An important expanding industry is the tourist safari tours to the many national parks. Big game hunting is now illegal in the country, but photo-safaris prove very popular in parks such as the Lake Manyara National Park. The Olduvai Gorge is probably the world's most famous prehistoric site.

Between 1970–76 the government, with Chinese help, built the Tanzam railway. This links Dar es Salaam on the coast with the Zambian Copperbelt and runs for 1,800 kilometres.

Below left: Zanzibar street scene, Tanzania. Most of the city is modernized, although the old city where slaves were sold still exists.

Below: Bagamoya beach, Tanzania. Bagamoya means "place where the heart lays down its burden", a most suitable name for this beautiful stretch of tropical coastline.

Seychelles

Area:	404 square kilometres
Population:	59,000
Capital city:	Victoria
Languages:	English and French
Currency:	Seychelles rupee

These islands, situated in the Indian Ocean about 1,760 kilometres east of the Kenyan coast, have a mixed population of French, Indians, Chinese and Africans. The islands gained their independence in 1976 but remained within the Commonwealth.

Commercial crops include coconuts, cinnamon, vanilla pods and patchouli (for oil). Salt fish are also exported.

In recent years the tourist industry has expanded rapidly, people being attracted by the tropical island climate, the bird life, and the coral reefs for diving and fishing.

St Helena

Area:	122 square kilometres
Population:	5,000
Capital city:	Jamestown
Language:	English
Currency:	Pound sterling

Below: The Seychelle Islands, Indian Ocean. Lying some 1,760 kilometres off the Kenyan coast, these islands are becoming very popular with tourists.

Napoleon Bonaparte of France lived on St Helena as a prisoner until his death in 1821. Today this island is a British Crown Colony and has the islands of Ascension and Tristan da Cunha as dependencies. It is an isolated volcano rising to 823 metres. Although the capital was established as an important port in the days of sailing ships, it is now only important as a cable station. The cable runs from Cape Town to Europe.

The pleasant climate is another factor in keeping the small population happy living on the island. Their cattle provide meat and they grow excellent potatoes, vegetables and fruit. Rope, string and lace are made from flax, and some is exported.

Angola

Area:	1,246,700 square kilometres
Population:	5,670,000
Capital city:	Luanda
Languages:	Portuguese and Bantu
Currency:	Kwanza

Although it is a large country, the population is sparse in this former Portuguese territory on the Atlantic coast of south-west Africa.

Bantu groups include the Ovimbundu. Bushmen live in the Kalahari Desert in the south. Here they live a nomadic life in small groups, hunting with sticks and bows for food. Their cave paintings are well known. The Hottentots are also found in this country, living a nomadic life, keeping their cattle and sheep. They speak a language of "click" sounds.

The dry lowlands of the coast rise eastwards to a plateau which averages 1,000 metres in height. Practically the whole of Angola is savanna land with a little dense forest along the river valleys. In the south, however, there are coastal semi-deserts which merge into the Kalahari Desert.

Coffee and maize are grown for

Above: Sa da Bandeira, Angola. The city is mainly an agricultural centre, surrounded by an extensive cattle-ranching and sheep-rearing region.

export, as well as sugar cane, sisal and cotton. Beans, cassava, and peanuts are grown for home consumption.

Oil and iron ore are the most important minerals nowadays, although diamonds mined in the north of the country used to be more important.

Cabinda is a small territory which lies between Zaire and Congo and is administered as a detached portion of Angola.

Zambia

Area:	752,620 square kilometres
Population:	5,140,000 (estimated)
Capital city:	Lusaka
Languages:	English and Bantu
Currency:	Kwacha

Zambia is a land-locked republic in Central Africa. It has been independent within the Commonwealth since 1964. Before then it was called Northern Rhodesia. Much of the country is a high plateau which ranges from 500 to over 1,200 metres above sea level. It is typical savanna country with tall grasses and detached stands of trees. The Zambezi River flows from west to east for some 2,736 kilometres before reaching the

Africa

Above: Young farmers in Zambia study the use of a flap-pump, which improves the supply of water

Below: Kitwe, Zambia. Copper ingots are loaded on lorries for transporting to Dar-es-Salaam, Tanzania, for export.

Indian Ocean. At one point the river plunges over Victoria Falls, a 160-metres-wide ledge, into a chasm over 100 metres below.

Zambia lies well within the tropics, but the climate is cooler because much of the country lies over 900 metres above sea level.

Although the official language of the country is English, six other major languages are spoken by the 70 or more ethnic groups.

About 70 per cent of Zambians work the land, many of them growing crops such as peanuts, maize, fruit and vegetables. The belt of land between Kalomo and Lusaka has better soil, and tobacco and cotton are grown here for export.

The country's main wealth comes from the mining and export of copper. Other minerals mined include lead, cobalt, coal, silver and zinc. Power is supplied by the hydro-electric scheme at the Kariba Dam, and from another built on the Kafue River.

Until 1975 Zambia's only rail link with the coast was through Zimbabwe-Rhodesia. A second outlet, known as the Uhuru or Tanzam railway, runs some 1,870 kilometres from Zambia to Dar es Salaam in Tanzania. An oil pipeline from this city also provides Zambia with fuel. Tourism is growing steadily, with the country's excellent wildlife national parks a main attraction.

Malawi	
Area:	118,484 square kilometres
Population:	about 5,310,000
Capital city:	Lilongwe
Languages:	Nyanja/Chewa, Tumbuka and English
Currency:	Kwacha

Malawi is a long, narrow, land-locked country in eastern Central Africa. It is 930 kilometres long, and between 80 and 160 kilometres across. Lake Nyasa stretches for 580 kilometres along

Above: A farmer in Malawi inspects his maize crop. Maize and rice provide the staple diet of Malawians. Tea and tobacco are grown for export.

its eastern border.

The African Rift Valley runs from north to south through the eastern part of the country and includes Lake Nyasa. West of the Rift Valley is a high plateau which rises to over 1,220 metres.

In the north of the country the Tumbuka is the major ethnic group. In the central and southern region the major ethnic group is the Nyanja/Chewa, while the Yao and the Lomwe live in the southeast. A few thousand Asians and Europeans also live in Malawi.

Much of the country is fertile and receives a high rainfall. This allows export crops such as tobacco, tea, peanuts and cotton to be grown. Sugar and coffee are grown as cash crops, with rice and corn providing the staple diet for the densely-populated country. Lake Nyasa supports a prosperous fishing industry. The country is poor in minerals, although there are deposits of coal and bauxite. Industries are only just being established.

Malawi became independent

Above: Tribal dances at Livingstone, the tourist capital of Zambia. Victoria Falls on the Zambian/Zimbabwe border are a short distance away.

within the Commonwealth in 1966. It was formerly called Nyasaland. Dr Hastings Banda has governed the country since independence.

Mozambique

Area:	784,961 square kilometres
Population:	10,000,000
Capital city:	Maputo (formerly called Lourenço Marques)
Languages:	Portuguese, Swahili and Ronga
Currency:	Mozambique escudo

Mozambique was formerly called Portuguese East Africa, only winning independence in 1975. It has a long coastline stretching for some 2,800 kilometres down southeast Africa.

The low-lying coastal plains rise to a plateau of between 250 and 600 metres. In the north of the country there are the Namuli Highlands which rise to above 1,800 metres. Several rivers flow through the country into the Indian Ocean including the Zambezi, Rovumba and Limpopo.

The coastal climate is hot and humid with cyclones (tropical storms) in the hot season from June to November. The rainfall decreases inland over the plateau.

About 70 per cent of the total labour force works the land. Maize, cassava, copra and tea are grown as cash crops with sugar cane, cotton and cashew nuts as commercial crops for export. A highly developed railway system and good ports favour trade.

The Comoros

Area:	1,862 square kilometres
Population:	217,000
Capital city:	Moroni
Language:	Swahili
Currency:	Central African franc

The Comoros are a group of three islands in the Indian Ocean between the north of Madagascar and the African mainland. They are Grand Comoro, Moheli and Anjouan. Most of the people are Muslims of mixed African-Arab descent. Formerly a French-ruled colony, the islands made a unilateral declaration of independence (U.D.I.) in 1975. The island of Mayotte, once part of the group, decided to become one of France's Overseas Departments.

These rugged islands are volcanic in origin and the soil is very fertile. Many tropical crops are grown including sugar cane, vanilla, cocoa beans, sisal, coffee, cloves and coconuts. Vanilla, copra and cloves are the main exports. But economic opportunities are limited on the islands.

Mayotte

Area:	374 square kilometres
Population:	38,000
Capital city:	Dzaoudzi
Languages:	Swahili and French
Currency:	French franc

The tropical island of Mayotte lies at the north end of the Mozambique Channel, between the Comoros and Madagascar. It first became a French colony in 1843. Since then it has been linked with the Comoros and Madagascar.

In 1976 the Comoros achieved independence but Mayotte decided to become an Overseas Department of France. The main reason for this split was religious: whereas the Comorans are mainly Muslim, Catholics are the main religious group on Mayotte.

Most of the people work on the land producing subsistence crops. Vanilla and copra are the main commercial crops and exports. Fishing is an expanding activity.

Below: Plants such as date palms can flourish in desert areas, as their deep roots reach water far underground.

Africa

Madagascar

Area:	594,180 square kilometres
Population:	8,000,000
Capital city:	Antananarivo
Languages:	Malagasy and French
Currency:	Malagasy franc

This republic consists of the huge island of Madagascar and several smaller islands. They are situated some 400 kilometres off the south-east coast of Africa. Madagascar is about 1,600 kilometres long and 580 kilometres wide at its widest point. A former French colony, the country still has many French residents, as well as Comorans, Indians and Taiwan-Chinese.

The island lies within the trade wind belt so that south-east winds prevail. They bring a heavy rainfall to the eastern side of the island and little to the west. Belts of evergreen rain forest cover the wetter areas of the east and north, with savanna and steppe on the central plateau and semi-arid vegetation on the drier western side. Much of the original rain forest has been cleared for agricultural land. This has destroyed much of Madagascar's unique wildlife.

Madagascar's economy is based on farming. Cassava, maize, rice and sweet potatoes are grown for home use. Crops grown for export include coffee, rice, sugar cane, vanilla and cloves. Cattle are reared on the plateau. Chromite is the most important mineral so far developed.

Réunion

Area:	2,516 square kilometres
Population:	476,700
Capital city:	Saint Denis
Languages:	French and Creole
Currency:	French franc

This French volcanic island is situated some 900 kilometres east of Madagascar in the Indian

Above: Mauritius, a volcanic island situated 800 kilometres east of Madagascar. Sugar cane, palms and steep mountains are typical landscape.

Ocean. The land rises to two peaks, the Piton de Neiges (3,069 metres) and the still active volcano, Fournaise. As the island is situated in the south-east trade wind belt there is moderate to heavy rainfall, with frequent tropical storms in the summer months.

The range of altitude makes it possible for a wide variety of crops to be grown. Sugar cane is the most important crop. Tea, cocoa, cassava, rice and vanilla are also grown. Wheat and temperate fruits are grown at higher levels. Small herds of pigs, sheep and cattle are kept. The main exports are sugar and rum.

Mauritius

Area:	1,865 square kilometres
Population:	about 881,000
Capital city:	Port Louis
Languages:	French, English and Mauritian Creole
Currency:	Mauritian rupee

Mauritius gained its independence in 1968, although it is still a member of the Commonwealth. It is situated some 800 kilometres to the east of Madagascar and almost on the direct line between South Africa and India. Large numbers of emigrants have come to the island from India. The population density is very high with over 470 people per square kilometre.

Mauritius is a volcanic island. It mountainous interior is surrounded by wide lowlands. The climate is tropical. Coconuts and sugar cane are grown on the coast lands. Sugar is the main export and sugar cane processing is the most important industry.

Namibia

Area:	824,269 square kilometres
Population:	909,000
Capital city:	Windhoek
Languages:	Afrikaans, English, Kwanyama and Herero
Currency:	South African rand

Namibia is a vast territory formerly called South-West Africa. It occupies the drier side of the African continent from the scrub lands of the Botswana border in the east to the absolute desert of the Namib in the south. The largest ethnic group is the Ovambo.

The central highlands rise to 2,500 metres above sea level. The high plateau of the east merges into the Kalahari Desert. The

Above: Boys of the Builders Brigade, Botswana, learn practical skills like painting and decorating. Few get jobs outside farming.

Namib stretches for some 1,600 kilometres along the coast. Rainfall here is less than 25 millimetres per year. The southern coastal areas have large deposits of diamonds.

Beef and dairy products are important commercially, as are Persian lamb pelts called Karakuls. Many foodstuffs are imported from South Africa. The fishing industry produces lobsters, fish oil, meal and tinned pilchards.

Botswana

Area:	575,000 square kilometres
Population:	630,000
Capital city:	Gaborone
Languages:	Setswana and English
Currency:	South African rand

Botswana, a country about the size of France, is situated in central southern Africa. The largest ethnic group is the Tswana.

The eastern and northern parts of the country are the best watered. The northern half of the country is the basin of Lake Ngami and the Okovango swamp. The southern half is essentially the Kalahari Desert. The climate is dry and sub-tropical.

Stock-raising is the most important activity where there is good grassland. Frequent droughts occur. Diamonds, copper and nickel are the leading exports.

Zimbabwe-Rhodesia

Area:	390,622 square kilometres
Population:	6,500,000
Capital city:	Salisbury
Language:	English
Currency:	Rhodesian dollar

Right: A view of Cape Town harbour, with Table Mountain in the background. Cape Town is a major port of South Africa.

Prior to 1964 there were two Rhodesias. The northern state became Zambia and the following year, the southern state illegally declared itself independent from Britain. For 14 years its minority white government has not been recognized by the rest of the world apart from South Africa. In 1978 it was agreed that the country would be called Zimbabwe-Rhodesia, and that a system of majority rule would be introduced during 1979.

The country consists of a broad belt of high plateau more than 1,200 metres above sea level running from south-west to north-east. The southern side drains to the Limpopo River while the northern side drains to the Zambezi River. The natural vegetation is savanna grassland with some open woodlands. The eastern border is mountainous.

Over 75 per cent of the people work the land, most being con-

Left: Part of the ruins of Great Zimbabwe, built in the Middle Ages. The Rhodesian African nationalists were the first to call Rhodesia Zimbabwe.

cerned with subsistence farming. On European farms, maize and cattle rearing, tobacco and citrus fruits are important. Cotton and sugar are also cash crops.

The economy of the country is based on rich mineral deposits, especially asbestos, chrome, copper and nickel. A very large coalfield exists at Wankie. The Kariba Dam, built across the Zambezi River, provides essential power for the mines, manufacturing industries and towns.

South Africa

Area:	1,177,854 square kilometres
Population:	26,000,000
Capitals:	Cape Town and Pretoria
Languages:	English, Afrikaans and Bantu
Currency:	Rand

South Africa is the most industrialized country of Africa. There are four distinct groups of peoples: Blacks, Whites, Coloureds and Asians. The Whites, who make up

Africa

15 per cent of the population, are mainly descended from the early French, Dutch, English and German settlers of the 17th to 19th centuries. The Blacks, who make up 70 per cent of the population, consist of several distinct ethnic groups including Zulus, Xhosas, Tswanas, Sothos, Swazis and

Above left: Mist rises in the early morning from a lake in Kruger National Park, South Africa.

Above right: A panoramic view of Table Bay, Cape Town.

Below: The Union Buildings at Pretoria, the administrative capital of South Africa.

others. Coloureds are of mixed descent.

There is a great variety of scenery to be found within the country but most of South Africa is a vast plateau, part of which is called the high veld. The low veld which includes the bushveld, is an area of low-lying, sub-tropical grasslands found in the north western, northern and eastern portion of the Transvaal and extending into Zululand. South Africa is flanked by the warm currents of the Indian Ocean on the east and the cool currents of the Atlantic on the west. Sandy beaches stretch for 3,000 kilometres around this coastline. The main mountain range of southern Africa is the Drakensberg. It extends for about 1,600 kilometres from the northern Transvaal to the Cape Midlands. Cape Town's Table Mountain, a famous landmark, is one of the peaks of the Cape Peninsula massif. The Great Karroo Desert lies in the south-west of the country.

South Africa's climate is generally sunny and temperate. Winters are usually mild although snow falls on the mountain ranges of the Cape and Natal. High veld winter nights are frosty but days are bright and sunny. Thunderstorms bring cool relief to the hot summers. Rain occurs mainly in the summer months between October and March.

Agriculture is very important. In

the Cape region, the farmlands are used mainly for wheat production. The drier south-western region is mountainous but in the valleys grapes are produced. Plums, apples and tobacco are also grown as well as winter crops of oats and barley. Other cash crops grown in the southern coastal regions include bananas, peanuts, pineapples and sugar cane.

Beef and mutton production are extremely important in South Africa as about 85 per cent of the land is not arable and suitable only for livestock. Today there is a flourishing cattle and dairy industry with over 30 breeds and cross-breeds making up the 13 million head of cattle in the country. Nearly 30 million sheep are also reared for their wool.

Gold is the strength behind the economy of South Africa. More than 400,000 men work in the South African gold mines, some working at depths of over 3,500 metres below the surface. The gold area is known as the Witwatersrand and lies in the north-east of the country. More than 55 per cent of the world's gold is mined here. Kimberley in the centre of the country is the place where diamonds are mined. South Africa is very rich in other minerals, including asbestos, chrome, coal, copper, iron ore and manganese.

Johannesburg is the main industrial city of the country. The majority of industries process the country's natural resources. Wool, iron, steel, chemicals and car assembly plants are important industries.

Swaziland

Area:	17,400 square kilometres
Population:	528,000
Capital city:	Mbabane
Languages:	English and Siswati
Currency:	South African rand and Emalangeri

Swaziland gained its independence in 1968. It is a small landlocked kingdom in southern Africa, completely surrounded by South Africa, apart from an eastern border with Mozambique. The main ethnic group is a Bantu people, the Swazis.

The country extends from the mountainous high veld of the west, which reaches over 1,000 metres, down to the low veld on the Mozambique border. Sugar is grown in these lowlands and is a major export. Maize, millet, rice and sorghum are grown for home use. Citrus fruits and cotton are other major cash crops. There are large plantations of pine and eucalyptus in the high veld.

Asbestos, iron ore and coal deposits are exploited. Tin ore and gold are also mined.

Lesotho

Area:	30,340 square kilometres
Population:	1,180,000
Capital city:	Maseru
Languages:	Sotho and English
Currency:	South African rand

This little mountainous state is completely surrounded by South Africa. It gained its independence from Britain in 1966, changing its name from Basutoland.

The mountainous relief of this country offers little arable land. Most people work the land but the farmers cannot grow enough food to feed the whole country. Maize, sorghum, wheat and vegetables are grown for home use. Cattle, Angora goats and sheep are reared on the rough pastures of the highlands. Wool from the sheep and mohair from goats form a major export.

Diamonds are the only major mineral. Small factories cut the diamonds. Other industrial products include candles and carpets.

The University of Botswana is established at Roma and provides an African alternative to the racially segregated education of the Republic of South Africa.

Below: A Swazi woman in her festive costume. Most of the Swazis are farmers growing maize, millet and rice for food.

Below: A Zulu dance. The Zulu people live in the Natal province of South Africa and number over four million.

Asia

South
China
Sea

Mekong

Guam

Amer

Pacific Islands

Pac

Nauru   Gilbert Islands

Papua New Guinea

Solomon Islands

Port Moresby   ● Honiara

Tuvalu

Wallis and Futuna

We

New Hebrides   Fiji
                         Suva ●   Niue

New Caledonia
                 ● Noumea

Indian Ocean

Ashburton

Australia

Diamantina

Murchison

Norfolk Island

Murray   Murrumbidgee   Canberra

Wellington ●

New Zealand

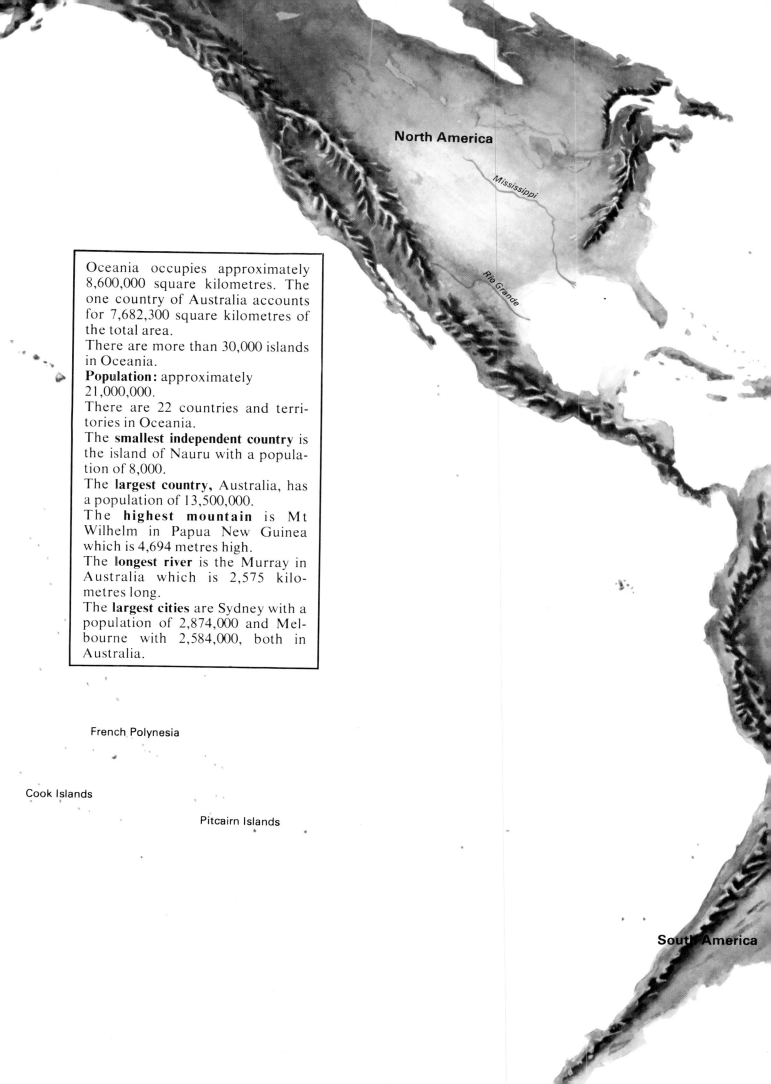

North America

Mississippi

Rio Grande

Oceania occupies approximately 8,600,000 square kilometres. The one country of Australia accounts for 7,682,300 square kilometres of the total area.

There are more than 30,000 islands in Oceania.

Population: approximately 21,000,000.

There are 22 countries and territories in Oceania.

The **smallest independent country** is the island of Nauru with a population of 8,000.

The **largest country,** Australia, has a population of 13,500,000.

The **highest mountain** is Mt Wilhelm in Papua New Guinea which is 4,694 metres high.

The **longest river** is the Murray in Australia which is 2,575 kilometres long.

The **largest cities** are Sydney with a population of 2,874,000 and Melbourne with 2,584,000, both in Australia.

French Polynesia

Cook Islands

Pitcairn Islands

South America

Oceania

Oceania covers millions of square kilometres of ocean, and comprises Australia, New Zealand, Papua New Guinea and thousands of islands in the Pacific Ocean.

More islands are found in this area than in all the rest of the world's seas, and the Pacific is the largest and deepest of all the oceans. Magellan described it in 1521 as "a sea so vast that the human mind can scarcely grasp it".

A continent of variety

Not surprisingly then, Oceania has a variety of environments, from the steaming humidity of the Solomons to the huge, dry deserts of Australia.

Some islands, like Canton and Johnston, are treeless, while the Solomons and Papua New Guinea have thick, often impenetrable vegetation.

Islands like Nauru are composed almost entirely of phosphate with little arable soil; while the Gilbert Islands and Tokelau can support some cultivation.

The majority of minerals are found in Australia, including iron ore, nickel, uranium, bauxite, lead, copper and zinc. New Caledonia has the world's largest known nickel deposits, copper is found in Papua New Guinea and gold is

Above: New Zealand offers very good grazing land for sheep. Wool and lamb are among New Zealand's main exports.

mined in Fiji. Offshore oil has also been discovered in parts of Oceania.

Economies vary from subsistence agriculture on many islands to the wealthy farming and industrial countries of Australia and New Zealand.

Discovery

Oceania was the last part of the globe to be discovered by Europeans, starting with Balboa and Magellan in the 16th century. The oldest inhabitants in the area are the Australoids and Negritos, who are believed to have migrated here 30,000 years ago. Their descendants are the native populations of Australia and part of Papua New

Left: The Australian Aborigines are steeped in ceremony and mythology. They daub their bodies with paint to take part in ceremonial rituals or *corroborees*.

Above: Increasingly, Australians and New Zealanders are taking to the ski slopes. This resort is in Perisher Valley in Australia.

Above: This Hawaiian girl is dressed in a traditional grass skirt costume that has changed little over the centuries.

Guinea, to name but two.

After later migrations, three main groups emerged each with its own language, culture and physical features, and each dominating a specific area.

Peoples

The Melanesians (from *melas*, meaning black, and *neesos* an island) occupy the chain of islands from Papua New Guinea east and south-east to the Solomons, the New Hebrides, New Caledonia and Fiji.

The Micronesians (*micros* = small) live on the islands to the north lying west of the International Date Line and close to the equator.

The Polynesians (from *poly* meaning many) inhabit an area stretching from Hawaii in the north to New Zealand in the south and from just west of Fiji in the east to Easter Island in the west.

Colonization

European colonization in Oceania made an enormous impact on the lives of the native populations, and some nearly died out. But they have since recovered to a certain extent and are now estimated to number nearly four million. But they are outnumbered by over 17 million Europeans and about 500,000 Asians.

Although most European descendants live in Australia and New Zealand, European culture prevails in the islands as well.

In some areas, however, such as the highlands of Papua New Guinea, tribal life remains as it was hundreds of years ago.

Independence

Although most of Oceania has won independence from its former colonial masters, the process is not yet complete. The New Hebrides, for example, are run by a unique Anglo-French Condominium (joint control). Many of the American territories have internal self-government, although the United States controls defence and foreign affairs.

Oceania

Australia
Area:	7,682,300 square kilometres
Population:	13,500,000
Capital city:	Canberra
Language:	English
Currency:	Australian dollar

Australia is bounded on the west and south by the Indian Ocean and by the Pacific on the east. It is the sixth largest country in the world, though its population of 13.5 million makes it one of the most sparsely populated. It is made up of six states and two administered territories. In the east, from north to south, are Queensland, New South Wales, the Australian Capital Territory where the Federal capital of Canberra is situated, Victoria and the island state of Tasmania. In the middle lie the Northern Territory and South Australia. Western Australia takes up the western part, covering 30 per cent of the whole continent.

Almost 75 per cent of the land mass is a vast, flat ancient plateau. Even the long mountain range, stretching the full length of the eastern coast, called the Great Dividing Range, has no peak higher than 2,230 metres. Between this range and the Pacific are the plains of the eastern seaboard, seldom more than 95 kilometres wide. The plateaus which stretch westwards to the Indian Ocean have a few tablelands and ridges such as the King Leopold, Hamersley, Macdonnell and Musgrave ranges.

There are huge deserts such as the Simpson and Gibson and large, inland lakes like Lake Eyre. Australia has some spectacular scenery, for example, Ayers Rock, a single boulder 347.3 metres high and 10 kilometres in circumference. Off the east coast lies the Great Barrier Reef, a fringe of coral stretching 2,000 kilometres.

Australia has its hottest weather in December and its coldest in

Above: An aerial view of Sydney, Australia's largest city, shows the famous Opera House and bridge.

July. In the north, the seasons are divided into two, the wet and the dry. The wettest weather occurs when it is hottest.

Travelling south, the climate ranges from sub-tropical to temperate with cooler weather in Victoria, south-west Australia and Tasmania. The coldest regions are in Tasmania and the south-east corner of the mainland where winter snowfalls occur.

The heaviest rain occurs in northern Queensland (up to 4,000 millimetres a year), but nearly 40 per cent of the country receives less than 250 millimetres a year.

The vegetation in fertile areas is colourful and varied although forests are small in area. The most distinctive plant is the eucalyptus tree with its 500 varieties. Australia also has some unusual animal life including the kangaroo, the platypus, the koala bear, marsupial mole and wombat. The continent boasts no great river system though the Murray, the largest river, drains a major part of New South Wales, most of Victoria and South Australia. Its important tributaries are the Darling and Murrumbidgee. There are vast underground water supplies but these are of limited value because of excessive mineralization.

The basis of the Australian economy has changed radically in the last two decades. For years a primary producing country, manufactured goods and mining have now greatly increased in importance. In 1962–63, for example, farm products accounted for 80 per cent of total export earnings, manufactured goods for 13 per cent and minerals for seven per cent. By 1976–77, the figures were 44, 20 and 29 per cent respectively. Australia's trading partners had also changed in importance. Between 1962 and 1977, Japan's share rose from 16 to 34 per cent, the United States' share fell from 12 to nine per cent and the United Kingdom's from 19 to five per cent.

Wool still accounted for 75 per cent of the gross value of pastoral production and 13 per cent of exports in 1976–77. Beef and dairy products supply both home and export demands and wheat is the most important crop. Australia's growing manufacturing industries now employ about 25 per cent of the civilian work force and contribute 24 per cent to her total home earnings. Food, beverages and tobacco are the biggest, followed by machinery, cars, chemicals and domestic appliances.

The biggest boom, however, has been in mining. The discovery of massive iron ore deposits in Western Australia in the 1960s overshadowed mineral discoveries of the past. The ancient rocks of the continent also yield a wealth of other minerals. Output of these has grown dramatically in the last 20 years. Nickel, uranium, bauxite, coal, lead, zinc and copper are among the other minerals found.

Above: An Australian Aborigine plays the *didgeridoo*, a long tube-like musical instrument made of wood.

Below: Sheep auctions attract large crowds in country areas. Wool is one of Australia's major exports.

Natural gas and oil are also found and the country is 70 per cent self-sufficient in petroleum.

Australia has a comprehensive state education system which is free and compulsory for children between the ages of six and 15.

There is also a substantial church-run, private education system.

For children in isolated areas, there is the unique School of the Air where lessons are conducted on a two-way wireless between teacher and pupils often 500 kilo-

Oceania

Above: The Flying Doctor Service takes medical care to people living on isolated Australian properties.

metres or more apart. Australia has 18 universities free to all except post-graduate students.

The original inhabitants are the Aborigines who, it is believed, arrived here 30,000 years ago. The first white settlement was a convict colony established by Britain in 1778 at Botany Bay near Sydney. Five other colonies with convicts and free settlers were later established. These six colonies administered themselves separately until 1901 when they federated to form the Commonwealth of Australia. The former colonies are now called states.

Except for Queensland which has one House of Parliament, all states and the Commonwealth Government in Canberra have two houses elected by the people. The main political parties are the Liberal and the Labor Party. A third party, the Country Party, has been aligned with the Liberal Party for over 30 years and this coalition has been dominant in the post-war years. Legislative power is invested in the parliaments and the British monarch who is represented by a Governor-General at Federal level and by a Governor in each state.

Most Australians – 85 per cent of them – live in urban areas, particularly the state capitals. Sydney, the capital of New South Wales, is the largest city with over three million of the state's 4,914,300 people. Of the 3,646,300 people in

Victoria, 2,603,500 live in Melbourne. Brisbane, Adelaide and Perth all have just under one million and Hobart, the smallest capital, has 162,059 people. The population is largely of British descent although massive immigration since 1945 has also brought other European settlers. In 1977, there were 106,000 Aborigines or part Aborigines.

Papua New Guinea	
Area:	75,300 square kilometres
Population:	2,829,000
Capital city:	Port Moresby
Language:	Pidgin English
Currency:	Kina

Lying between the equator and northeastern Australia, Papua New Guinea comprises the eastern half of a large island, of which the other half is West Irian, administered by Indonesia. It also comprises a number of smaller islands, including Bougainville, New Britain and New Ireland.

The climate is hot and humid. Temperatures average between 22° and 33° centigrade, and rainfall is heavy. Vegetation is so lush that much of the country is almost impenetrable. Some areas have yet to be explored. Fast-flowing rivers, such as the Fly and the Sepik, have wide swampy deltas.

The mainland is divided by mountain ranges, the main ones being the Owen Stanley in the south and the Star Mountains and Bismarck, Hindenburg and Schraeder ranges in the north. The highest peak is Mount Wilheim, at 4,754 metres.

Ine country was formed by merging the territory of Papua, under Australian rule since 1906, and the trust territory of New Guinea, a former German colony, administered by Australia since 1914. It won full independence in 1975, and has a National Parliament elected every five years.

Above: A view of the business area of Port Moresby, the capital of Papua New Guinea. Its population of 76,507 makes it the largest city.

Executive power is invested in the British monarch.

The official language is Pidgin, a form of English, though over 700 other languages are spoken. More than 90 per cent of the population's work is subsistence agriculture. Only 76,507 people live in the capital, Port Moresby.

Among the extensive mineral resources that have been discovered are copper, gold, silver and petroleum. Copper accounted for 35 per cent of the country's export earnings in 1976–77. Its trading partners are Australia, Japan (who occupied the country from 1942–45) and Germany.

Isolation makes social services difficult to administer and only 50 per cent of children attend primary schools.

Above: Every year in Papua New Guinea a tribal festival is held at Mt. Hagen. The costumes are very colourful.

Solomon Islands

Area:	29,785 square kilometres
Population:	197,000
Capital city:	Honiara
Language:	English
Currency:	Australian dollar

The Solomon Islands comprises the major islands of Choisaul, Santa Isabel, New Georgia, Malaita, Guadalcanal and San Cristobel and many smaller islands. Most of the islands are covered with dense tropical rain forest with grasslands on the northern plains of Guadalcanal.

Whalers, traders and missionaries began arriving on the islands from Europe in the 19th century and they became a British Protectorate in 1893, governed from Fiji until 1952. The Solomons have had a Legislative Council since 1960, and were granted internal self-government in 1976 and full independence in 1978. They are a member of the Commonwealth.

Until recently, the economy was based almost solely on copra but since the late 1950s there have been various attempts to diversify. Rice and cattle farming have been introduced and fishing and timber industries are now established. Mineral exploration has been extensive: bauxite has been found and an estimated 10 million tonnes of phosphate exist on Bellona Island.

The Solomons' two ports, Goza and Honiara, are on regular shipping routes between Australasia, New Zealand, Hong Kong and Japan.

Education is both state-run and private with most private schools run by the churches. There are 266 state-aided and 78 private primary schools and ten secondary schools. Over 30,000 children attended school in 1975. A further 20 secondary schools are being built.

New Hebrides

Area:	14,760 square kilometres
Population:	97,000
Capital city:	Vila
Languages:	French and English
Currency:	New Hebrides franc and Australian dollar

The New Hebrides is an archipelago of 70 islands ranging in size from 25 hectares to 3,600 square kilometres. The larger ones have rugged interiors and narrow coastal strips where most of the population live.

This unique Anglo-French Condominium was established in 1906, with each European power responsible for its own citizens. There is also a fully elected Representative Assembly. This has led to there being two official languages, two police forces, three public services, three courts of law, two currencies, three budgets and two resident commissioners. Attempts are being made to draw up a constitution for independence in 1980.

More than 60 per cent of the people are engaged in subsistence farming. Copra, coffee and cocoa are the main exports, and 46,520 tonnes of manganese were exported in 1975.

There are 8,000 pupils at French schools and 10,000 at British schools. Education is not free but the charge is nominal; therefore, schools are well attended.

New Caledonia

Area:	19,103 square kilometres
Population:	133,000
Capital city:	Noumea
Language:	French
Currency:	Franc du Pacifique

New Caledonia is a long narrow island south of the New Hebrides. It has a mountainous interior. Its population is mixed and comprises 40 per cent indigenous Melanesians, 40 per cent Europeans (mainly French), with some Asians and Polynesians making up the rest.

A French territory since 1853, it has had an elected Territorial Assembly since 1956 although a French commissioner retains

Below: Village huts in the New Hebrides, a group of 70 islands jointly administered by the British and the French.

191

Oceania

control of French national departments and the police.

New Caledonia has the world's largest-known nickel deposits. Nickel exports account for almost all the foreign earnings. Coffee, copra, maize and vegetables are the most important crops.

There are 240 primary schools and eight secondary schools.

New Zealand

Area:	268,704 square kilometres
Population:	3,150,000
Capital city:	Wellington
Language:	English
Currency:	New Zealand dollar

New Zealand lies in the South Pacific Ocean 1,800 kilometres south-east of Australia. It is made up of two major islands — the North and South Islands — and the smaller Stewart Island off South Island.

The mountain system is its dominating geographical feature. The Southern Alps run almost the entire length of the South Island with no fewer than 16 peaks exceeding 3,000 metres, the highest being Mt Cook at 3,764 metres. The mountains of the North Island cover 10 per cent of the total area. In the west are most of the active volcanoes, hot springs and geysers, as well as the largest lake, Lake Taupo.

Forests cover nearly 25 per cent of the country, and swift flowing rivers abound. The longest in the North Island is the Waikato at 425 kilometres and the 322-kilometre Clutha River is the longest in the South Island. Several hydro-electric power stations have been built alongside such rivers.

New Zealand's temperatures average 12° centigrade except in the warmer far north. Rainfall is high throughout the year. The only areas receiving less than 600 millimetres a year are those east of the Southern Alps. Peaks in the South Island are frequently covered with snow and there are some spectacular glaciers. The Tasman Glacier on Mt Cook is the largest. The economy is heavily

Above: Sheep, important to New Zealand's economy, graze on plains with snow-capped mountains behind.

dependent on pastoral and agricultural industries. Wool, meat and dairy produce account for over 75 per cent of exports and 13 per cent of the total home earnings. The United Kingdom is still New Zealand's biggest customer, taking over 20 per cent of her exports in 1976–77. Other customers are Australia, the U.S.A., other EEC countries and Japan.

Expanding industrial production accounts for 12 per cent of exports. Forests supply timber for a growing pulp and paper industry. Nearly 25 per cent of the work force are employed in manufacturing.

Coal is sufficient for local needs, and iron and silica sands are mined. There is an inland gas field at Kapuni in the North Island and natural gas deposits have been found at Maui.

New Zealand's people are of predominantly British stock with a large minority – 230,000 – of Maoris, the Polynesian inhabitants who came to the islands in successive waves in A.D. 900 and 1300.

British whalers and missionaries began to arrive in the first half of the 19th century. In 1840 New Zealand was annexed as a British colony, and granted dominion status in 1907.

Left: The kiwi has become a national symbol for New Zealand. It is a shy bird which only comes out at night.

About 80 per cent of the population live in urban areas, particularly on the North Island. The capital, Wellington, has 350,950 people and Auckland, the largest city, 801,200. The biggest city on the South Island is Christchurch with 327,200. There is a comprehensive social welfare system which includes a national health scheme and compulsory schooling between six and 15.

New Zealand is a member of the Commonwealth. Executive power is vested in the British monarch as head of state represented by a Governor-General. The House of Representatives has 87 members including four Maoris, elected for three years. There are two major political parties, the National Party and the Labour Party.

Fiji
Area:	18,272 square kilometres
Population:	588,000
Capital city:	Suva
Languages:	English, Hindustani, Fijian
Currency:	Fijian dollar

The 800 islands of Fiji – only 100 of which are inhabited – lie nearly 2,000 kilometres south of the equator, and some distance north of New Zealand. Most of the larger islands are high with some flat coastal land. Viti Levu, where the capital Suva is situated, is the third largest island in the Pacific.

The climate is tropical with temperatures ranging from 16° to 32° centigrade. The economy is largely agricultural with sugar as the main crop. Tourism is the second largest source of foreign earnings followed by gold and coconut products. The United Kingdom is Fiji's main trading partner. Fiji is the centre of communications in the south-west Pacific, lying on the main sea and air routes from the U.S.A. to Australasia.

Nearly half the population are

Above: A climbing party negotiates the icy slopes of Mt Cook, which is a peak in the Southern Alps, South Island, New Zealand.

Oceania

Indian, 44 per cent Fijian and most of the rest British.

Education is neither free nor compulsory although it is subsidized by the government. In 1976 there were 641 state primary schools and 109 secondary schools. The University of the South Pacific attracts students from other Pacific Islands.

Fiji was ceded to the United Kingdom in 1874 and was a Protectorate until independence in 1970. Parliament has two houses – an appointed Senate (22 seats) and an elected House of Representatives (52 seats). Fiji is a member of the Commonwealth.

Tonga	
Area:	700 square kilometres
Population:	90,000
Capital city:	Naku'alofa
Languages:	Tongan and English
Currency:	Pa'anga

The Kingdom of Tonga, lying 640 kilometres east of Fiji, is made up of 169 islands, 36 of which are inhabited and which are divided into three main groups, Vava'u, Ha'apai and Tongatapu. The capital, Naku'alofa, is on Tongatapu.

The climate is mild (between 15° and 21° centigrade for most of the year) and the soil is fertile. The economy is agricultural with bananas and coconuts being the chief crops. Agriculture employs 74 per cent of the working population. Oil was discovered offshore in 1977 although the extent of the deposits is not yet known. Tonga is a member of the Commonwealth.

Education is free and compulsory for all children aged between six and 14 years. In 1975, there were 180 schools with over 40,000 pupils. There are several technical and vocational schools and one teachers' training college. Tonga has three public hospitals and 27 doctors.

A former British Protected State, Tonga has been a monarchy since the mid-19th century. The present monarch is King Taufa'shau Tupou IV. The king is head of state and government. He appoints and presides over a Privy Council. The Legislative Assembly also includes seven hereditary nobles and seven elected representatives.

American Samoa	
Area:	197 square kilometres
Population:	31,000
Capital city:	Fagatoga
Language:	Samoan
Currency:	U.S. dollar

The seven islands of American Samoa lie in the south-central Pacific, 3,700 kilometres southwest of Hawaii. A former German colony, the islands were ceded to the United States between 1899 and 1904, and were administered by an appointed governor until 1977 when the governor was elected. A House of Representatives is also elected and a Senate is elected by local chiefs.

Employment is provided largely by a U.S. naval base, a fish canning plant, and the growing of crops such as coconuts and bananas.

American-style education is free and compulsory up to 16 years old.

Tuvalu	
Area:	24 square kilometres
Population:	5,900
Capital city:	Fanafuti
Language:	English
Currency:	Australian dollar

The nine islands of Tuvalu, formerly known as the Ellice Islands, are scattered over one million square kilometres south of the equator, close to the International Date Line.

Once part of the British Crown Colony of the Gilbert and Ellice Islands, in 1974 the people voted to form a separate colony. A British appointed Commissioner is responsible for external affairs, defence and finance. An elected assembly governs internal affairs.

The people live mainly by fishing and growing coconuts. There are eight primary schools and one secondary school.

Right: Gilbert Islanders live by growing crops and by fishing. Here, a large group of them have gathered together for an evening of song.

Gilbert Islands

Area:	857 square kilometres
Population:	51,932
Capital city:	Tarawa
Language:	Gilbertese
Currency:	Australian dollar

The 33 coral atolls of the Gilbert Islands are set in a staggering five million square kilometres of ocean. The group was once a part of the Gilbert and Ellice Islands which were governed from the Solomons, but split up in 1975. The Gilberts were granted internal self-government in 1977 and full independence is expected in 1979. They are a member of the Commonwealth.

The islands' major source of income is phosphate mining on Ocean Island. The only other export is copra.

Guam

Area:	549 square kilometres
Population:	105,000
Capital city:	Agana
Languages:	Chamorro and English
Currency:	U.S. dollar

Guam, the largest of the Mariana Islands, was colonized by Spain in 1668, and ceded to the U.S. in 1898. It is now under the jurisdiction of the U.S. Department of the Interior. It has an assembly of 21 elected members and an elected governor. A referendum in 1976 voted for more autonomy but maintenance of close links with the U.S.

The economy is largely geared to servicing the important U.S. army base – but the growing number of tourists is forcing it to cater for civilians. Education is compulsory and there are both private and state schools. There is also a university, largely financed by the U.S.A.

French Polynesia

Area:	4,200 square kilometres
Population:	137,000
Capital city:	Papeste
Language:	French
Currency:	Franc du Pacifique

French Polynesia comprises the Society, Tuamotu, Austral, Gambier, Marquesas and Repa groups of islands.

Tahiti, the largest single island, was proclaimed a French Protectorate in 1842 and a colony in 1880. The other groups were annexed by 1900. Since 1977, a High Commissioner has presided over an elected council, and France is responsible for foreign affairs, defence, finance and justice.

The economy is based on services for army bases and grow-

Left: Many Pacific islands are volcanic in origin like Mangareva which is situated in the Tuamotu Archipelago in French Polynesia.

Oceania

ing coconuts. Education is compulsory and free up to 14 years old.

Cook Islands

Area:	241 square kilometres
Population:	18,000
Capital city:	Avarn
Language:	English
Currency:	New Zealand dollar

The 15 Cook Islands are of two types; the Northern Cooks are atolls and the Southern are volcanic.

A British protectorate in 1888, the islands became part of New Zealand in 1901 and a self-governing territory in 1965. Their isolation has caused severe economic difficulties since the export of fresh fruit is hindered by a lack of shipping, but there are now fruit-canning and clothing factories, and tourism is increasing.

Education is free and compulsory from six to 16.

Nauru

Area:	21 square kilometres
Population:	8,000
Capital city:	Nauru
Language:	Nauruan
Currency:	Australian dollar

Nauru is made up almost entirely

of phosphate rock, the mining of which is its only industry. In 1975–76 Nauru earned $A 45 million from its phosphates, although the phosphate is due to run out in 1992.

A former German colony, Nauru has been administered by Australia since 1918 and has been self-governing since 1968. It has a special relationship with the Commonwealth.

Most foodstuffs have to be imported. For the future, the possibility of shipping soil to the island is being investigated. Nauru also hopes to derive economic security from shipping and civil aviation services. There are 10 primary and two secondary schools on Nauru.

Niue

Area:	259 square kilometres
Population:	4,000
Capital city:	Aiofi
Languages:	English and Polynesian
Currency:	New Zealand dollar

The coral island of Niue has had internal self-government since 1974, with an elected assembly. It is still an overseas territory of New Zealand, its people having free entry there. Its 1976 population showed a 23 per cent decrease since 1971 and it is estimated that twice as many Niueans live in New Zealand as on the island.

Vegetables, fruit, copra and handicrafts are the main products as well as a small forestry industry. Uranium was discovered in 1977 but the size of the deposits is not yet known.

Norfolk Island

Area:	35 square kilometres
Population:	1,600
Capital city:	Kingston
Language:	English
Currency:	Australian dollar

Norfolk Island lies between Australia and New Zealand and is a single island eight kilometres long and 4.8 kilometres wide. Its economy is based largely on tourism with 18,807 visitors coming to the island in 1974–75. The economy is otherwise agricultural with bean seed, kentia palm, fruit and vegetables being grown.

Norfolk Island was established as a convict colony in 1788 and was a separate Crown Colony until 1897 when it became a dependency of New South Wales. In 1913, it was transferred to the Australian Government.

Wallis and Futuna

Area:	96 square kilometres
Population:	10,000
Capital city:	Mata-Uta
Language:	French and Wallisian
Currency:	Franc du Pacifique

A self-governing French Overseas Territory, the Wallis and Futuna colony consists of two groups, taking its name from the major island of each group. About 7,000 of its mainly Polynesian inhabitants live on Wallis Island and 3,000 on Futuna. Some 11,000 islanders live in New Caledonia

Right: An island hospital surrounded by palm trees has been built from local woods with coconut thatching for its roof.

and the New Hebrides.

Coconuts, yams, taros and bananas are cultivated and exported.

An elected Territorial Assembly governs the islands. There are nine state-financed schools.

Pacific Islands

Area:	1,813 square kilometres
Population:	125,000
Capital city:	Saipan
Languages:	English and nine languages in the Malayo-Polynesian group
Currency:	U.S. dollar

The 2,000 islands of the U.S. Trust Territory of the Pacific Islands include the Palau group, the Western Carolines, Eastern Carolines, the Marshall Islands and the Marianas.

Formerly Spanish, Japanese and German possessions, the islands have been administered by America since World War Two.

In recent years the tourist industry has become increasingly important, and is now the islands' main source of income.

Pitcairn Islands

Area:	5 square kilometres
Population:	65
Capital city:	Adamstown
Languages:	English and Tahitian
Currency:	New Zealand dollar

The Pitcairn Islands comprise Pitcairn Island and three uninhabited islands which lie half-way between Panama and New Zealand. Most of its small number of inhabitants are descendants of the Bounty mutineers, but their total is gradually dwindling.

The island is administered by the British High Commission in New Zealand. The High Commissioner acts as governor in consultation with a council of four elected, five nominated and one ex-officio members.

Industries are agriculture, fishing and some handicrafts.

Tokelau

Area:	10 square kilometres
Population:	1,600
Languages:	English and Tokelauan
Currency:	New Zealand dollar

Tokelau comprises three atolls – Atufa, Nukunonu and Fakaofo – of which Nukunonu is the most populated. The poor economic prospects of the islands have led many people to move to New Zealand in recent years.

A British protectorate since 1877, Tokelau was included in the Gilbert and Ellice Islands colony until 1927. Since then it has been a separate colony administered by New Zealand. Each atoll has an elected *faipula* who presides over a Council of Elders. There is a school on each atoll.

Western Samoa

Area:	28,421 square kilometres
Population:	151,275
Capital city:	Apia
Language:	Samoan
Currency:	West Samoan dollar

The four high volcanic islands of Western Samoa lie in the South Pacific 2,400 kilometres north of New Zealand. The Samoan language is believed to be the oldest form of Polynesian in existence. An intricate hierarchy of graded titles remains despite European influence since 1830. Western Samoa was administered by New Zealand from 1920 until independence in 1962. It is a member of the Commonwealth. Cocoa, coconuts and bananas are the main crops. There is also some light industry.

There are 213 schools with nearly 48,000 pupils.

North America, together with Greenland, occupies 21,515,335 square kilometres.

Population: approximately 240,000,000.

Two large countries, Canada and the United States of America, dominate North America. The island of Greenland, and the tiny French island of St Pierre and Miquelon are the other two countries included in North America.

Canada is the larger of the two countries occupying 9,976,140 square kilometres but the United States has the largest population with 216,820,000 people.

The **highest mountain** is Mt McKinley in Alaska at 6,194 metres.

The **longest river** is the Missouri which measures 4,368 kilometres. It is a tributary of the Mississippi which is 3,779 kilometres long.

The **largest lake** is Lake Superior, also the largest freshwater lake in the world, covering 82,413 square kilometres.

The **largest cities** are New York with 11,571,000 people, Los Angeles with 7,032,000 and Chicago with 6,979,000.

North America

Above: An Indian reservation in the arid west. The women are skilled in the weaving of multicoloured rugs using the wool from their flocks of sheep.

North America is the world's third largest continent. It extends from the Arctic Ocean in the north to the Isthmus of Panama in the south. It is bounded by the Atlantic Ocean on the east and the Pacific Ocean on the west. In shape North America is roughly an upside-down triangle. The narrow point looks towards South America while the wide base sprawls along the Arctic Circle. At its most northwesterly point the continent is separated from Asia by only a narrow channel of water, the Bering Strait. The superpowers, U.S.A. and U.S.S.R., are face to face.

The bulk of this great land mass is occupied by three countries – Canada, the United States and Mexico. Greenland, St Pierre, Miquelon, the islands of the West Indies and the small countries of Central America make up the rest of it. Due to the differences in history, culture and economy, Mexico, Central America and the West Indies are dealt with in a separate section. What is described on this page is the remaining part of the continent.

Canada and the United States

The size of North America is vast. At its widest, from Newfoundland to British Columbia, it is over 6,000 kilometres across. From its most northerly point on Ellesmere Island to the southern tip of Florida, almost at the Tropic of Cancer, it measures 6,400 kilometres. The total area is 21,500,000 square kilometres. The population is approximately 240 million.

North America is often referred to as the "New World". The original Americans were Indians and Eskimos who came from Asia via a "land bridge" across the Bering Strait at a time when the sea level was lower than at present. For thousands of years these settlers simply adapted their way of life to the prevailing natural environment that they found.

In the last 300 years the coming of settlers of European origin has transformed North America into the most highly developed, wealthiest continent in the world. North America is extremely well endowed with natural resources, rich

Above: The American Civil War was one of the bloodiest wars in history. This painting shows the Battle of Gettysburg in June 1863.

farmlands, vast forests, valuable mineral and power supplies. There are still great stretches of empty land in the north, in the Rockies and the deserts of the south-west. Almost everywhere else the signs of human activity are plain to see.

Below: In the early days the stage coach was the only means of transport across the continent. The journey must have been very uncomfortable.

Right: Vancouver nestles at the foot of the Rocky Mountains. It has a magnificent harbour and a mild, wet climate. It is Canada's third largest city.

Canada
Area:	9,976,140 square kilometres
Population:	23,000,000
Capital city:	Ottawa
Languages:	English and French
Currency:	Canadian dollar

In area, Canada is the world's second largest country. It is situated in the northern part of the continent of North America occupying 50 per cent of the total area. Canada is bounded by the Arctic Ocean to the north, the Atlantic Ocean to the east and the Pacific Ocean to the west. There are a great many offshore islands. The southern boundary with the U.S.A. runs along the 49° line of latitude

Left: Toronto's new town hall. Modern architecture is a feature of many Canadian cities, although it does not always blend with the existing designs.

and then through some of the Great Lakes and along the St Lawrence Valley.

The settlement of Canada
Before the arrival of European settlers in Canada, the country was inhabited by Indians and Eskimos. They were primarily hunters and gatherers living in many different tribal groups and speaking different languages.

Although North America was first visited by the Vikings as early as the 11th century, lasting European settlement did not begin until very much later.

In 1496 John Cabot brought news to Europe of rich fishing grounds off the coast of Newfoundland. Fishermen from many European countries began working these grounds in the summer months. The catch was dried or salted and shipped back home before the winter storms set in. Many of the fishermen landed on the coast for short periods to obtain water and timber and, eventually, small settlements were set up at the heads of inlets.

In 1608 the French established the first major settlement at Quebec on the St Lawrence River.

Fur trapping was one of the occupations of the early settlers and the French established a fur trading post at Montreal in 1642. By 1670 the Hudsons Bay Company was founded and British traders operated from the Nelson River. Much of Canada was explored through the activities of these two rival groups.

Unfortunately the early colonies suffered the same conflicts as their parent countries in Europe. During the first half of the 18th century Britain captured all the French colonies and in 1763 France formally ceded her Canadian territory to Britain. In 1867 Canada separated from the United States to become an independent country.

Relief and climate
The physical heart of Canada is the Canadian Shield which lies in a great arc around the Hudson Bay. It is composed of extremely ancient rocks and has an undulating surface which slopes gently towards Hudson Bay. The outer edges of the shield stand at over 600 metres and are marked by the St Lawrence Valley and Great Lakes in the south and by a line of lakes in the west. The largest lakes are Lake Winnipeg, Lake Athabasca, Great Slave Lake and Great Bear Lake. The shield has been severely glaciated. Much of the north is bare rock while to the

North America

Left: Spectacular scenery in the Rocky Mountains. Rugged peaks project above the snowfields. The Rockies are a barrier to east-west communications.

west, south and east are deposits of ground-up rock debris. The area is studded with thousands of lakes.

The climate of the shield is severe. Winters are long and extremely cold, but summers although short are surprisingly warm. However, this season is marred by the appearance of millions of mosquitoes and flies. During the summer months, the surface soil thaws and becomes marshy as a permanently frozen subsoil prevents the water from draining away.

The natural vegetation of the shield reflects the climatic conditions. Coniferous forest (or taiga) predominates. Spruce, pine and fir are the only trees that can withstand the extreme winter cold. Northwards trees become sparser and eventually they give way to tundra vegetation. This may be grasses or mosses and lichens. However during winter the tundra

is covered by snow and ice.

West of the Canadian Shield lie the great interior plains. The northern part, the Mackenzie lowlands, are covered by coniferous forest and are economically linked with the shield. The southern part of the plains is known as the Prairies. This is an area of level or undulating land, but it is not low-lying, standing at over 600 metres. Although the prairies have fertile soils, the climate is continental and one of extremes. Summers are very hot and winters bitterly cold. The range of temperature between the two seasons can be up to 45° centigrade. Annual rainfall is below 500 millimetres and water conservation is a necessity. Despite this, the prairies are the richest farmlands in Canada.

Western Canada is a region of spectacular mountain scenery. Nearly everywhere along the Pacific coast mountain ranges descend steeply to the ocean and there is little flat land available for large scale farming. Most of the coast is indented with deep narrow inlets known as fjords. Offshore a line of hilly islands lie parallel to the coast. These are the remnants of a former mountain chain which has been engulfed by the ocean. Fishing is an important activity in the sheltered waters protected by these islands.

Right: Sledges pulled by husky dog teams are still the best way to travel in the frozen Arctic. Motorized sledges are slowly being introduced.

The climate of the Pacific coast is kept mild by warm sea currents. The prevailing winds are from the south-west and they bring a plentiful rainfall to the area. These mild moist conditions favour the luxuriant growth of large conifer trees such as the Douglas fir and the western red cedar.

Inland the coast ranges are backed by an area of high plateaus and intermontane basins. Some of the latter are used for farming. The land then rises again to the high peaks of the Rocky Mountain ranges. Tourism is important in this region of outstanding natural beauty and there are a number of national parks.

Along the Atlantic coast in the Maritime Provinces and Newfoundland are remnants of the older Appalachian Mountains. The climate in this area is affected by moist cool winds from the north Atlantic. Winters have cold and overcast weather and summers are cool and wet.

Natural resources

Canada has a great many natural resources. These include rich mineral deposits, valuable forests, fishing grounds and an abundance of power resources. These have

resulted in the country having a well diversified economy.

Canada is a leading producer of iron, nickel, copper, zinc, gold, silver, lead, uranium, molybdenum and asbestos. Minerals account for 28 per cent of Canada's exports. Iron ore has been mined for some time around Skeep Rock at the western end of Lake Superior. More recently vast reserves have been found around Schefferville in Labrador. A railway has been built to carry the ore to the coast. Much of the ore is exported to the U.S.A.

North of Lake Huron lie the biggest nickel and platinum mines in the world. In the prairies there is oil and natural gas and large deposits of potash for making fertilizer. Uranium is found in the Mackenzie Basin.

The ancient rocks of the Canadian Shield are a vast storehouse of mineral deposits, which until recently have been inaccessible. But with modern communications and transport, some remote areas are being developed.

Forestry and fishing

Over 30 per cent of Canada is forest. In the west there are excellent stands of timber which are mainly felled for constructional timber (planks and beams). In the east, the colder climate results in smaller trees which are felled for pulp and paper. Timber products are a major export from Canada. Although road transport of felled timber is increasing in the east there is still much reliance on the use of rivers to float the timber downstream following the spring thaw. The saw and pulp mills are all on river or coastal locations.

There are still large reserves of timber in Canada but some are hard to reach. Felling is strictly controlled and the forest allowed to re-seed itself, to conserve resources.

Valuable fur pelts are another product from the taiga. There is still some traditional trapping mostly in the hands of American Indians and half-breeds who live in log cabins scattered along the rivers. However, much Canadian fur, particularly mink and fox, now

North America

comes from fur farms.

There are rich fishing grounds off both coasts. On the Pacific coast, salmon are trapped in the fjords during their spawning run in the summer. Most of the catch is canned and exported.

On the Atlantic coast fish abound on the Grand Banks around Newfoundland. Cod is found in great quantities here but haddock, halibut, hake and flounder are also caught.

Agriculture
Less than 10 per cent of the total land area of Canada is agricultural. Yet this small proportion is very productive and 11 per cent of Canadian exports are agricultural products.

The prairies are the largest continuous area of agricultural land. Wheat is the chief crop grown

here, and about 50 per cent is exported. The wheat is planted in spring. Fields are often left fallow in order to retain the precious moisture for the following year. Crop rotation is practised to keep the soil in good condition. Fodder crops are grown as part of the rotation and cattle, pigs and poultry kept at many prairie farms.

Other important agricultural regions in Canada are scattered. The St Lawrence Valley is the country's chief dairying district and the surplus milk is converted to butter and cheese for export. Dairying is also important in the Lakes peninsula between Lakes Huron, Ontario and Erie. The shores of Lakes Ontario and Erie have a mild climate. Tree crops and soft fruits are grown and even grapes can be grown in sheltered areas. Apples are an important crop in British Columbia and Nova Scotia.

Industry
Manufacturing industries employ two million people in Canada. Manufacturing and primary industries such as mining, use large amounts of energy and the country is fortunate in possessing plenty of energy resources. The high rainfall, many rivers and slope of the land make ideal conditions for hydro-electric power production. One industry that has developed as a direct result of an abundance of cheap electricity is aluminium smelting, although the raw bauxite and alumina have to be imported. Aluminium is smelted at Kitimat

on the west coast and Arvida in the Saguenay Valley. The pulp and paper industries also rely heavily on hydro-electric power.

Oil and natural gas are found on the prairies. Edmonton is the main centre of production and has petro-chemical industries. The oil is piped to refineries at Vancouver and on the Great Lakes.

At Sydney in Nova Scotia there is an immense steel plant. There is a large local coalfield here and the iron ore is brought from Labrador.

Many engineering industries are to be found in Canada. These range from shipbuilding at the ports to lighter electrical engineering at some of the inland centres. Food processing, textiles and clothing are also important.

Canada's main trading partners are the U.S.A., Britain, Japan and a number of European countries.

Communications

In a country the size of Canada good communications are vital.

Canada has two major rivers, the Mackenzie and the St Lawrence. The Mackenzie is the longest river in Canada. It flows northwards from the Great Slave Lake, which is fed by other rivers, to the Arctic. This part of Canada is very sparsely populated. The winter freeze makes the river impassable for at least five months of the year and it is not heavily travelled.

Left: Communication complex on the St Lawrence Seaway. Road and rail routes converge while a bulk cargo freighter passes along the ship canal.

Above: McGill is one of Canada's best known universities. Many campuses have attractive parkland settings in the middle of cities.

The St Lawrence river, draining the Great Lakes, is one of the greatest waterways in the world. The Great Lakes stand at different heights and a complicated network of ship canals and locks is necessary to enable ships to pass from one lake to another. In 1959 the St Lawrence Seaway was opened. This project improved navigation on the river above Montreal, allowing seagoing ships to travel right into the Great Lakes in the heart of the North American continent to pick up wheat from the prairies. But the Great Lakes and the St Lawrence may freeze in winter. In contrast, the Gulf Stream keeps the ports of Nova Scotia ice-free.

Railways played an important part in the settlement of Canada. There are two great transcontinental systems, the Canadian National and the Canadian Pacific Railways. They begin at Halifax and St John respectively, take different routes across eastern Canada to Winnipeg, then take different routes across the prairies, cutting through the barrier of the Rockies by spectacular passes to converge again at Vancouver, on

the west coast of the continent.

The road network is well developed in the more densely populated parts of Canada but is poor elsewhere. The Trans-Canada Highway crosses the country from coast to coast, and other major roads are being developed.

However it is air transport that is really helping to open up the empty lands of Canada. In addition to international airports most cities have their own airports and small landing strips abound.

The people of Canada

Of the 23 million people in Canada, 9.5 million are of British origin, 6 million of French origin and 1.25 million of German origin. Almost all those of French origin are descended from those who came to Canada before 1763. Most of them settled in the area that became the province of Quebec, where French is still the main language, and French influence and culture are very strong. Montreal is the second biggest French-speaking city in the world.

Many British immigrants arrived in this century. Between 1900–1914 the Canadian government encouraged immigration while opening up the prairies. Many people of Slavic origin arrived during this time and the Ukrainian language is second to English on the prairies. There was another major wave of immigration after World War Two which was dominated by Slavs and Germans.

Forty-six per cent of Canadians are Roman Catholic and 40 per cent are of Protestant and other Christian faiths. There is a small proportion of Jews and the rest belong to minority religious groups.

Of the indigenous inhabitants there are still 282,800 American Indians and 18,000 Eskimos in Canada. Many Eskimos still live in the far north of Canada and follow their traditional way of life. The American Indians have been absorbed more successfully into the American way of life, but many still live in the remote areas, follow-

North America

ing the traditions of their ancestors.

The most densely populated part of the country is the St Lawrence Valley. Over 75 per cent of the population live within a narrow 300-kilometre-wide belt that stretches along the U.S. border. Here too are found the largest cities, Vancouver, Winnipeg, Toronto, Ottawa, Montreal and Quebec.

Government

Canada is a monarchy, with Queen Elizabeth II of the United Kingdom as Head of State. The Queen is represented in the country by a Governor-General. There is a democratically elected government which has a federal constitution. The government meets in Ottawa, the capital.

Canada is divided into ten provinces. These are British Columbia, Alberta, Saskatchewan, Manitoba, Ontario, Quebec, New Brunswick, Nova Scotia, Prince Edward Island and Newfoundland. Each province has its own legislature and government which meet in provincial capitals. The least populated parts of Canada are divided into two territories, the Yukon and North West Territory, which are administered by councils.

St Pierre and Miquelon	
Area:	242 square kilometres
Population:	6,100
Capital city:	St Pierre
Language:	French
Currency:	French franc

St Pierre and Miquelon are the largest of a group of eight small islands about 20 kilometres off the south coast of Newfoundland.

They were claimed for France in 1535 and are administered by a French appointed governor.

Miquelon, with an area of 216 square kilometres, is the largest island. But the population is only about 600. St Pierre is 26 square kilometres in area but has a population of about 5,500.

The islands are mainly barren rock with only a poor soil cover and are unsuitable for agriculture. But, like Newfoundland, they are able to tap the rich fishing grounds of the Grand Banks. Fishing is the mainstay of the islands' economy.

Greenland	
Area:	2,175,600 square kilometres
Population:	49,700
Capital city:	Godthab
Languages:	Greenlandic and Danish
Currency:	Danish krone

Greenland is a large island. It lies in the Arctic Ocean only 400 kilometres from the Canadian coast. A Danish territory, in June 1953 it became an integral part of Denmark with the same rights as any other Danish county.

Most of the country lies within the Arctic Circle, and of the total area some 1,833,900 square kilometres are covered by ice cap. Most of the ice-free land is barren rock. Until 1900 hunting land and sea mammals was the principal activity. During this century fishing has replaced hunting as the chief occupation.

Greenland has rich mineral deposits, but the climate makes mining difficult. Cryolite, lead, zinc and silver are all mined.

Most of the inhabitants are Eskimos, living in small communities along the west coast.

United States of America

Area:	9,363,353 square kilometres
Population:	216,820,000
Capital city:	Washington D.C.
Language:	English
Currency:	U.S. dollar

The United States of America is the world's fourth largest country in area and population. It is also the richest and most powerful country in the world. But it is a land of contrasts. In the extreme north-west are frozen Arctic wastelands, in the south scorching deserts. In the west are high mountain peaks, and in the south-east low-lying sub-tropical swamps. Many of its people enjoy the highest standard of living in the world, while others live in poverty.

The country is not one continuous land mass. The bulk of the United States occupies the southern part of the North American continent. It lies between Canada in the north and Mexico in the south and stretches across the continent from the Atlantic to the Pacific Ocean. Two parts of the country are separated from the rest. Alaska, situated in the far north-west of the continent, is separated from the rest of the United States by Canada. The Hawaiian islands lie 3,860 kilometres to the west in the middle of the Pacific Ocean.

Hawaii is a group of Pacific islands whose geography has little in common with the mainland. It was formed by volcanoes and is very mountainous. There are still active volcanic peaks on Hawaii called Mauna Loa and Mauna Kea. Its tropical climate makes the islands a favourite tourist resort. It is also a large producer of sugar cane and tropical fruits.

The United States is a federation of 50 individual states including Alaska and Hawaii. Each state has its own democratically-elected governor, legislature and state government which operate from the state capital. Each state con-

Above: The Lincoln Memorial, Washington. Abraham Lincoln was elected the 16th President of the United States in 1860.

trols its own internal affairs and has certain powers that the federal government is unable to revoke.

The federal constitution of the United States is partly the result of the piecemeal manner in which the country was built up. The original

13 colonies of the east coast became the junior version of the United States after the American War of Independence in 1783.

In 1803 the United States bought a large area of French settled territory from Napoleon as he needed money to finance his war in Europe. This was known as the Louisiana Purchase and it included much of the Mississippi Valley. In 1845 Texas was admitted to the Union and three years later California became part of the country after a short war with Mexico and the following treaty. Later in 1867 Alaska was purchased from Russia for the sum of seven million pounds. As each area of land was added to the United States there was a demand for a degree of state autonomy and independence from the centralized government.

Each of the 50 states elects two senators and between one and 43 congressmen, depending on the state's population. Senators serve for six years, congressmen for two.

In addition to the state governments there is an elected federal government which has control over national and international affairs.

The federal government is divided into three branches: the executive (President), the legis-

Below: The Americans still have their pioneering spirit which has led them to great achievements in all aspects of modern space exploration.

North America

lative (Senate and House of Representatives) and the judicial (courts). The constitution provides for checks and balances between the three. The President and Vice-President are elected for four years.

The seat of the federal government is in the nation's capital at Washington D.C. on the east coast. D.C. refers to the federal District of Columbia, an area of 180 square kilometres created out of Maryland and Virginia and belonging to neither. This was set up in order to free the federal government from any pressure from the states. The President, Congress and Supreme Court are all located in Washington. Here too are the headquarters of federal government departments and agencies and a large foreign diplomatic corps.

Historical background

The history of the United States is one of immigration. Even the supposed "native" Indians were immigrants entering the continent from Asia during the Ice Ages 25-40,000 years ago. Prior to the arrival of the European settlers there were probably about 800,000 Indians in the United States, all speaking different languages. Each tribe adopted a different way of life to suit the area in which it lived. The plains Indians were nomadic,

Above: Many Americans enjoy the outdoor life. Fishing and shooting are favourite pastimes and many families own campers for their holidays.

following the great herds of buffalo which they hunted for food and clothing. Others lived in permanent settlements and cleared patches of woodland to cultivate squash, beans and corn.

The Spanish established settlements in Florida in the 16th century. They introduced the horse into the continent. In 1607 the British founded their first colony at Jamestown in Virginia. This was followed by the Pilgrim Fathers settlement in New England in 1620. Throughout the 17th and 18th centuries immigration continued slowly and many more settlements were established along the east coast. The Appalachian Mountains were a barrier to the westward spread of settlers. By 1800 it is estimated there were only about 5.5 million people in the whole of the United States.

From the 1840s the population of the United States began to soar as wave after wave of British, Irish, Germans, Scandinavians, Dutch, Russians, Greeks and Italians flooded into the country. Hard times, famine, wars, religious or political persecution forced millions to leave their homelands in Europe to seek a new life elsewhere. The United States offered

Left: Phoenix lies at the heart of Arizona's ranching country. Rodeos are a chance for the cowboys to demonstrate the skills they possess.

them work, cheap land and the opportunity to prosper. The immigrants landed first on the east coast but soon the pioneers crossed the Appalachians and poured into the empty heartland of the country. They travelled by improvized river craft, by covered wagons and later by rail. The discovery of gold and policies such as the Homestead Act which gave free land to anyone who would settle and farm it, helped encourage the immigrants. The peak of immigration was reached in 1907 when 1,285,000 people arrived in the United States.

One group of immigrants came to the country without any choice. They were the black slaves transported from West Africa to work on the cotton, tobacco and sugar plantations of the south. The American Civil War of 1861–5 abolished slavery, but many of the freed slaves remained on the plantations as share croppers.

The social upheavals in Europe caused by the First and Second World Wars would undoubtedly have started further waves of immigration. But, foreseeing this, the government set up a quota system which strictly limited the number of people coming to the United States. The era of easy immigration was over.

Relief and climate

The physical structure of the United States is broadly a central

Above: The familiar skyline of New York. Because the roads are so crowded, the quickest way to the airport is by helicopter.

area of plains and lowlands, bounded to the east and west by mountains.

The Appalachians stretch for over 2,000 kilometres along the east coast from the St Lawrence Valley to Alabama. They are some 600 million years old and have been heavily eroded. Their average height is about 1,200 metres.

East of the Appalachians is a coastal plain. This is narrow in the north and drained by a number of rivers including the Hudson, Delaware and Potomac.

The coastal plain becomes wider and lower to the south until in Florida it lies at no more than 30 metres above sea level. The shore here is a network of marshes and swamps, the most famous being the Everglades.

The whole of this eastern region receives about 1,000 millimetres of rain annually. Temperatures

Left: "The Loop", Chicago's central business district, gets its name from the elevated railway that forms a loop round the area.

increase towards the south. The coastal plain is heavily settled and intensively cultivated.

The whole of the western United States is an area of spectacular scenery, for example the Rocky Mountains. Some 70 million years old, they have a rugged outline and many peaks rise to over 4,000 metres. Most of Alaska consists of a continuation of the Rockies. The highest ridge is the Great Divide. It separates east flowing rivers from those draining west into the Pacific. Farther west are the Sierra Nevada, the Cascades and Coast Ranges.

Between the ridges lies a complicated area of high plateaus, basins and valleys. Although the ridges receive a high rainfall from the prevailing westerly winds, the basins lie in the rain shadow. Aridity increases to the south and here in the Great Basin are deserts, such as Death Valley, the Mojave and Colorado Desert. Daytime temperatures soar to over 30° centigrade in summer, but drop rapidly at night. Winters are

North America

Above: Much of the United States valuable forest land lies within the National Parks.

there are low-lying flatlands about 300 metres in height. The climate is less severe here and becomes sub-tropical along the swampy coastal plain of the Gulf of Mexico. Almost the whole of this central area is rich farmland.

In the north-east of the United States lie the five Great Lakes: Superior, Michigan, Huron, Erie and Ontario.

Agriculture

The United States is fortunate in possessing an abundance of rich farmland. In the last 300 years, forests have been cleared, the plains ploughed up and some arid semi-desert areas irrigated and brought into cultivation.

The typical American farm is large and highly mechanized. It produces a high yield with only a small labour force. Scientific methods of farming, selective stock breeding, irrigation and the widespread use of fertilizers, weed killers and insecticides all help account for the high productivity.

Below: New York is the largest and busiest port in the U.S.A. Major ocean liners can dock close to the city centre.

Above: American farming is scientific and highly mechanized. New, fast-growing grain crops can be grown in the short Alaskan summer.

The most extensive area of farmland in the United States is to be found on the Great Plains and the central lowlands of the Mississippi basin. Crops can be cultivated over such large areas that a number of crop belts exist.

cold. The spectacular Grand Canyon is in the Great Basin. Here the Colorado River has cut a gorge 1,700 metres deep into the surrounding desert plateau.

East of the Rockies lie the Great Plains, where the height of the land decreases eastwards by three great "steps". The Great Plains are a vast stretch of gently undulating land. They have a continental climate with very hot summers and cold winters. The temperature range lessens towards the south. The rain-bearing winds from the east have lost much of their moisture by the time they reach the plains, and the rainfall continues to decrease farther west.

Eastwards the plains dip gently to the Mississippi Valley. Here

Above: Heavy industry, although vital to the economy, inevitably means ugly industrial landscapes and pollution. This is an iron and steel works.

On the Great Plains cattle ranching predominates in the west, wheat cultivation in the east. The different land use is a direct result of the climate as rainfall decreases steadily towards the west. Scorching summer temperatures evaporate much of the valuable moisture. Years of adequate rainfall are followed by several years of drought. Strong winds sweep unchecked across the level treeless plains. In winter they bring blizzards.

The fertile soils of the eastern plains are ideal for wheat cultivation. Unfortunately during the early years of settlement, rising wheat prices led the farmers to push farther and farther into the drier west. When the drought years came, the exposed topsoil turned to dust and was blown away by the strong winds. A useless "Dust Bowl" was left covering much of Nebraska, Kansas and Oklahoma.

Modern plains farmers now take greater care of the land. In the west, many of the natural pastures have been replaced by more nutritious sown grasses. Irrigation allows the growth of fodder crops such as alfalfa.

In the east although wheat is the major crop, other grain and fodder crops are grown in rotation. Farmers try to prevent soil erosion by planting shelter belts of trees and cropping the land at right angles to the prevailing winds.

In the central lowlands the crop belts run from east to west. Soils are fertile. The northern part has a covering of boulder clay. Throughout the region summers are very warm. In the south winters are short and mild. Rainfall is over 750 millimetres annually, decreasing slightly to the north.

South of the Great Lakes, in Minnesota, Wisconsin and Michigan, is the hay and dairying belt. There is a great demand from the nearby industrial cities for milk and dairy products. South of this lies the famous "corn-belt" centred on the states of Iowa, Illinois and Indiana. Although corn (maize) is the main crop, hay, soya beans and other grain crops are also grown. Pig rearing is a major activity on the corn belt. The corn is used to feed the pigs. Farmers earn more money from selling pigs than selling corn.

South of the corn belt the great cotton belt stretches across the central lowlands from Texas east to Georgia and the Carolinas. Traditionally these states have been the main cotton producers in the world. Unfortunately years of single cropping have exhausted the soils and now cotton is only grown in the most favoured areas. The exhausted soils have been planted with pasture for beef and dairy cattle. New crops such as peanuts, soya beans, sweet potatoes, fruit and vegetables are also grown in the cotton belt. Meanwhile cotton growing has moved westwards and now a great deal is grown under irrigation in Arizona, New Mexico and California.

In Virginia and North Carolina the growing season is too short for cotton. Tobacco and peanuts are the main crops.

The Gulf coastlands are too wet and swampy for cotton cultivation, but ideal for growing rice and sugar cane.

The whole of the eastern coastal plain is a vast fruit and vegetable growing area. Potatoes are grown in the colder north. Dairying and market gardening predominate in

Below: The United States uses so much energy that it is turning increasingly to nuclear power.

the central part. These supply the huge local urban areas. The south specializes in market gardening (especially early salad crops) and fruit. Citrus fruits flourish in the sub-tropical climate of Florida.

Farming land in the western United States is very limited with the notable exception of California. California is the biggest food-producing state in the country. Irrigation is essential, but the mildness of the climate means that fruit and vegetables can be grown all year round. Citrus fruits are most important, but grapes and many other "Mediterranean" fruits are grown. A complete range of vegetables is produced and

cotton, wheat, barley, rice and fodder crops are also grown.

Forestry and fishing

Despite the amount of felling by the early settlers, there are still extensive areas of valuable forest in the United States. These lie mainly in the mountainous west, in the states of Washington, Oregon, Idaho and Montana. The wet and humid climate of the coastal areas encourages the growth of massive firs and pines such as the Douglas fir. This area essentially produces sawn timber rather than pulp and paper. In Idaho and Montana much of the timber finds an immediate market in the local mining

centres. Alaska has vast reserves of softwood timber.

The Gulf-Atlantic lands are another important lumbering region. Hardwoods felled here are destined for the furniture industry. The southern pines yield turpentine, resin and pulp for paper making.

The most valuable fisheries of the United States lie off the Pacific coast and the Gulf of Mexico. Salmon is caught in abundance off the coasts of Alaska and the northwest states. Shellfish are the main catch off the Gulf coasts.

Raw materials and industry

The United States has just over five

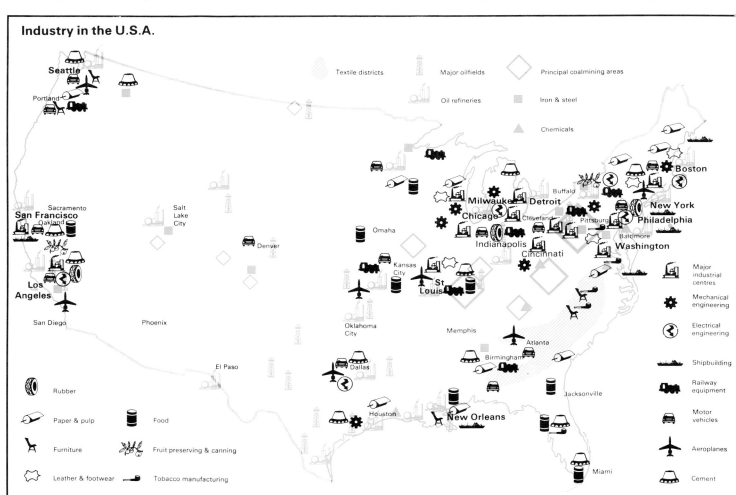

Industry in the U.S.A.

This map shows the chief industries within the United States. Over 31 per cent of the total population works in industry. The range of manufactured goods produced is enormous –

machinery, motor vehicles, aircraft, chemicals, timber, electrical equipment. There are large iron and steel works, particularly in the Pittsburg area, while most of the

oilfields are located further south in Texas. In recent years, the U.S. government has been very concerned about future energy supplies and the need to conserve fuel.

per cent of the world's population yet produces about 30 per cent of all manufactured goods. The country is richly endowed with natural resources. In addition to valuable farmland and forests, there are vast reserves of mineral deposits and energy resources.

The Rocky Mountains, including Alaska, are a vast treasure house of minerals. The days of the lone prospector who panned the rivers for alluvial gold washed out of the solid rock are long past. The minerals now have to be mined, which is a difficult and expensive operation. Many occur in complex combinations and have to be separated before they can be used. Mining today is in the hands of very large companies. There are still precious metals such as gold, silver and platinum found in the Rockies. But the industrial metals are now more valuable. These include copper, lead, zinc, molybdenum, uranium and iron.

For the last 100 years the main source of iron ore in the United States has been around the western end of Lake Superior. The huge ore bodies found here were the main reason for the growth of the great iron and steel plants along the shores of the lower lakes. Unfortunately the best of these deposits are nearly worked out and high-quality ore now has to be imported from Labrador via the St Lawrence Seaway.

The United States has some of the biggest coalfields in the world. One huge coalfield lies on the Allegheny plateau in the northern

Above: The assembly line method of manufacturing was pioneered by Henry Ford when he built his Model "T"

part of the Appalachians. The coal occurs in thick seams close to the surface. It can be easily reached by shaft mining or by stripping away the overlying soil. Some 70 per cent of all United States coal comes from here.

The United States is the world's third largest producer of oil after the U.S.S.R. and Saudi Arabia. The main oilfields occur in Texas, Louisiana, Oklahoma and California. There are also vast reserves in Alaska.

Hydro-electric power is well developed in the west of the United States, where almost every major river has been harnessed to generate electricity. With the great demand for energy the United States has turned more and more to nuclear power. The necessary uranium is found both in the

Left: Cotton harvesting in Arkansas. The cotton gin, which separates the cotton fibre from the seed, was invented by Eli Whitney in 1793. Today, the cotton industry is highly mechanized.

Right: A vast array of articles fills the shelves of an American supermarket.

United States and Canada.

The most heavily industrialized area of the United States is located in the north-east and around the Great Lakes. The close proximity of iron ore, coal and limestone (from the Michigan peninsula) have made the Great Lakes area one of the greatest iron and steel making centres in the world. Huge quantities of iron and steel are produced at cities such as Gary, Cleveland and Buffalo. Pittsburg is also a major steel-producing city.

Because of the abundance of steel, the Great Lakes area has important engineering industries. Detroit is the biggest car-making city in the world. Chicago makes agricultural machinery, Cincinnati specializes in the manufacture of machine tools and also has rubber and chemical industries.

On the north-east coast are situated the three large cities of New York, Philadelphia and Baltimore. All stand on navigable estuaries and are major ports. New York is the financial capital of the United States. Many banks and insurance companies have their head offices here on Wall Street. New York is also the centre of the nation's clothing industry. Although there is little heavy industry in New York itself, south of the city and elsewhere on the Atlantic seaboard are shipbuilding industries, oil refining, smelting of imported ores, chemicals, engineering and textiles. Textile industries and specialized light engineering are also found in New

North America

Left: American elections are noisy, exciting occasions. Banners, hats, T-shirts and badges all proclaim which candidate the individual supports.

Right: Las Vegas is the gambling capital of the United States. All the casinos have these gaudy façades.

England on the east coast.

The southern states have experienced an industrial boom since World War Two. The manufacture of cotton textiles is traditional in this area, but chemicals, oil refining, petro-chemicals (including plastics and synthetic fibres), engineering, aluminium and tin smelting are all recent developments. Florida has become one of the centres of space technology. Fort Worth and Dallas in Texas are major aircraft centres. Los Angeles in southern California is also noted for its aircraft and space industries.

The people and ways of life

The inhabitants of the United States are racially very mixed. To the native Indians have been added Europeans, Negroes, and Asians. Large numbers of Chinese and Japanese moved onto the west coast in the latter half of the 19th century. California still has a sizeable Chinese population. In the last ten years thousands of Vietnamese refugees, victims of the Vietnam War, have been allowed to settle in the United States. The United States has often been described as a "melting pot" because so many nationalities have merged into one distinctive American society.

However, even today remnants of individual cultures are still to be found in the United States. National dance and folk groups abound. Some cities have distinctive zones where one particular culture is dominant. These prove to be great tourist attractions. New Orleans has a colourful historic French Quarter. Chinatown is an exciting sector of San Francisco. New York is especially interesting

as it is a series of communities within one city. Here one can visit Little Greece or Little Italy. Brooklyn is the home of many of the city's Jews and the Negro quarter of Harlem is well defined.

Of all the people to be found in the United States the American Indians and Negroes have been least assimilated into the American society. Indian tribes who once roamed free over the entire country were pushed slowly into remoter areas as settlers moved into their traditional farming and hunting grounds. In the face of much conflict, the government finally set aside resettlement areas known as reservations. Unfortunately these are usually in the least productive parts of the country. Many of the 750,000 Indians still live on the reservations although their old ways have all but died out.

At the end of the Civil War most of the Negro population was confined to the plantations of the south-east. In the years immediately following their freedom

Above: Americans are proud of their revolutionary heritage. This band is playing at the restored 18th-century village of Williamsburg.

Above: The hamburger is practically the national dish of the United States. Convenience foods play a large part in the American diet.

many remained on the plantations working as share croppers. However, in time, they came to realize there was better paid work available in the growing industrial cities of the north. So began a great migration which has resulted in as many Negroes now living in the north as in the south. Today there are nearly 27 million black Americans. Their social and economic status still varies considerably from state to state.

The largest religious group in the United States are Protestant and associated Christian faiths. They make up about 32 per cent of the population. Another 23 per cent are Roman Catholic. Jews represent a small but important three per cent of the total. There are a number of minority religious groups in the country, such as the Mormons who live around Salt Lake City in Utah. However, some 37 per cent of the population claim no religious ties.

About 75 per cent of all Americans live in or near the big cities. This is reflected in the distribution of population across the country. The most densely populated areas are the industrial regions: the

Below: All policemen in the United States are armed and many people carry firearms for their own protection.

north-east between Boston and Washington, the southern Great Lakes around Chicago, Detroit and Pittsburg and southern California around Los Angeles. The least populated regions are Alaska, the mountains of the west and the deserts of the south-west.

There are 33 cities with over one million inhabitants. The three giants are New York (11,571,000), Los Angeles (over 7,000,000), and Chicago (just under 7,000,000).

A typical American city has a built-up business centre of skyscrapers, hotels, high-rise apartments and parking lots. This is called "downtown". Surrounding it are often poorer inner-city sections and older residential areas. Further out are the suburbs. They are newer, mostly built since World War Two and relatively wealthy people live there. They may stretch for many kilometres.

North America

Above: The United States produces more cars than any other country, both for export and for the home market.

Each family here owns its own house, a car or two, an enormous range of material possessions and enjoys one of the highest standards of living in the world.

However there is another side to the coin, for there are poor Americans. The share croppers of the southern states who work small plots of land and have to pay part of their crop as rent, have little opportunity to improve their living standard. In isolated districts of the southern Appalachians are to be found the "hillbillies". Many still live in small wooden shacks with no piped water or proper sanitation. They practise subsistence farming on severely eroded hill lands, and frequently go hungry.

Not all poor Americans are confined to the rural areas. Unemployment in the industrial areas has resulted in many inner city districts becoming poverty stricken.

Communications and trade

Good communications are vital in a country the size of the United States. Indeed its excellent transport system has helped the country's economic development.

The major American rivers are navigable for much of their length, and many have been improved or extended by canalization. The Erie Canal was the first to be constructed in 1825. This joins the Hudson River to Lake Erie, thus providing a continuous waterway from New York to the Great Lakes. It was a major factor in the growth of the port of New York. Since it was first constructed, the canal has been enlarged and is now known as the New York State Barge Canal.

The Great Lakes in the northeast of the United States are so enormous they are more like inland seas than lakes. They provide an invaluable routeway to the north of the industrial heart of the United States. Unfortunately the lakes stand at different heights, so shipping has to pass from one to another via canals and locks. The Soo Canals link Lakes Superior and Huron but the height difference here is only seven metres. However, Lakes Erie and Ontario are joined by the Niagara River and Falls. The total fall of the Niagara River is 108 metres in 42 kilometres. This great drop is by-passed by the Welland Canal, but eight locks are necessary and the passage takes hours.

The Great Lakes are joined to the Atlantic by the St Lawrence River. Rapids on the upper river are by-passed by the St Lawrence Seaway, a series of locks and canals. These enable ocean-going vessels to sail right into the Great Lakes. Since it was opened in 1959, the Seaway has turned cities such as Chicago, Milwaukee and Cleveland into busy ports.

The Great Lakes–St Lawrence Seaway is vital to the economy of the United States. It is the route by which iron ore from Labrador reaches the steel mills of Lakes Michigan and Erie. It is also the route by which the products of the interior are exported to cities

Below: Many American cities have multiple-lane highways, flyovers, underpasses and huge parking lots.

Below: Railways in the U.S.A. are fast, and comfortable, but fewer people use them today than in the past.

all around the world.

Other inland waterways such as the Mississippi, Missouri and Ohio rivers allow large bulky loads to be shipped from the interior to the coast easily and cheaply.

The railway network is well developed in the United States. There are a number of transcontinental routes. Chicago is the undoubted railway centre of the country with no fewer than 22 major railways converging on the city. The coming of the railways was an important factor in the settlement of the country. They brought many settlers to the plains attracted by offers of cheap land. They were the main carriers of overland freight and for years provided the only reliable and fast way to cross the country. Now, however, their importance has much declined. They still carry a sizeable proportion of freight, especially livestock, but the coming of the airlines has drastically reduced the passenger traffic.

Americans fly more than any other people. Over 30 per cent of all the world's air traffic arises in the U.S.A. New York and Chicago airports are the two biggest in the world. Even small towns have airports that link them to other cities.

With the distances involved in travelling in the United States the time saved by flying off-sets the cost.

The United States has a superb road network. There are over 65,000 kilometres of fast interstate highways linking all major towns in the country. It is possible to drive from coast to coast without ever leaving these first class roads. The United States is the world's biggest car manufacturer. Over 70 million cars crowd the vast, multiple-lane highways.

Trade

Although the United States is so well endowed with natural resources, it is by no means self-supporting in its needs. Many Americans are ardent conservationists and believe in using their own resources at a limited rate so that there will be sufficient left for the future. The major imports are therefore raw materials, particularly mineral ores and oil, and foodstuffs, mostly those things that cannot be grown at home such as

coffee, tea, cocoa and sugar.

The country's major exports are a whole range of manufactured goods, foodstuffs, which the country grows in abundance, and raw materials.

The United States' main trading partners are Canada, Britain, Japan and Western European countries.

International relations

Being such a powerful country the United States plays an important part in international affairs. The country is for example a member of the UN, OAS (Organization of American States), NATO and OECD (Organization for Economic Co-operation and Development). In addition its statesmen often try to help in conflicts between other countries, usually by acting as advisers or go-betweens.

Florida

Gulf of Mexico

Nassau ● **11**

Havana ●

12

1

32

Belmopan
2

13

Kingston ●

5

● Tegucigalpa

an Salvador

6

Managua ●

San Jose ●

7

Pacific Ocean

9 ● ● Panama City
Balboa

8

8

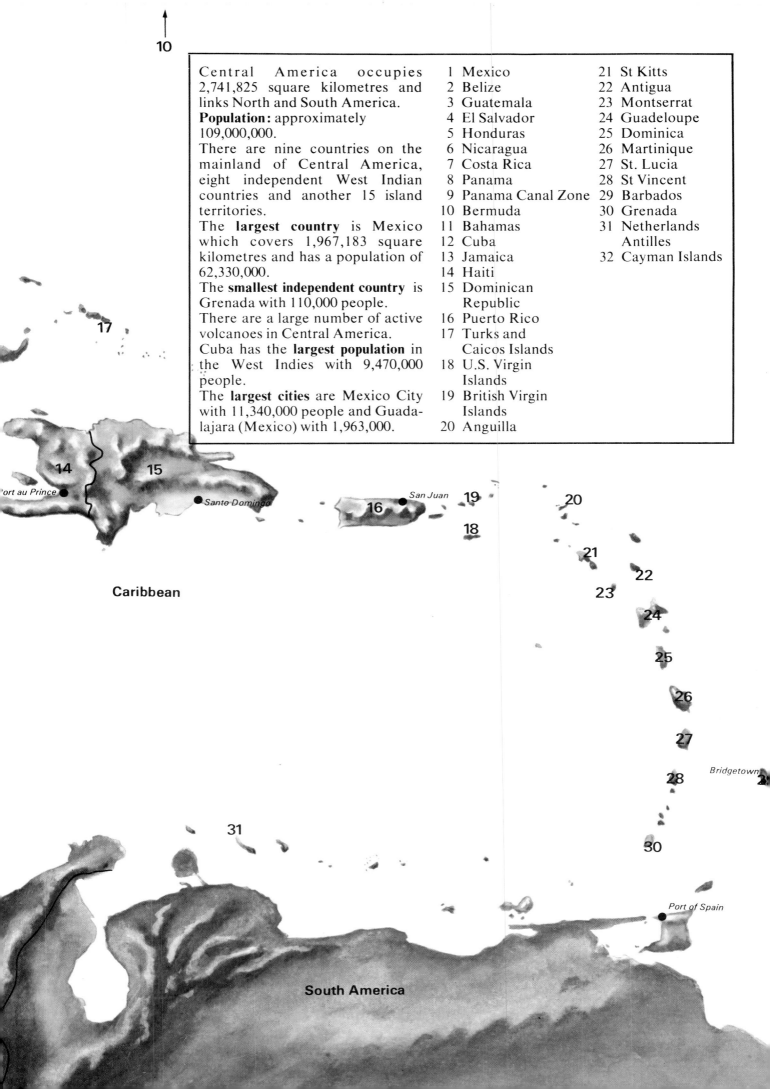

10

Central America occupies 2,741,825 square kilometres and links North and South America.
Population: approximately 109,000,000.
There are nine countries on the mainland of Central America, eight independent West Indian countries and another 15 island territories.
The **largest country** is Mexico which covers 1,967,183 square kilometres and has a population of 62,330,000.
The **smallest independent country** is Grenada with 110,000 people.
There are a large number of active volcanoes in Central America.
Cuba has the **largest population** in the West Indies with 9,470,000 people.
The **largest cities** are Mexico City with 11,340,000 people and Guadalajara (Mexico) with 1,963,000.

1 Mexico	21 St Kitts
2 Belize	22 Antigua
3 Guatemala	23 Montserrat
4 El Salvador	24 Guadeloupe
5 Honduras	25 Dominica
6 Nicaragua	26 Martinique
7 Costa Rica	27 St. Lucia
8 Panama	28 St Vincent
9 Panama Canal Zone	29 Barbados
10 Bermuda	30 Grenada
11 Bahamas	31 Netherlands Antilles
12 Cuba	32 Cayman Islands
13 Jamaica	
14 Haiti	
15 Dominican Republic	
16 Puerto Rico	
17 Turks and Caicos Islands	
18 U.S. Virgin Islands	
19 British Virgin Islands	
20 Anguilla	

17

14   15

Port au Prince   Santo Domingo   San Juan   19   20
16   18
21
22
23
24
25
26
27
Bridgetown
28
30
Port of Spain

Caribbean

31

South America

Central America

The mainland of Central America and the wide arc of islands in the Caribbean Sea were first settled by Indian peoples – Aztecs, Mayans, and Caribs – who were all at different stages of civilization when Columbus landed in the Bahamas in 1492.

Europeans, mainly Spanish at first, but later French, British, Dutch and Danish, arrived to exploit their new colonies, bringing African and Asiatic Indians to help them. The pure native Indian peoples were much reduced in number by disease and ill-usage and now very few pure Indians are left. The present population of the area is a mixture of American Indians, Europeans, Africans and Asiatic Indians.

The mainland was under Spanish control until the 1820s when most of the separate republics were set up. Many of the Caribbean islands remained European colonies until fairly recently and some of the smaller ones still rely on British, French or Dutch support. European languages, religions and cultures still dominate the area.

Above: Shanty town shacks in Port-of-Spain, Trinidad. Living standards are low for most people here and lack of sanitation, no piped water or electricity and overcrowding are common.

The U.S.A. now exerts the most important political and economic influence in the area, though there are exceptions, notably Cuba.

Natural hazards like earth-quakes, volcanic eruptions, and hurricanes can wreak enormous havoc throughout Central America and the Caribbean. But as most of the area lies within the Tropics it enjoys a warm climate, and tree and crop growth is lush where soil

Above: Poor farming methods and the growing of one crop year after year without fertilizing the soil have led to hillside erosion in Jamaica.

and rainfall conditions are suitable. Unfortunately poor farming methods, unequal sharing of land and lack of investment in agriculture have led to low output of foods in many states of Central America. Most ordinary people still live in the countryside making a poor living from the land. The most productive farming is carried out on the plantations – often foreign-owned – which specialize in growing single crops for home use and export to other countries.

Manufacturing industry is not well developed in the area, except in Mexico. Though many countries have mineral and energy resources, their populations are not large, rich or skilled enough to support industry. So they have

Above: Cuban soldiers in Angola. Cuba has been closely allied to the U.S.S.R. since 1959. It gives military help to groups in Africa sympathetic to communist ideas.

tended in the past to export their minerals and other resources in a raw state.

One modern industry that is growing rapidly and becoming an important income earner, especially in the Caribbean, is tourism. The warm tropical climate, bright sunshine, beautiful forest and mountain scenery, white sandy beaches and clear warm waters teeming with life attract visitors in increasing numbers every year. The fact that the U.S.A. is so close has helped this development, but the industry now has a world-wide appeal.

Throughout the whole area the population is growing rapidly, and at a faster rate than the output of food. Jobs are not increasing fast enough to employ the large numbers of young people and many have had to emigrate to find employment and a better standard of living.

Right: Colourful processions and carnivals are a main feature of life in many parts of Latin America. Here people dressed as Aztecs take part in a music and dance festival.

Central America

Mexico

Area:	1,967,183 square kilometres
Population:	62,330,000
Capital city:	Mexico City
Language:	Spanish
Currency:	Peso

Mexico is the largest of the states lying between the continents of North and South America. The Aztec and Mayan empires flourished here before they were conquered by the Spanish under Cortes in 1521.

When asked what the country was like, Cortes crumpled a piece of parchment, released it and said, "that is the map of Mexico". The bulk of the country is a high plateau, narrowing to the south and flanked on either side by parallel ranges of high mountains that rise steeply from narrow coastal plains. Most of the plateau is at least 2,000 metres above sea level and split into tilted blocks and basins with volcanoes such as Popocatapetl rising up to 5,452 metres. Here is where most Mexicans live. The only lowlands are in the south and west, plus the Yucatan Peninsula jutting out into the Gulf of Mexico.

The climate is tropical or subtropical everywhere with differences due to altitude. The lowlands are hot and wet with dense tropical forest, the plateau cooler and drier with scrubland thinning out towards the north. True hot desert is found on the Pacific coast in the north-west.

Four out of ten Mexicans work in agriculture, some producing

Above: American tourists are attracted to Acapulco by its warm Pacific rollers, ideal for surfing.

coffee, cotton and sugar for export, but the majority on small subsistence farms. Except in irrigated areas yields are low and only about 15 per cent of the land is suitable for cultivation. Most of this is on the rich volcanic soils of the basins on the central plateau. Grazing cattle, sheep and goats is the main type of farming in the drier north.

Mexico's population is increasing by 3.5 per cent or 1.5 million a year. It has more Spanish speakers than any other Latin American country. With 50 per cent of all Mexicans under 20 years old and with no growth in farming employment, future jobs must be found in manufacturing or service industries. These are based mainly in the towns which are growing rapidly. Mexico City, for instance, with a population of over nine million people, gains another 1,100 every day.

Industry is now the most important sector of the Mexican economy, producing steel, cars, chemicals and textiles for home and export.

Besides being the world's largest producer of fluorspar and the second largest of silver, Mexico is rich in non-ferrous metals such as lead, zinc and copper. There is little coal, but fairly large oil and

Left: Aztec dancers at Guadalupe Basilica. Aztec dancing is formal and controlled, producing some of the loveliest of all Indian dances.

gas fields have been found.

Further recent discoveries of large oil and gas reserves in the southern Gulf coastlands should ensure self sufficiency and also allow an increase in exports, chiefly to the U.S.A.

Belize

Area:	22,965 square kilometres
Population:	135,000
Capital city:	Belmopan
Languages:	English and Spanish
Currency:	Belizean dollar

The former British Honduras, this British colony became self-governing in 1964 and changed its name to Belize in 1973. Britain retains control of defence and foreign affairs, especially since Guatemala still claims the territory.

Belize has a hot, wet climate, with dense forests of hardwoods such as mahogany and rosewood.

Since 1970 Belmopan, a small town 50 kilometres inland, has been the capital. Before then the main port of Belize City was the capital, but it lies on a swampy coast and is liable to hurricane damage. The population is a racial mixture of Europeans, Indians and Negroes.

Belize is an ''empty'' poor country. Most people work on the two per cent of the land that is cultivated. The main exports are agricultural products, sugar and citrus fruits, and timber.

Guatemala

Area:	108,889 square kilometres
Population:	6,300,000
Capital city:	Guatemala City
Languages:	Spanish and Indian dialect
Currency:	Quetzal

Guatemala is the most populous of the small republics of Central America, though not as densely populated as El Salvador.

Dense tropical forests in the lowlands to the north are sparsely settled, though once the centre of Mayan city life. Most Guatemalans live in the rugged mountains, steep valleys and basins in the south, even though the area is subject to violent earthquakes. The most recent in 1976 severely damaged the capital.

American Indians predominate in the population, eking out a living growing maize, wheat, beans and rice, and providing seasonal labour on commercial plantations. Only about ten per cent of the land is cultivated.

Apart from a recently developed nickel mine in the east there is little mineral wealth, nor is manufacturing important.

El Salvador

Area:	21,040 square kilometres
Population:	4,260,000
Capital city:	San Salvador
Language:	Spanish
Currency:	Colón

El Salvador, hemmed in along 260 kilometres of the Pacific coast by Honduras and Guatemala, is the only Central American republic without a coast on both oceans. It has the highest population density in Central America with almost 200 people per square kilometre.

Pressure on the land has ensured that as much as possible is cleared and cultivated intensively, in contrast to most of its neighbours.

The economy is dependent on high grade coffee grown on the deep layers of volcanic ash and lava in the mountains. Coffee is by far the biggest export and provides employment for nearly 50 per cent of the work force. El Salvador is also important as the world's

Left: The open-air market at Toluca. Craftware such as this pottery is made in the surrounding villages and sold here, often to tourists.

Central America

Above: Harvesting maize by hand. Maize is the staple crop of many people in Central America.

main source of medicinal gum, balsam.

It is probably the most highly industrialized of the Central American states, exporting textiles, chemicals and fertilizers.

Honduras

Area:	112,088 square kilometres
Population:	2,830,000
Capital city:	Tegucigalpa
Language:	Spanish
Currency:	Lempira (peso)

Honduras has fertile soils, rich timber resources and mineral wealth – yet it is the poorest of the Central American republics. A history of civil wars since the end of Spanish rule lies at the root of the country's poverty.

Poor peasants of mixed ancestry, mainly Mestizos of Indian and Spanish descent, make up 90 per cent of the population. Along the Caribbean coast are large numbers of Negroes, while a small number

Right: This Haitian boy is descended from African negroes who were brought to the Caribbean by Europeans. They were made to work as slaves on the plantations.

of families of pure Spanish descent make up the ruling class.

Most Hondurans live in the western half of the country on the broad plateaus, fertile valleys and small basins that lie between the mountain ranges.

Bananas, grown on the northwest coast, account for 40 per cent of exports. Coffee and timber account for 12 per cent each. Mining for silver, gold, lead and zinc, though declining, is still important.

Nicaragua

Area:	148,000 square kilometres
Population:	2,500,000
Capital city:	Managua
Language:	Spanish
Currency:	Córdoba

Nicaragua is the second largest of the Central American republics and the most thinly populated. The hot humid lowlands in the east and the mountains rising from them contain dense forest but few people. To the west of the moun-

Above: Sugar cane is still one of the main plantation crops in the Caribbean. It used to be cultivated by hand but now machines are used.

tains is a narrow depression, containing two large lakes and providing an easy link between the two oceans.

Between the depression and the Pacific live 90 per cent of the people. Volcanoes rise above the valley. Managua was severely damaged by earthquakes in 1972 and 1978.

Like all the other small states, Nicaragua is mainly agricultural. Coffee, cotton and sugar are produced for export, and cattle raising is becoming more important in the highlands. Copper, gold and silver are mined, but mining development in the future will depend on better transport.

Costa Rica

Area:	50,900 square kilometres
Population:	2,000,000
Capital city:	San Jose
Language:	Spanish
Currency:	Colón (peso)

Costa Rica is a narrow strip of country traversed by two mountain ranges. Between them lies a tableland, the heart of the republic, at about 1,200 metres, which has a mild temperate climate.

Over 50 per cent of the land is cultivated and 30 per cent forested. The economy is based on the export of coffee, bananas, meat, sugar and cocoa. Industry, based on energy from water power, is well developed, with food processing, chemicals and plastics being most important.

Costa Rica is politically stable, and has the lowest illiteracy rate in Central and South America. It enjoys the highest living standards in Central America.

Panama

Area:	75,650 square kilometres
Population:	1,700,000
Capital city:	Panama City
Language:	Spanish
Currency:	Balboa (equivalent to the U.S. dollar)

The isthmus of Panama, 48 kilometres at its narrowest, is one of the great crossroads of the world. It bridges the gap between two continents and between two oceans. Spanish treasure trains crossed its "Royal Road" in the 16th century, its railway was built to take gold seekers to California in the 1850s and then the canal was made.

The area was part of Colombia until 1903 when it became an independent republic.

Less than 25 per cent of the land is inhabited, being mountainous with humid, unhealthy lowlands.

Panama is very dependent on the canal for income and jobs. The other main source of revenue is a large registered merchant fleet.

Attempts to lessen this dependence are being made by developing its fertile but empty areas, its forest wealth, and its copper, gold, silver and coal deposits.

Panama Canal Zone

Area:	1,676 square kilometres
Population:	42,000
Capital city:	Balboa

The Panama Canal Zone is a strip

Above: The sandy secluded beaches fringed by tropical trees and warm clear waters are typical of the Caribbean islands. Naturally, they are a popular haunt for tourists.

of land eight kilometres wide on either side of the canal. The U.S.A. controls it until the end of the century.

The canal, opened in 1914, is 12 metres deep, 150 metres wide and 82 kilometres long.

Bermuda

Area:	54 square kilometres
Population:	53,000
Capital city:	Hamilton
Language:	English
Currency:	Bermudan dollar

Bermuda, the oldest British colony, is situated 1,280 kilometres south-east of New York in the western Atlantic Ocean. It is a group of coral islands and tiny islets, only 20 of which are inhabited.

The ten largest islands form a narrow chain linked together by bridges and causeways. There are no rivers on the islands and drink-

Right: Coral islands like Bermuda are built up from the shells of millions of tiny sea creatures. The islands may take thousands of years to form.

ing water is either rainwater or distilled sea water.

Bermuda has one of the highest densities of population in the world. About 60 per cent of the people are Negroes, the rest are of English or Portuguese origin.

There is abundant sunshine, coral islands, beaches and surf which attract tourists throughout the year. Catering for these people, mainly North Americans, is the main activity of the islands. And there is no income tax in Bermuda.

Bahamas

Area:	13,935 square kilometres
Population:	218,000
Capital city:	Nassau
Language:	English
Currency:	Bahamian dollar

The Bahamas are a long narrow arc of about 1,700 coral islands, which stretch 960 kilometres south-east from the Florida coast to north of Cuba.

Columbus made the first landfall in America in 1492 on Watling's Island, one of the most easterly of the Bahamas. Only the largest 25 islands are inhabited.

Central America

Warmed by the Gulf Stream in winter and cooled by sea breezes in summer the climate is ideal for tourists. The fact that the U.S.A. is so near is another asset for this industry.

Tourism is the mainstay of the economy, but tropical fruit growing is also an important industry. A large oil terminal and refinery, opened in 1974, has given further variety to the economy. The Bahamas have been an independent state within the Commonwealth since 1973.

Above: The warm waters of the Caribbean are famous for fishing. Here, a swimmer spears a crayfish.

Above: A street seller in Latin America. Many people are now moving into the cities, although few find work.

Cuba

Area:	114,524 square kilometres
Population:	9,470,000
Capital city:	Havana
Language:	Spanish
Currency:	Cuban peso

Cuba is the largest of the islands of the Greater Antilles. Most of it is an undulating plain below 150 metres. Rich, well-watered soils provide more farming land than elsewhere in the region.

Farming, which is the mainstay of the economy, is dominated by two crops, tobacco and sugar. Sugar and sugar products provide 80 per cent of all exports. Cuba is also rich in nickel, iron ore, chrome, manganese and copper deposits.

Since the communist revolution in 1959 the Cuban economy has been fully state-controlled, and trade links switched from the U.S.A. to the U.S.S.R. and Eastern European countries.

The legacy of former American investments is shown in the excellent road and rail system. Despite recent moves to encourage rural growth, about 50 per cent of the population still live in towns.

Below: A modern, luxurious hotel in the Caribbean. In some areas the contrast between the facilities for rich tourists and the poverty of the local people can cause sharp feelings of resentment against the tourists.

Jamaica

Area:	10,991 square kilometres
Population:	2,080,000
Capital city:	Kingston
Language:	English
Currency:	Jamaican dollar

Jamaica, the largest of the former British colonies in the West Indies, became an independent member of the Commonwealth in 1962.

The island is scenically beautiful with mountains, forests, springs, rivers and white sandy beaches. While sugar, grown on large plantations, is the main export crop, Jamaica produces a wide range of other tropical fruits such as bananas, coffee, cocoa, tobacco and oranges, as well as maize and rice for subsistence.

Most of the population are Negroes, descendants of African slaves brought to work on the sugar plantations.

Jamaica is the world's second largest producer of bauxite (the source of aluminium). This, together with agriculture, tourism and fishing, helps to make it one of the more prosperous islands of the West Indies.

Haiti

Area: 27,750 square kilometres
Population: 5,200,000
Capital city: Port au Prince
Language: French
Currency: Gourde

Haiti occupies the western part of the island of Hispaniola. It is the only French-speaking republic in Central America. With its growing population and primitive farming methods, it is likely to remain one of the poorest countries in the area. The largest group of the population are negroes.

There are some agricultural exports, and bauxite and copper are sold to North America.

Below: Bauxite works in Jamaica. Jamaica is the world's second largest producer of bauxite.

Dominican Republic

Area: 48,734 square kilometres
Population: 4,697,000
Capital city: Santo Domingo
Language: Spanish
Currency: Peso

The Dominican Republic occupies the eastern portion of the island of Hispaniola. Unlike Haiti, its culture is Spanish and its people a mixture of Europeans, Africans and Indians. It has higher living standards and there is much American investment in the sugar industry.

Sugar accounts for about 50 per cent of its exports, but efforts have been made to encourage coffee and cocoa production, the development of minerals such as iron, bauxite and copper, and the introduction of light industry.

Puerto Rico

Area: 8,891 square kilometres
Population: 3,213,000
Capital city: San Juan
Languages: Spanish and English
Currency: U.S. dollar

Above: Tall palm trees and low scrubland grow in the sub-tropical climate of the West Indies.

Discovered by Columbus in 1493, Puerto Rico was a Spanish colony until 1898 when it was handed over to the U.S.A. after the Spanish-American war. Now it is an outlying territory of that country and its predominantly Spanish population are American citizens.

It is similar in structure to Cuba and Hispaniola: high volcanic ridges form the core of the island, fringed by narrow coastal plains.

The poor soils cannot support all the people, and there are few other resources so there has been much emigration to the United States mainland.

The economy has traditionally been based on agriculture, particularly sugar production for export, but recent U.S. investment in coffee, orange production, tourism and light industry is helping to broaden the base of the economy.

Turks and Caicos Islands

Area: 430 square kilometres
Population: 7,000
Capital city: Grand Turk
Language: English
Currency: U.S. dollar

Only seven of the 30 small islands in this British colony are inhabited. They lie east of the Bahamas, and north of Hispaniola. Fishing and tourism are the main activities.

Central America

Virgin Islands (U.S.)

Area: 344 square kilometres
Population: 92,000
Capital city: Charlotte Amalie
Language: English
Currency: U.S. dollar

The largest, most easterly islands of this group were bought by the U.S.A. from Denmark in 1917.

British Virgin Islands

Area: 153 square kilometres
Population: 10,030
Capital city: Road Town
Language: English
Currency: U.S. dollar

The main activities of these small volcanic islands are fishing and farming, but tourism is developing. The islands are a British colony.

Anguilla

Area: 91 square kilometres
Population: 8,500
Capital city; The Valley
Language: English
Currency: East Caribbean dollar

Anguilla, a member of the Commonwealth, is the smallest of the Leeward Islands. It has cotton, sea salt, fishing and tourist industries.

St Kitts-Nevis

Area: 267 square kilometres
Population: 48,000
Capital city: Basse Terre
Language: English
Currency: East Caribbean dollar

These two Leeward Islands are both mountainous and volcanic. Together, they are a member of the Commonwealth.

Antigua

Area: 442 square kilometres
Population: 70,000
Capital city: St John's
Language: English
Currency: East Caribbean dollar

This low-lying coral island is the largest and most developed of the Leeward Islands. Sugar and cotton are grown. Tourism is important.

Montserrat

Area: 98 square kilometres
Population: 12,162
Capital city: Plymouth
Language: English
Currency: East Caribbean dollar

This mountainous island with volcanic springs has a rich soil. Cotton, limes and sugar are grown. There is a tourist industry.

Guadeloupe

Area: 1,779 square kilometres
Population: 354,000
Capital city: Basse Terre
Language: French
Currency: French franc

Above: A small coastal settlement in the Netherlands Antilles, with moorings for small boats.

Guadeloupe and Martinique, discovered by Columbus in 1493 and settled by the French in 1635, are the last of the once extensive French colonies in the Caribbean. They are now full departments of France and have members in the French Parliament.

Guadeloupe is made up of two very different islands separated by a narrow bridged channel. The larger is forested and mountainous with an active volcano rising to nearly 1,500 metres. The smaller is low-lying and made up of coral limestone. Most people are Negro descendants of African slaves.

Sugar and rum are still the main products, but cotton, bananas and pineapples are also exported.

Dominica

Area: 751 square kilometres
Population: 78,000
Capital city: Roseau
Language: English
Currency: East Caribbean dollar

The volcanic island of Dominica is the largest of the Windward Islands. It is the last place where a small group of Caribs – the original people of the area – still survive.

Left: Many people still travel by mule or donkey. Unpaved roads become unfit for cars in the wet season.

Above: Small wooden fishing boats drawn up on Silversands beach in Barbados.

Martinique

Area:	1,102 square kilometres
Population:	325,000
Capital city:	Fort de France
Language:	French
Currency:	French franc

Martinique is a heavily forested mountainous island.

St Lucia

Area:	616 square kilometres
Population:	114,000
Capital city:	Castries
Languages:	English and French patois
Currency:	East Caribbean dollar

First colonized by the French, St Lucia changed hands 14 times, becoming independent in 1979.

St Vincent

Area:	389 square kilometres
Population:	110,000
Capital city:	Kingstown
Language:	English
Currency:	East Caribbean dollar

St Vincent produces arrowroot, sugar, cocoa and bananas.

Barbados

Area:	431 square kilometres
Population:	260,000
Capital city:	Bridgetown
Language:	English
Currency:	Barbados dollar

Barbados lies by itself 160 kilometres to the east of the arc of the volcanic Windward Islands. It differs from them as it is low-lying and composed mainly of coral limestone which has weathered to give fertile soils.

Barbados is sometimes called "Little England" for since 1625 it has had continuous links with Britain, first as a colony and since 1966 as an independent member of the Commonwealth.

Tobacco was the original basis of the economy but sugar is now the main crop providing nearly 60 per cent of the total exports. Tourism is the other major industry.

A high proportion of the island is cultivated but as it is one of the most overcrowded islands in the world many Barbadians have emigrated since the early 1950s.

Grenada

Area:	344 square kilometres
Population:	110,000
Capital city:	St George's
Language:	English
Currency:	East Caribbean dollar

Grenada specializes in growing nutmegs and cloves. It became independent from Britain in 1974.

Netherlands Antilles

Area:	993 square kilometres
Population:	242,000
Capital city:	Willemstad
Languages:	Dutch and Spanish patois
Currency:	Antillean guilder

Curaçao is the largest of the six islands. Petro-chemical works dominate the economy.

Cayman Islands

Area:	259 square kilometres
Population:	13,000
Capital city:	Georgetown
Language:	English
Currency:	Cayman Island dollar

These coral islands base their economy on tourism and finance.

Below: Fishermen in Grenada draw in their nets from a small boat. Fish are an important source of protein here as many poor people exist on a diet of mainly starchy food.

Atlantic Ocean

Pacific Ocean

Caracas

6

2

Orinoco

Georgetown

Bogota

3

Paramaribo

4

5

Cayenne

1

Quito

Amazon

8

Xingu

Lima

Sao Francisco

Lake Titicaca

10

Brasilia

9

11

Asuncion

Parana

Santiago

13

14

Buenos Aires

Montevideo

12

Colorado

15 Stanley

South America covers approximately 17,855,000 square kilometres.

Population: approximately 220,000,000.

There are 15 countries in South America.

The **smallest country** is the Falkland Islands which are 11,961 square kilometres with a population of 1,900.

The **largest country,** Brazil, covers almost 50 per cent of the continent and is 8,511,965 square kilometres. Its population is 110,100,000.

The **highest peak** is Mt Aconcagua in the Andes, at 6,960 metres.

The Andes are the highest mountain chain after the Himalayas of Asia.

The **longest river** is the Amazon which is 6,437 kilometres long and has the greatest flow of water of any river in the world.

The world's **highest uninterrupted waterfall** is the Angel Falls in Venezuela. It drops 979 metres.

1 Colombia
2 Venezuela
3 Guyana
4 Surinam
5 French Guiana
6 Trinidad and Tobago
7 Ecuador
8 Peru
9 Bolivia
10 Brazil
11 Paraguay
12 Chile
13 Uruguay
14 Argentina
15 Falkland Islands

South America

South America can be divided into three main physical areas. The high rugged Andes Mountains running the whole length of the western coast are the continent's most striking physical feature. Earthquakes and volcanic eruptions can occur over their whole length and because of their height, steepness, and deep ravines they are a formidable barrier to movement.

To the east are the vast lowlands in the basins of the Orinoco, Amazon and Paraguay/Uruguay system of rivers.

Farther east are the tablelands, made of old sedimentary and volcanic rocks of the Brazilian and Guianan Highlands and the Patagonian plateau.

The continent has such an extent of latitude and such a range of altitude, that climates range enormously, from equatorial to tundra. Every type of natural vegetation, from rain forest to lichens or mosses of a glacial valley, can be

Above: Yungay, Peru, before the avalanche of 1970 which destroyed the area. Avalanches of rock often sweep down from the Andes.

Above: The interior of South America is an empty area of forests and plains. Roads are being built to exploit the area's resources.

Above: The beautiful church of Sao Francisco convent in Salvador, Brazil. Roman Catholicism was introduced by the Spanish and Portuguese, and churches were often paid for by wealthy landowners.

found and the range of crops that can be grown extends from rice and sugar to oats and potatoes. A great variety of animals can be grazed.

The early Spanish and Portuguese settlers were given grants of huge areas of land and control over the local people living on them. Their descendants still hold these lands today, and in many countries these small groups of families retain political and economic power in governments. American Indian peoples play little or no part in national affairs.

Many of the countries in South America are vulnerable to changes in world prices, over which they have little control. Attempts have been made to diversify their economies and encourage trade within the continent. Trading groups, such as L.A.F.T.A. (Latin American Free Trade Association) have been set up. But the richer countries with well-developed economies like Brazil, Argentina and Venezuela have not always had the same aims as the

Above: The tourist attractions in South America include ruins of Inca civilizations in the Andes of Peru, and this famous statue of Christ which overlooks Rio de Janeiro, on the Atlantic coast of Brazil.

Above: Few of the original peoples of South America have survived and retained their traditional life-styles since the arrival of the Europeans.

poorer states like Bolivia, Paraguay and Ecuador.

Population is growing rapidly and all the biggest cities are experiencing massive immigration from the countryside. Most people live within 300 kilometres of the coast, leaving the interior almost empty.

A task for the future is to open up these lands, especially the Amazon Basin. The dangers of careless exploitation of a fragile, complex environment such as the Amazon Forest are not yet fully understood – but all the states in the area have already built or plan to build roads and airstrips to link up these remote areas with their centres of population. They will also be able to develop the mineral and forest wealth, as well as the agricultural potential.

South America

Colombia

Area:	1,138,618 square kilometres
Population:	25,050,000
Capital city:	Bogota
Language:	Spanish
Currency:	Peso

The republic of Colombia, situated in the north-west of the continent, is the only South American state with a coastline on both the Pacific and Atlantic oceans.

The heartland of the country is in the west, made up of three high Andean ranges rising to over 7,500

Below: A self-help scheme in Colombia. Governments and international bodies provide aid to help raise living standards.

metres. These divide near the border with Ecuador and run south-north, dipping to the lowlands along the Caribbean coast. In the deep valleys between the ranges and on the plateaus and basins of the highlands live over 90 per cent of the people.

Climates and vegetation are linked closely to altitude. They vary from hot, humid rain forest along the coasts and Amazon lowlands rising through tropical grasslands, cool temperate forests to thin pastures on the high plateau and to permanent snowfields on the Andean peaks. In such varied conditions a very wide range of subsistence and commercial crops can be grown, from pineapples to potatoes, from rice to barley.

The majority of people work on the land which provides the main exports, especially high quality coffee, bananas and cocoa. Large-scale cattle grazing is being developed on the tropical grasslands of the eastern lowlands. Manufactured goods such as textiles and chemicals are becoming increasingly important in Colombia's economy.

About 35 per cent of the adult population is illiterate. Most of them live in the rural areas where living standards – income, health, housing and education – are lower than in the towns.

Venezuela

Area:	912,050 square kilometres
Population:	12,400,000
Capital city:	Caracas
Language:	Spanish
Currency:	Bolivar

When the first Spanish explorers arrived in Lake Maracaibo in 1499 the native Indian houses built on stilts above the water reminded them of Venice and they gave the country the name Venezuela – "Little Venice". Today it is the richest country on the South American continent, with the

Above: A typical shanty town in Bogota, Colombia. Flimsy shacks house the people who have flocked into the cities.

highest standard of living.

The core of the country, where over 70 per cent of the people live, is in the Venezuelan Highlands which are a continuation of the Andes. These mountains, rising steeply to over 2,500 metres, have within them wide, shallow basins with rich soils. The location of these basins high in the mountains moderates the temperature, making them suitable for cultivation and settlement.

To the south are the low, rolling, grassy plains of the Orinoco valley, the Llanos. These plains suffer extensive flooding in the hot wet season, but in the dry season the ground is baked hard. South of the Orinoco are the Guiana Highlands, rounded, forested hills rich in minerals. This area is almost uninhabited and much is unexplored.

Native farming on tiny plots to produce maize, beans and rice is not very efficient, but commercial crops of coffee, cotton, sugar and cocoa are exported.

Venezuela's wealth is based on minerals, notably oil which

accounts for over 90 per cent of total exports. Since 1917, when oil was first discovered, Lake Maracaibo has been the main area, but production is increasing in the Llanos region, farther east.

Venezuela is planning future prosperity when the oil reserves run out by improving farming in the highlands and the Llanos, by further tapping the iron, manganese, bauxite, gold and diamond wealth of the Guiana Highlands, and by developing modern steel, chemicals, aluminium and other manufacturing industries.

Guyana

Area:	210,000 square kilometres
Population:	800,000
Capital city:	Georgetown
Language:	English
Currency:	Guyana dollar

The Guianas and Surinam are three countries on the north coast of South America. They are the

only large areas of the continent colonized by people from northern Europe — the British, Dutch and French. Guyana was first settled by the Dutch between 1616–1621. It became a British colony in 1814, an independent member of the Commonwealth in 1966 and since 1970 has been a republic.

Although nearly as large as Britain almost 90 per cent of the country is empty, the home of small, wandering groups of American Indians. They live by hunting, fishing and shifting cultivation in the dense rain forest that covers much of the interior in the Guiana Highlands.

Most Guyanese live within 12 kilometres of the coast on a flat, marshy coastal plain that is prone to flooding from the rivers and the sea. The Dutch began the task of draining the area by building canals and dykes, and reclamation is still taking place.

Less than one per cent of the total area is cultivated, mostly on the coastal strip. Since 1820, sugar has been the main crop, grown on plantations originally worked by African slaves. After slavery was abolished, immigrant Chinese and Indian paid-labourers replaced the Negroes. This has resulted in a mixture of peoples in Guyana – native Indians, Negroes, Asiatic Indians, Chinese and Europeans.

The world's largest deposit of bauxite is found in the interior near Mackenzie on the Demerara River, and this accounts for over 33 per cent of Guyana's foreign earnings. Small-scale gold and diamond workings are found in the Guiana Highlands but the vast tropical forest resources there are not exploited because of lack of transport. Guyana's coastal plain is overpopulated, and even if the interior of the country were to be opened up the country could probably not support more people.

Left: The dense undergrowth in the rain forest makes travel over land very slow. The easiest mode of transport is by boat on the rivers.

Surinam

Area:	163,265 square kilometres
Population:	414,000
Capital city:	Paramaribo
Languages:	Dutch and English
Currency:	Surinam guilder

Surinam is the middle of the three Guiana states on the north-east coast of South America. It was settled by the British in the 1630s.

After changing hands several times the territory was handed to the Dutch in 1667 in exchange for New Amsterdam – now called New York. It remained a Dutch colony until 1948 and since 1975 it has been an independent republic.

Physically, the country is like the other Guianas. From the coast southward there are three regions.

First, there is a low, marshy coastal tract varying in width between 25–80 kilometres, followed by a strip of undulating plain covered with savanna grassland about 30 kilometres wide.

In the south are dense rain forests of the Guiana Highlands which have been cut into deep ravines by the rivers. Temperature and humidity are high all the year and onshore trade winds bring heavy rains.

The cultivated areas on the drained part of the coastal plain produce rice which is the main food crop and chief food export. Other crops such as oranges, sugar, cocoa and bananas are also grown here. An industry which is expanding rapidly from being very small is cattle raising on the savanna grasslands. The timber resources of the interior are important exports.

By far the largest export is bauxite which has been worked since 1916 and exported in a raw state, mainly to the U.S.A.

Oil has been discovered in the coastal area, and iron ore inland. Both await development.

The population, like Guyana's, is a mixed one, and 90 per cent of them live around the capital or in the other coastal settlements.

South America

Above: A Trinidad limbo dance. Many visiting tourists try to copy this dance, but few are successful.

French Guiana
Area: 91,000 square kilometres
Population: 52,000
Capital city: Cayenne
Language: French
Currency: French franc

Devil's Island – the French equivalent of Britain's convict colony at Botany Bay – is French Guiana's best known landmark. It lies ten kilometres offshore north-west of Cayenne, and French criminals were transported to its prison until as recently as 1949.

The territory was first settled by the French in 1667, captured by the British during the Napoleonic wars in 1809 and handed back to France in 1814. It is now governed as a full department of France and its citizens have full French citizenship.

Like the other Guianas the country has been neglected by its European government, and it is the poorest of the three. Gold mining has long dominated the country's economy to the neglect of the other mineral resources, which are known to exist in the interior. These include iron ore, copper, lead and bauxite, none of which has been exploited.

There is little agricultural deve-lopment. Less than one per cent of the total area is cultivated. Manioc, maize and bananas are produced for home consumption, and sugar, rum, cocoa and a little coffee for export. Some tropical hardwood is also exported, but the vast forest reserves have not yet been significantly tapped.

Imports are far greater than exports and the economy has to be balanced by money from France. This imbalance could be checked if the mining, stock-raising, timber and agricultural resources of the country were expanded. The road system badly needs improvement. Tourism is being encouraged. In 1965 the French government set up a scientific centre for space research in the territory.

Most of the people are "Creoles", a mixture of African, Asian and European blood. Over 50 per cent of the people live in the capital, Cayenne, which is built on an island in the mouth of the Cayenne River.

Trinidad and Tobago
Area: 5,128 square kilometres
Population: 1,070,000
Capital city: Port of Spain
Language: English
Currency: Trinidad and Tobago dollar

Trinidad and Tobago are the most southerly of the West Indian islands and are similar in structure to the continental mainland. Trinidad, the largest island, lies eleven kilometres off the coast, just east of the Orinoco delta. Tobago is 31 kilometres north-east of Trinidad.

Trinidad was discovered by Columbus on his third voyage in 1498, and remained Spanish till 1802 when it came under British control. The two islands became

Right: Barbados Bay, Tobago. Since the 1960s tourism has become the mainstay of the economy of many islands in the Caribbean.

an independent member of the Commonwealth in 1962 after the collapse of the Caribbean Federation. Since 1976 they have been a republic.

Trinidad is shaped rather like Wales. In the north a mountain range which is a continuation of the Venezuelan Highlands, rises to over 900 metres and runs east-west. In the south, there is a parallel lower range.

Between, in the centre, is an undulating lowland with some coastal swamps. Temperatures are high all the year but the onshore trade winds that bring heavy rain-fall to the northern mountains help to reduce the humidity. Soils are rich, and support a luxurious tropical vegetation. About 33 per cent of the island is cultivated and the chief crops for export are sugar and cocoa. Coconuts, coffee, bananas and food grains are also grown.

Trinidad's minerals are the mainstay of its economy. Oil and gas provide 90 per cent of the export earnings, and there is a large oil refinery which also handles oil from other South American states.

There is a curious lake of asphalt/pitch in the south of Trini-dad, which seems to be an in-

Above: Many of the Indian peoples in the Andes have their own languages and are unaffected by Western culture.

exhaustible supply, for as soon as any is removed more oozes up from underground. Manufacturing industries have been introduced and encouraged since the 1960s, and tourism is growing rapidly on both islands.

Ecuador

Area:	283,560 square kilometres
Population:	6,500,000
Capital city:	Quito
Languages:	Spanish and Quechua
Currency:	Sucre

Ecuador divides into three separate regions which run nearly north to south. Each is different physically, economically and socially.

The coastal lowlands in the west contain about 52 per cent of the population. The north is hot, wet and heavily forested but towards the south it gets drier, merging into hot desert on the Peruvian border. People are moving to this region which contains the country's largest city and port, Guayaquil.

Agriculture is well organized, producing the main export crop, bananas, as well as cocoa, coffee and rice. Oil is produced and refined, and manufacturing industries are developing.

The Andes rise sharply from the lowlands to over 6,000 metres. The highland region – the Sierra – is made up of two volcanic ranges on the east and the west separated by high level basins about 2,000 metres above sea level. It has a climate like perpetual spring, with small seasonal differences, though temperatures vary greatly between night and day. The Spaniards who settled in the Sierra, founded the capital here. The 45 per cent of the population who live in this zone are mainly poor, non-Spanish-speaking American Indians. Most work as farm labourers for the large estate owners producing potatoes, wheat and barley, and grazing sheep and llamas.

Only three per cent of the population live to the east of the Andes on the steep mountain slopes, and the hot, humid lowlands of the Amazon Basin. Oil has recently been discovered and is piped over the Andes to the coast for export. New roads are being built to the area in an attempt to colonize this frontier region and link it more easily with the Sierra and the Pacific coastlands.

Below: Villagers in the Peruvian Andes meet to plan the rebuilding of

Peru

Area:	1,285,216 square kilometres
Population:	15,620,000
Capital city:	Lima
Languages:	Spanish and Quechua
Currency:	Sol

Peru, like Ecuador and Colombia, straddles the Andes and is similarly structured, with Pacific coastlands, Andean ranges, and Amazon lowlands. But Peru's coastal strip is much narrower than Ecuador's and receives hardly any rain. The mountains are more rugged, with towering peaks, high bare plateaus and basins, and very deep gorges carved by streams flowing east to the Amazon.

Peru was the centre of Spain's South American empire. The Spaniards overcame the Inca civilization that flourished in the highlands and exploited its silver and gold mines.

About 40 per cent of the people live in the coastal region. Here, oil and hydro-electric power provide

roads and their village after an earthquake had destroyed them.

South America

Above: Slums, called *favelas*, cling to the steep slopes above the centre of Rio de Janeiro, at one time capital of Brazil. Brasilia, the new capital city, is in a better, more central position for governing the whole country.

energy for industries such as steel and copper smelting.

Short Andean streams water ribbons of rich irrigated agricultural land along the valleys, producing sugar, cotton, rice, vines and fruit. The cold Peruvian current offshore supports vast numbers of anchovies which are processed into fishmeal and exported. Sometimes a warm water current intrudes from the north and the fish disappear – as has happened since the early 1970s.

The highland region, where 50 per cent of the population live, is more backward than the coast. Transport is difficult. Copper, lead, zinc and silver are mined and subsistence farming is practised. Sheep, llamas and alpaca are raised, and some wool is exported.

The greater part of Peru lies to the east of the Andes yet has only ten per cent of the people. Oil has been discovered and timber and agricultural resources are yet to be developed.

Bolivia

Area:	1,098,581 square kilometres
Population:	5,950,000
Capital city:	La Paz
Language:	Spanish
Currency:	Peso

Bolivia is named after Simon Bolivar who freed the country from the Spanish in 1825. Its territory once extended to the Pacific but during the war with Chile in 1882 it lost its access to the sea. The country is isolated and inaccessible so Bolivia has difficulties in developing her resources. Her exports to the rest of the world are dependent on the goodwill of her neighbours, Chile, Peru, Argentina and Brazil.

Bolivia is a land of high mountains, cold, bare high plateaus where the Andes are at their widest, and semi-tropical lowlands in the east.

The broad plateau of the Andes some 4,000 metres high is called the Altiplano. It is the traditional core of the country where most Bolivians live. Seventy per cent of the people are American Indians who live in small towns and villages. They make a living from mining tin, copper, lead and zinc, and some practise subsistence farming, grazing llamas, alpaca and sheep on the poor pastures.

The slopes and valleys on the eastern flanks of the Andes are the best areas for farming. The warm humid conditions are ideal for growing tropical fruits, cocoa,

coffee and sugar.

Farther east there are plains which cover 70 per cent of the country. Oil and gas are produced here and efforts are being made to bring people from the Altiplano to settle and open up this area for cattle ranching, and cotton and sugar production.

Mining has always been the mainstay of Bolivia's economy. Gold and silver were mined from Potosi under Spanish rule. Now tin and oil are important. Together, these minerals make up over 90 per cent of all Bolivia's exports.

The native Indians play little part in the country's affairs and until they do its wealth will not be realized. Bolivia has a long history of internal unrest and this helps to explain the relative poverty of the mass of its people.

Brazil

Area:	8,511,965 square kilometres
Population:	110,100,000
Capital city:	Brasilia
Language:	Portuguese
Currency:	Cruzeiro

Brazil is a vast country that includes a wide variety of environments and peoples with different standards of living. It is the fifth largest country in the world, bigger than the mainland of the U.S.A. It occupies nearly 50 per cent of the South American continent and contains nearly 50 per cent of its peoples.

It was discovered by the Portuguese explorer Cabral who landed on the north-east coast in 1500. The first capital of the colony was at Salvador but in 1763 Rio de Janeiro became the capital. It remained so until 1960, when the new capital Brasilia, with its impressive architecture and well-

Left: An Indian of the Bolivian Altiplano. A broad-brimmed hat shades his eyes from the sun's harsh glare. Thick cloaks are needed at night.

Right: Part of the huge sprawl of Sao Paulo. A busy industrial city, it has problems of congestion, poor housing and foul air pollution.

Right: Part of the huge sprawl of Sao Paulo. A busy industrial city, it has problems of congestion, poor housing and foul air pollution.

planned layout, was established in the interior.

The country can be divided into two lowland and two highland regions. North of the Amazon is a small part of the Guiana Highlands, rising to over 2,500 metres. To the south is the vast lowland which makes up 40 per cent of the total area of Brazil, drained by the Amazon, the world's largest river system. South and east of the Amazon Basin are the Brazilian Highlands made up of ancient sedimentary and volcanic rocks. They form a tableland rising to over 2,000 metres which has been uplifted on the east and tilted inland. This makes a steep slope facing the Atlantic, which has always been a barrier for people trying to move to the interior from the narrow coastal plain. Finally, there are rolling lowlands to the west in the valleys of the Paraguay and Parana rivers that drain into the River Plate.

In a country which extends from 5° North to 33° South, a range of equatorial and tropical climates can be found. It is hot and humid all year round in the Amazon valley, producing the dense rain forest of the Selvas. Farther south, tropical climates with alternating wet and dry seasons give rise to the savanna grasslands and forests of the Brazilian Highlands. In the far south, warm temperate conditions give rise to rich pampas grassland.

The original Indians, a few of whom still survive in the forests of the north, Europeans and Negroes are the three groups of people who have intermarried to make up Brazil's peoples. Nearly 50 per cent of the population live within a narrow coastal band, less than 100

Right: Indians in the Amazon rain forest hollowing out a tree trunk to make a canoe. They live by fishing and primitive cultivation.

South America

Above: The waters of the Rivers Amazon and Negro meet. Ocean-going ships can travel over 3,000 kilometres up the Amazon.

With such rich resources it is not surprising that Brazil is a growing industrial power, and manufactured goods make up 40 per cent of her exports.

Industry is best developed in the south-east, between the cities of Sao Paulo, Rio de Janeiro and Belo Horizonte. Sao Paulo, one of the fastest growing cities in the world, has over eight million people. It is the main commercial and industrial centre. Over 50 per cent of all Brazil's manufactured goods are produced here.

The new capital, Brasilia, is a symbol of where Brazil sees its future. It is in the development of its vast interior away from the coast, which has for so long dominated the nation's affairs. New roads, such as the 5,000 kilometre "Trans-amazonica" from the Atlantic coast west to the Peruvian frontier, have been built. This will open up the interior and bring it up to the standards enjoyed by people living along the coast.

Brazil has its problems: a rapidly growing population; and the relative backwardness of much of its agriculture. It is also a country of contrasts, between poverty and wealth, between rural backwaters and urban bustle, but it is a country with a promising future.

kilometres from the Atlantic.

Brazil is one of the world's largest farming countries and is self-sufficient in all foods except wheat. Not all farms yield equal quantities of crops. In the south and south-east farming is very efficient producing coffee, sugar, grains and soya beans, but in the north and east farming methods are generally less efficient.

The grasslands of the interior are suitable for large-scale cattle grazing but further developments are still needed. Agricultural exports are important, especially coffee (Brazil is the world's largest producer), sugar, cocoa and soya beans.

Minerals have played a large part in the country's development.

Gold and diamonds in Minas Gerais encouraged settlement of the interior in the 17th and 18th centuries, and Brazil has rich deposits of iron ore, manganese, bauxite and tin. Because many of these deposits are located in the west and in the Amazon Basin they cannot be fully exploited till better communications have been built.

Besides mineral wealth Brazil has a huge potential of hydro-electricity. Many rivers flow off the highlands into the River Plate, and the Amazon system is enormous. The world's largest hydro-electric power station is being built at Itaipu on the River Parana. It will supply the south-east with electricity in the 1980s.

Paraguay

Area:	406,752 square kilometres
Population:	2,750,000
Capital city:	Asuncion
Languages:	Spanish and Guarani
Currency:	Guarani

The republic of Paraguay is one of the most under-developed and backward states in South America. This is partly due to its location in the upper part of the River Paraguay Basin, 1,450 kilometres inland from Buenos Aires on the coast. Transport on the river is slow, costly and difficult as the river twists and turns and the channel is subject to constant shifting.

The River Paraguay flows north to south and divides the country in two. To the west are the dry barren plains of the Chaco. These stretch across 50 per cent of the country, then rise up into the Andean foothills. On the east are rolling wooded lowlands and a level forested plateau of 300-600 metres.

Paraguay has a pleasant subtropical climate with a warm wet summer and a warm dry winter.

The people are a mixture of Guarani Indians and Spanish stock, and nearly all of them live in the south and east of the country. The Chaco is very thinly settled. The lowlands are extensively flooded in the wet season but the soils here and in the forest clearings are fertile. Sugar, citrus fruits, cotton and soya beans as well as manioc, the staple crop, are grown here. However, the majority of the people get a poor living from the three per cent of the total area that is cultivated.

Rearing sheep and cattle for meat and hides is an important part of the economy, especially on the Chaco. The forests are also a very important source of wealth.

Meat packing, sugar refining and saw-milling are Paraguay's main industries. Hydro-electric power stations are also being built along the River Parana, so modern industries like steel and aluminium will grow. Surplus electricity will be exported to her neighbours. Because of Paraguay's isolated position, improved transport links are needed to develop resources to the full.

Chile

Area:	741,767 square kilometres
Population:	10,400,000
Capital city:	Santiago
Language:	Spanish
Currency:	Peso

Chile occupies a narrow strip of land 4,200 kilometres long from north to south and only about 180

Above: The rugged, glaciated coastline of southern Chile. It suffers some of the world's harshest weather.

kilometres wide from east to west between the crest of the Andes and the Pacific. It is cut off from the rest of the continent by a desert to the north and mountains to the east which rise to over 6,000 metres. Chile is a land of contrasting scenery with a relatively small population. It has many resources – rich farming land, forests, fish and minerals – but they have yet to be properly exploited.

From the coast inland there are three zones which run parallel to one another. The coast ranges consist of steep, high cliffs rising to about 2,000 metres. They are separated from the Andes by a long valley depression, the central valley. In the south the cliffs have been cut into by the sea and the central valley drowned. A maze of islands and channels is left, thus communication is difficult. The whole of Chile is prone to earthquakes.

The different regions of Chile experience different climates. In the north no rain falls on the hot Atacama Desert. The centre of the country has a Mediterranean climate of warm wet winters and hot dry summers. This is the most

productive area of Chile, where over 80 per cent of Chileans live. To the south the climate becomes cooler, wetter and stormier and there are forests, snowfields and glaciers.

The fertile soils of the central valley heartland, watered by Andean streams, produce a wide range of grains, fruits, vines and fodder crops. This area could support a larger population, but as farming methods are poor, yields are not high and Chile has to import foods. Forest products in the south, and fisheries are important but mineral wealth forms the basis of the economy. Copper makes up 60 per cent of all exports. Iron ore, coal, nitrates from the desert, and oil and gas from the far south, are also produced.

Uruguay

Area:	186,926 square kilometres
Population:	2,760,000
Capital city:	Montevideo
Language:	Spanish
Currency:	Peso

Uruguay is the smallest and politically the most stable state in South America. It is located north of the River Plate estuary between the two largest countries in the continent, Argentina and Brazil.

The territory was first settled by

Below: Gauchos of the Uraguayan Pampas in traditional dress. Beef cattle and sheep graze on the rich Pampas.

South America

the Spanish from Argentina, but then the Portuguese advanced southwards from Brazil to gain a natural boundary at the River Plate. Disputes inevitably arose about who should control the area. The two countries agreed to a British suggestion to set up a "buffer" state and the independent republic of Uruguay came into being in 1828.

The landscape is a low undulating plain, reaching its highest point in the north at just over 600 metres. It has a pleasant temperate climate with few extremes of temperature or rainfall, warm summers and short mild winters. The climate and the fertile black soils produce rich grasslands which form the basis of the country's economy.

Most of the people are white descendants of Spanish or Italian immigrants from the last century. The British were at that time putting money into farms, railways, roads and public services. This was really the beginning of Uruguay's modern economy based on stock raising and cultivation.

Ninety per cent of the total area is used for sheep and cattle, and wool, frozen meat and hides make

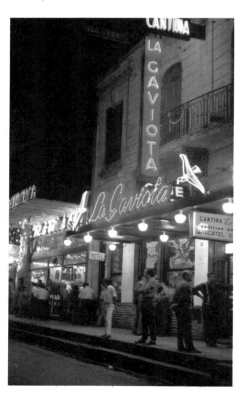

Above: The relatively high living standard of the Argentinians is based on the richness of her farmlands.

Above: The centre of Buenos Aires, the capital of Argentina, has fine modern buildings and leafy squares.

up 75 per cent of all exports by value. Wheat, maize, sunflowers and linseed are also grown for export on big ranch-type farms.

Meat canning and freezing are important industries, but Uruguay's efforts to widen her industry base are hindered by her lack of minerals and fuel which have to be imported.

Argentina	
Area:	2,807,560 square kilometres
Population:	25,060,000
Capital city:	Buenos Aires
Language:	Spanish
Currency:	Peso

The federal republic of Argentina is a wedge-shaped country that occupies most of the southern part of South America east of the Andes crest. It is the second most important country on the continent, after Brazil. Its peoples enjoy a standard of living second only to Venezuela's in South America.

The area was colonized first in the north-west by Spaniards advancing south from Peru and Bolivia in the 16th century. It was of little importance to a Spanish empire ruled from Peru, and the

Left: Buenos Aires at night. The city is the centre of Argentinian life and dominates the country's affairs.

war-like American Indian deterred large-scale settlement. Even Buenos Aires was a tiny, isolated outpost throughout 200 years of Spanish control. In 1816, when the Spanish were overthrown, Argentina became an independent republic.

There are three main physical regions. To the west are the Andes and the foothills, which merge with the plains of the Chaco and the Pampas, and the southern plateau of Patagonia. The Chaco, as in Paraguay, is hot, with alternately wet and dry seasons. It is a sparsely settled region of poor ranching and irrigated cotton cultivation.

The Pampas, extending in a wide arc for 600 kilometres from Buenos Aires, is a flat treeless plain with extremely fertile, stoneless soils. It has a temperate climate of warm summers and mild winters. It forms the heart of the country where 75 per cent of the people live on about 20 per cent of the total land area.

Patagonia, a cool windswept plateau about 600 metres high, stretches from latitude 40° South to the Straits of Magellan. It is a dry region being in the rain shadow of the Andes. Rainfall decreases westwards throughout Argentina.

The country's wealth and importance result from the produce of her soils, particularly the Pampas, one of the richest farming areas in the world. Farm products – mainly meat, wool and wheat – make up 80 per cent of Argentina's exports by value.

In colonial times the Spanish grazed cattle on the Pampas for their hides, tallow and salt beef. When refrigerated ships were introduced in the late 19th century the open grasslands began to be fenced. The stock improved and high-quality frozen meat could be produced for export to European countries. Large-scale immigration of Italians and Spaniards began too. They came to work on the large *estancias* (ranches) that were being developed with the help of British investments in railways, port facilities and telegraphs.

Today, farming on the Pampas uses a system of crop and stock rotation producing wheat, maize, flax, sorghum and alfalfa grass, as well as cattle and sheep. The fertility of the Pampas has been maintained and the area could even increase its output of foodstuffs should the need arise.

Agriculture is also important in the north and north-west in the Andean foothills. Fruit, vines, sugar and cotton are grown here using irrigation from mountain streams. Patagonia's thin pastures are grazed by sheep reared mainly for their wool.

Argentina is not rich in minerals, though some gold, silver, copper and tin are found in the Andes. She has considerable reserves of gas and coal, and produces 85 per cent of her oil needs. But these deposits are in areas remote from the heartland on the estuary of the River Plate. Coal, oil and gas occur in Patagonia, and oil and gas in the foothills area of the west and north-west. Pipelines have been built to carry the oil and gas to Buenos Aires where most industries are based. Plans are being made to increase the production of hydro-electricity on some Andean streams, and on the Uruguay and Parana rivers. These schemes have been planned jointly with neighbouring countries. This power will help to increase Argentina's production of steel and chemicals, as well as food processing, textiles and other light industries.

It is perhaps strange in a country so dependent on farm produce for her prosperity as Argentina, that 75 per cent of her people live in towns. Over 25 per cent of them live in and around Buenos Aires, the second largest city in the southern hemisphere.

Buenos Aires is the centre of Argentina's industrial, cultural and commercial life and the hub of a dense network of railways that fan out over the Pampas. It is also the country's main port on a wide shallow estuary – the channel has to be constantly dredged to remove the sand and mud brought down by the rivers. The city centre is built on a planned rectangular grid pattern, with many parks, wide avenues and skyscrapers.

Argentina has a well-educated population and reasonable resources yet is beset by internal unrest. This prevents her from becoming a truly prosperous nation.

Below: The Spaniards brought horses to the Pampas in the 16th century. Since then, horses and cowboys have been familiar features of the area.

Falkland Islands	
Area:	11,961 square kilometres
Population:	1,900
Capital city:	Stanley
Language:	English
Currency:	Pound sterling

The Falkland Islands lie in the South Atlantic, about 600 kilometres off the coast of Patagonia.

The landscape has been heavily glaciated and the climate is similar to that of north-west Britain: cool, cloudy, windy and changeable. This makes crop ripening difficult but grass grows well and sheep grazing is the main activity. Wool and sheepskins are the sole exports.

Most of the people are of British stock and take pride in the British link. The islands are a British colony but Argentina claims them. Stanley, the main port, services whaling ships returning from the hunting grounds in the Antarctic.

The Poles

At the northern and southernmost parts of the world lie two of the coldest areas of all, the Arctic and the Antarctic. Beyond 66°30' North and 66°30' South the sun never rises high in the sky, even in mid-summer, although for part of the year it stays above the horizon for 24 hours each day. These are the lands of the midnight sun. In winter, the sun never rises above the horizon so there is a long period of darkness.

Left: Most famous of all Arctic animals is the polar bear. It may look lovable but is, in fact, a ruthless and very powerful hunter.

A large ocean covers about 14 million square kilometres of the Arctic. This is surrounded by the northern parts of a number of countries. Ice always covers the coldest central parts of the Arctic Ocean. Each winter this ice sheet grows larger and the seas along the shores of many of the surrounding countries freeze over. There are also islands within the Arctic region, including Greenland, which are covered by large ice caps.

The weather in both polar regions is usually cold and often

Right: In northern Canada, beyond the forests, is a windswept landscape of tundra and lakes. Dwarf plants flower briefly each spring in this area.

Bering Sea

Arctic Ocean

North America

U.S.S.R.

● North Pole

Greenland

Spitzbergen

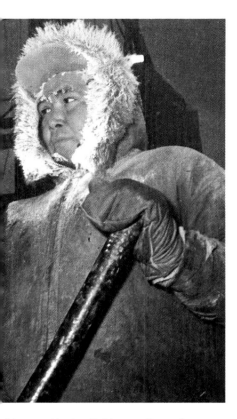

Above: Native Eskimos, Canadians and Americans all brave savage weather to exploit the crude oil found in America's far north.

unpleasant. Arctic temperatures, though low, are not quite as bad as in the Antarctic. The Arctic region also has surprisingly little fresh snow each year.

The snow and ice of both polar regions do not go on piling up for ever. They slowly move away from the centre towards the warmer margins. Some of them then melt and water flows into the seas; some of the ice breaks off the main sheet and floats into the oceans as icebergs.

Far more people live in the Arctic region than the Antarctic. Where ice does not permanently cover the lands of the Arctic, mosses, lichens, poor grass and small trees are found. A number of animals including seals, Arctic foxes, reindeer and polar bears also live there. A few hardy peoples like the Chukchees of Siberia, the Eskimos of northern Canada, Alaska and Greenland and the Lapps of northern Scandi-

navia live by herding animals, hunting, fishing or trading. There are a number of valuable minerals in the rocks, including iron ore, coal, oil, nickel and copper. Many people from other places now live in the Arctic to work in the mines and the oilfields.

Above: Weather observations are made even in uninviting places like this blizzard-swept spot in Alaska.

Below: Bright Arctic summer sunlight is deceptive; warm clothing, windproof tents and sturdy sledges are essential for survival.

The Poles

A large land mass covers about 13.2 million square kilometres of the Antarctic. This, and the oceans surrounding it, are covered with ice and snow. Scientists have found that this ice is over 3,000 metres thick in places, and that the land beneath is mountainous. The highest peaks rise to over 5,000 metres above sea level and in places stick up above the level of the ice cap. Scientists have also worked out that 90 per cent of the world's permanent ice and snow is in Antarctica.

Even in summer, during December and January, the average temperatures in Antarctica only just rise above freezing on the coasts. Inland they are far lower. In the winter, during June and July, the average temperatures fall as much as 60° centigrade below freezing point. Strong winds and blinding blizzards are common.

The two polar regions were among the last parts of the world to be explored. There is still much that we do not know about them. Only since about 1900 have people really been able to travel in these bitter areas. Norwegians and Americans explored the Arctic whilst Norwegians and Britons led Antarctic exploration. Captain Scott is, perhaps, the most famous polar explorer of all. He reached the South Pole in January 1912 a few days after his Norwegian friend and rival, Amundsen, and then died with his companions on the return journey.

The Antarctic has very few plants and not that many animals. Emperor penguins and skuas live there and whales, seals and fish live in the surrounding seas. But people cannot make a living from these. The only inhabitants of this southern polar region are the scientists who study such things as the weather, the ice, the land scapes beneath the ice and the rocks. Some valuable mineral have been found but they are no yet being mined. Whaling is a important industry around the sub Antarctic islands.

Travel in polar regions present a special challenge even today The Lapps, Eskimos and othe native peoples of the Arctic stil use traditional methods such a skiing and sledging. Where the ic breaks they use skin-covered kayaks, or canoes. In Antarctica ships and aircraft are used to brin supplies to the scientific station Tracked vehicles, light aircraft and helicopters are used by the

Right: The stark beauty of the Antarctic is usually marred by raging gales and blinding blizzards. Crystal-clear air and tranquillity is rare.

Falkland Islands

Indian Ocean

Norwegian Antarctic Territory

Weddell Sea

Bellingshausen Sea

British Antarctic Territory

Australian Antarctic Territory

● South Pole

Amundsen Sea

Ross Sea

Pacific Ocean

scientists for their local travel.

Antarctica has been divided into sectors, rather like different sized slices of a cake, and each one has been claimed by different countries. But these claims, some of which were disputed, were put aside in 1959. In that year, a 30 year treaty was signed leaving the continent free for any nation to carry out peaceful scientific research.

Nigel Collins

Index

Index

Index

Acknowledgements

The publishers have made every effort to trace the ownership of all copyrighted material in this publication and to secure permission from the holders. Photographs have been credited by page number and position: (T) top, (C) centre, (B) bottom, and combinations, for example (TR) top right.

The publishers would like to thank the following:

Actualit: 49R, 77B, 78, 79T
Afa Colour Library: 93
Ardea: 29BR
Art Institute of Chicago: 42B
Australian News & Information Bureau: 190TL, 191T
Automobile Association: 22
BP: 50-51
Berolina Travel: 86T
Nick Birch: 105
Bo Bojesen: 99, 102BR, 103TL TR B, 104T
Dr Booth: 24BR; front cover TL
Douglas Botting: 240T
Brazilian Embassy: 239T
British Aircraft Corporation: 58T
British Hovercraft Association: 58BL
British Tourist Authority: 71T
Camera Press: 41, 56TR, 85B, 153T
Tim Canadine: 148B, 149T B
J. Allan Cash: 44C, 47, 48L, 54-55T, 69T, 76T, 84T, 127T, 163T, 165, 169T B, 170, 174B, 206T; front cover C
Roger Clare: 160B, 209B
Bruce Coleman Ltd: 28BR, 29T
D. Collins: 34R
Colorific: 214L
Colour Library International: 90B, 91T
Consolidated Gold Fields: 49B
Czechoslovak Tourist Office: 100
Daily Telegraph Colour Library: 52BR, 202B, front cover CR; (S. Donovan) 236B; (Nicholas Guppy) 191B; (L. L. T. Rhodes) 190TR, 190TL
Glyn Davis: 201B, 205B
Tony Duffy: 119B
Edistudio: 96
Mark Edwards: 137B
Robert Estall: 203B, 206B
Ethiopian Tourist Office: 164L
FAO: 25BL, 130T, 167, 172T, 234BL, 237B
Finnish Tourist Office: 68T B
Ford Motor Co: 53B, 213T
Fotolink: 207T
Peter Fraenkel: 30-31, 44B, 162T B, 168B, 176BR, 177T, 179B, 182TR; back cover BR
Henry Grant: 118BL
Sally and Richard Greenhill: 148T
Greyhound Bus Lines of America: 217T
Peter Haabjoem: 84B; back cover BL
Sonia Halliday: 45T, 70, 72, 92T, 94B, 95T, 106 B, 121B, 124, 126 B, 127B; Robert Harding Associates: 136, 202T, 244TR; (Jon Gardey) 56BL
Ed Harriman: 107TL
Brian Hawkes: 176T
N. Heitkotter: 32B
Alan Hutchinson Library: 48R, 163B, 172B, 174, 220TR
Anthony Hutt: 158CR, 159T
Icelandic Photos: 66L
Indian Government Tourist Office: 125B
Jacana: 73

Jamaican Tourist Office: 124T, 151B, 226B
Japanese Embassy: 57B
Japan Information Centre: 52BL
Joyce Jason: 205T
Dalu Jones: 166, 175BL
Victor Kennett: 137T, 139T
Cathy Kilpatrick: 182TL
Keystone: 82, front cover BL
Tom Lonsdale: 54B, 160T, 161T
Macquitty Collection: 50C
Malaysian Rubber Bureau: 145T
Mansell Collection: 28BL
Janet Marchpenny: 151T, front cover BR
John Massey Stewart: 120B
Middle East Archive: 130B
Denis Moore: 19, 56TL, 64C R, 71B, 74L R, 75TB, 77T, 111, 112B, 113B, 117T, 118TL TR BR, 156B, 159B, 171, 210B, 215B, 216BL, 228B, 238T
Dr Pat Morris: 35C, 164BR
Morrocan Tourist Office: 158T BL
Margaret Murray: 43L R, 168T, 175T
NASA: 17, 18, 21, 207B, 217B
National Parks Service of America: 210TL
National Tourist Organization of Greece: 107TR B
Natural Science Photos: 35TL
NHPA: 34C; (Greenaway) 32T; (Neil Habgood) 31BR; (Brian Hawkes) 30BL
New Zealand High Commission: 35TR, 186T
Chris Niedenthal: 98, 102BL T
Norwegian Tourist Office: 67T
Novosti: 114-5, 115T B, 119TL
Oxfam: 25BR
Sheila Padget: 144B
Phillippines Embassy: 24BL
Photri: 239B
Pictor: 83T, 85T, 124C, 211T, 215TL, 232T
Picturepoint: 46T C, 55B, 91B, 187T, 214R
Dr R. M. Polhill: 173
Renault: 57T
Rex Features: 50B
G. R. Roberts: 45B, 69B, 188, 189T, 204T B
Sabena: 76B
SAS: 56BR, 66T
Satour: 181B 182B, 183BL
Nick Scott: 20
SEF: 64L, 129, 138T, 139B, 161B, 178B
Shell Photo Services: 245TL TR
Ronald Sheridan: 125T, 222TR, 223
Francis Skinner: 150T, 152T B
Society for Cultural Relations with the USSR: 113T, 117B
Solarfilma: 13
M. Storm: 220C
Swiss National Tourist Office: 86B, 87B
Tate Gallery, London: 52T
Thomson Holidays: 92B
Transworld Feature Service: 40
United Nations: 49L
T. Usborne: 24T, 176BL
U.S. Travel Service: 208B, 216BR
USIS: 46B, 209T
Varig Airlines: 232BL, 233BL TR
Keith Wicks: 175BR
Brian Woodrift: 112T, 119TR, 120T
Yugoslav Tourist Office: 101
Zefa: 44T, 65, 67B, 79B, 87T, 88, 89, 97T B, 116B, 128, 131T B, 132T B, 133T B, 134T B, 135T B, 140, 141T B, 142T B, 143T B, 144T, 145B, 146T B, 147, 150B, 177B, 179T, 180T, 181T, 183BR, 186B, 189B, 194, 195T, 196T B, 201T, 203T, 221, 222BL, 229T B, 232BR, 242B, 243; back cover CR

Consultant Editor
Brian P. Price, B.Sc., F.R.G.S.

Contributors and Advisors
Arnold Bell
David Elcome
Cathy Kilpatrick
Sheila Padget
Brian P. Price
Stephanie Thompson
Nicolas Wright

Title page: New York
Endpapers: The earth from space